THE NEW MIDDLE AGES

BONNIE WHEELER, *Series Editor*

The New Middle Ages is a series dedicated to transdisciplinary studies of medieval cultures, with particular emphasis on recuperating women's history and on feminist and gender analyses. This peer-reviewed series includes both scholarly monographs and essay collections.

PUBLISHED BY PALGRAVE:

Women in the Medieval Islamic World: Power, Patronage, and Piety
edited by Gavin R. G. Hambly

The Ethics of Nature in the Middle Ages: On Boccaccio's Poetaphysics
by Gregory B. Stone

Presence and Presentation: Women in the Chinese Literati Tradition
by Sherry J. Mou

The Lost Love Letters of Heloise and Abelard: Perceptions of Dialogue in Twelfth-Century France
by Constant J. Mews

Understanding Scholastic Thought with Foucault
by Philipp W. Rosemann

For Her Good Estate: The Life of Elizabeth de Burgh
by Frances A. Underhill

Constructions of Widowhood and Virginity in the Middle Ages
edited by Cindy L. Carlson and Angela Jane Weisl

Motherhood and Mothering in Anglo-Saxon England
by Mary Dockray-Miller

Listening to Heloise: The Voice of a Twelfth-Century Woman
edited by Bonnie Wheeler

The Postcolonial Middle Ages
edited by Jeffrey Jerome Cohen

Chaucer's Pardoner and Gender Theory: Bodies of Discourse
by Robert S. Sturges

Crossing the Bridge: Comparative Essays on Medieval European and Heian Japanese Women Writers
edited by Barbara Stevenson and Cynthia Ho

Engaging Words: The Culture of Reading in the Later Middle Ages
by Laurel Amtower

Robes and Honor: The Medieval World of Investiture
edited by Stewart Gordon

Representing Rape in Medieval and Early Modern Literature
edited by Elizabeth Robertson and Christine M. Rose

Same Sex Love and Desire among Women in the Middle Ages
edited by Francesca Canadé Sautman and Pamela Sheingorn

Sight and Embodiment in the Middle Ages: Ocular Desires
by Suzannah Biernoff

Listen, Daughter: The Speculum Virginum *and the Formation of Religious Women in the Middle Ages*
edited by Constant J. Mews

Science, the Singular, and the Question of Theology
by Richard A. Lee, Jr.

Gender in Debate from the Early Middle Ages to the Renaissance
edited by Thelma S. Fenster and Clare A. Lees

Malory's Morte D'Arthur: *Remaking Arthurian Tradition*
by Catherine Batt

PARADIGMS AND METHODS IN EARLY MEDIEVAL STUDIES

Edited by

Celia Chazelle and Felice Lifshitz

First published in 2007 by
PALGRAVE MACMILLAN™
175 Fifth Avenue, New York, N.Y. 10010 and
Houndmills, Basingstoke, Hampshire, England RG21 6XS
Companies and representatives throughout the world.

PALGRAVE MACMILLAN is the global academic imprint of the Palgrave Macmillan division of St. Martin's Press, LLC and of Palgrave Macmillan Ltd. Macmillan® is a registered trademark in the United States, United Kingdom and other countries. Palgrave is a registered trademark in the European Union and other countries.

ISBN-13: 978–1–4039–6942–2
ISBN-10: 1–4039–6942–6

Library of Congress Cataloging-in-Publication Data

Paradigms and methods in early medieval studies / edited by Celia Chazelle and Felice Lifshitz.
    p. cm.—(New Middle Ages series)
Includes bibliographical references and index.
ISBN 1–4039–6942–6
    1. Civilization, Medieval—Study and teaching. 2. Middle Ages—Study and teaching. 3. Europe—Civilization—Study and teaching. 4. Europe—History—To 476—Study and teaching. 5. Europe—History—476–1492—Study and teaching. I. Chazelle, Celia Martin. II. Lifshitz, Felice, 1959–

CB353.P29 2007
909.07—dc22   2007012020

A catalogue record for this book is available from the British Library.

Design by Newgen Imaging Systems (P) Ltd., Chennai, India.

First edition: November 2007

10   9   8   7   6   5   4   3   2   1

Printed in the United States of America.

To Caroline Bynum and colleagues in the Medieval Studies colloquium, Institute for Advanced Study, 2005–2007

CONTENTS

FIGURES, MAPS, AND TABLE

Figures

Maps

Table

PREFACE

This volume grew out of a lively discussion on the listserv, the Early Medieval Forum, of the research strategies currently defining early medieval studies. The electronic exchanges, among scholars in North America, Europe, and other parts of the world, led to the organization of sessions at the Medieval Academy of America annual meetings in 2004 and 2005, in which some of the US-based members of the listserv participated. Conversations with participants and attendees of the two conferences made clear to us the need for a collection of essays that would explore the issues discussed there in greater depth.

We owe our thanks to many who have helped this project come to fruition. First of all our contributors, for promptly and willingly responding to our requests for revisions and for their patience with editing delays. Second, we are very appreciative of the Institute for Advanced Study in Princeton, NJ, where Celia was a Visitor in 2005–2006 and Felice a Member and Visitor in 2006–2007. In particular, we are grateful to Caroline Bynum and the participants in her Medieval Studies colloquium at the Institute for their comments on and criticisms of an earlier draft of our Introduction, and for also stirring our thoughts through lively discussions of topics in medieval studies over weekly lunches. We have learned much from our Institute colleagues, and the volume is deservedly dedicated to them.

We have accumulated a number of other institutional debts during the past two and a half years, as we put together this volume. Celia wishes to thank The College of New Jersey for release time from teaching and for a sabbatical leave in 2005–2006, and the National Endowment for the Humanities for a full-year fellowship in 2005–2006. Felice would like to thank the Alexander von Humboldt Stiftung for a fellowship renewal during the summer of 2006, as well as the Institut für Mittelalterforschung of the Austrian Academy of Sciences in Vienna, and the Historisches Seminar of the Universität Frankfurt, where she was offered ideal working conditions by Walter Pohl, Helmut Reimitz, and Max Diesenberger

(Vienna, in summer 2004) and Gundula Grebner and Johannes Fried (Frankfurt, summer 2006). Felice would also like to acknowledge Florida International University for a sabbatical leave in 2006–2007. Our deep gratitude goes as well to Bonnie Wheeler, Farideh Koohi-Kamali, Julia Cohen, Kristy Lilas, our copyeditor Maran Elancheran, and the other staff at Palgrave Macmillan who have worked so hard to expedite the publication process for us.

Finally, we register our enormous gratitude to our families for their willingness to share, once again, the frustrations as well as the joys of scholarly labor.

Princeton, New Jersey
December 8, 2006

LIST OF ABBREVIATIONS

CCSL	Corpus Christianorum Series Latina
CLA	*Codices Latini Antiquiores*, ed. E.A. Lowe, 12 vols. (Oxford: Clarendon Press, 1934–1971)
MGH	Monumenta Germaniae Historica
Conc.	Concilia
DD	Diplomata
Epp	Epistolae
SS	Scriptores
SSrG	Scriptores rerum Germanicarum in usum scholarum separatim editi
SSrL	Scriptores rerum Langobardicarum et Italicarum
SSrM	Scriptores rerum Merovingicarum
TMR	The Medieval Review: http://www.hti.umich.edu/t/tmr/

CHAPTER 1

INTRODUCTION: EARLY MEDIEVAL STUDIES IN TWENTY-FIRST-CENTURY AMERICA

Celia Chazelle and Felice Lifshitz

When the University of North Carolina administration commissioned a study of humanities teaching at UNC in the early 1940s, it turned to Loren MacKinney, the author of a book on European medicine between 600 and 1100—the "early medieval" period, as he designated it—to lead the project.[1] Published in 1945, the review eloquently pleaded for the importance of a humanities curriculum, ascribing to it the power to prevent dictatorship, among other attributes.[2] In 1943, Charles Rufus Morey, founder of the Index of Christian Art (1917) and chair of Princeton's Department of Art and Archaeology from 1924 to 1945, who had also published in early medieval European history, joined other scholars of the humanities at the symposium, "Approaches to World Peace," to explore how their disciplines could foster international unity. An article Morey subsequently published in 1944, amidst "the horrors of the present war," predicted that "medieval culture will play its part in the formation of a new humanism, as custodian of values whose worth becomes more clear as the disaster of modern materialism develops the fullness of its catastrophe."[3] Morey spoke in glowing terms of the state of medieval art history in the United States, praising such specialists of the early Middle Ages as George H. Forsyth, Kenneth John Conant, and Richard Krautheimer. American medieval scholarship, he thought, would move increasingly toward an emphasis on the early period. The public, too, he believed, was showing new appreciation for this fascinating period, as evident, in his view, from the reception of the 1937 exhibition, "Art of the Dark Ages," at the Worcester Art Museum in Worcester, Massachusetts.

These anecdotes not only attest the shared sense of MacKinney and Morey that humanities scholarship in the United States had genuine political relevance, they point to the significance of early medieval studies within this larger domain, in the first half of the twentieth century. Even if we leave aside the contributions of a great number of European emigrés, the importance of American early medieval studies before as well as after World War II is evident. The career of the Carolingian historian Richard E. Sullivan may serve as an illustration. Although Sullivan's intellectual grandfathers and great-grandfathers (the medievalist teachers of his teachers, including Benjamin Stites Terry, James Westfall Thompson, Charles Howard McIlwain, and Charles Holt Taylor) primarily studied the later Middle Ages, his undergraduate and doctoral supervisors at the Universities of Nebraska and Illinois, Edgar Nathaniel Johnson and Charles E. Odegaard, published books on early medieval subjects in the 1930s and 1940s.[4] Among their contemporaries were F.W. Buckler[5] and Charles Edward Russell; the latter scholar was a Pulitzer prize-winning journalist, Socialist politician, member of a presidential delegation under Woodrow Wilson, cofounder of the NAACP, and author of *Charlemagne: First of the Moderns*.[6] Sullivan's own generation, if we count scholars who began to publish between the late 1950s and the early 1970s, includes such innovative historians and art historians educated in this country as Karl F. Morrison,[7] Ann Freeman,[8] Archibald Ross Lewis,[9] Bernard S. Bachrach (a contributor to this volume),[10] Katherine Fischer Drew,[11] Ilene Forsyth,[12] Richard L. Crocker,[13] and too many others to name. Sullivan himself spent most of his career at Michigan State University, where he was the graduate supervisor of (among others) John Contreni and Thomas F.X. Noble. Contreni is currently dean of the College of Liberal Arts and professor of History at Purdue University; Noble is director of the Medieval Institute at the University of Notre Dame. Both these historians, too, have guided the graduate work of many younger scholars in the field who now hold positions throughout the United States.

Despite this impressive roster, however, medievalists, even those who concentrate on the earlier centuries, sometimes seem unaware of the long-standing strength of early medieval studies in this country. The question that a major early medievalist in Europe posed to one editor of this volume, as recently as 1995, of why there are no "good" American early medievalists, represents a commonly held view in medievalist circles. A few years later the other editor was told, at a reception following the opening lecture in Medieval Studies at Princeton University (delivered by a later medieval historian), that early medieval history in the United States was a rapidly dying field.

Early medieval studies are definitely more prominent in institutions in Europe, where national genealogies and transnational organizations such as the European Union have been traced back to early medieval peoples and polities.[14] It is thus not surprising that early medievalists hold some of the most prestigious European research appointments: chairs and professorships, for example, at King's College, London, the University of Cambridge, and the University of Vienna, and the directorship of the Institute for Austrian Historical Research.[15] In contrast, insofar as medieval Europe has figured in the imaginary of U.S. lineage, the focus has been France and England in the eleventh and following centuries.[16] Scholars of this period and these regions have generally been more numerous on the American academic scene,[17] and perhaps more importantly, they have played key roles in the public sphere.[18] The lesser visibility of early medieval studies in the United States relative to later medieval history (as of the medieval history of other regions besides France or England, such as Spain),[19] may help clarify the obvious disconnect between scholarship on the early Middle Ages and beliefs about the era common within the wider American public. In many ways, the situation seems little changed from what MacKinney described in a lecture delivered in 1936:[20]

> All in all, the trend of the most reliable opinion of our day seems to be toward the view that the early middle ages were not centuries of primitive violence or stagnation, but of cultural progress.... With so many eminent scholars expressing themselves favorably concerning the dark age, it is surprising to find that the average student [and] professor.... [is] at least a quarter of a century behind the latest findings in scholarship, for it takes years for new information to seep down to the text book, high school and grammar-grade levels.

Still today, seventy years later (almost one hundred years after the "latest findings" to which MacKinney alludes), notions of the early Middle Ages as a "Dark Age" characterized by chaos, violence, and cultural stagnation persist. The comparisons of the "primitive" designs on jewelry worn by "conquering hordes" with "the exquisitely refined classical adornments relished by the vanquished Romans," in a *New York Times* review of a 1985 show of early medieval artifacts, can be matched by countless statements in American high school and college textbooks and books for general audiences, and by representations in cartoons such as *Far Side*, Hollywood movies, and TV programs, such as (to offer but one example) a soon-to-be-aired History Channel special, "The Dark Ages."[21]

Viewed in light of these circumstances, it is noteworthy that every contributor to the present volume has pursued his or her scholarly career in this country.[22] While Florin Curta and Celia Chazelle came from Romania and Canada, respectively, to do graduate work at American universities, and Michael Kulikowski went from the United States to undertake his doctorate at the University of Toronto, they and the other contributors have all immersed themselves in professional contexts in the United States. This feature distinguishes our book both from journals such as *Early Medieval Europe* and from most collections of essays in early medieval studies;[23] far more frequently, articles by America-based early medievalists appear alongside, indeed are often outnumbered by, those by scholars from Europe. The series American Early Medieval Studies, of which three volumes were published in 1991, 1992, and 1999, is indicative of this tendency. In her introduction to the series, Catherine Karkov asserted that it was meant to respond to the "pressing need in this country for swift professional publication in early medieval studies..." created by high publisher backlogs and market costs.[24] Karkov did not aim to help only American early medievalists, yet it is remarkable, considering the series title, that the majority of its essays were revised versions of papers delivered at the International Congress of Medieval Studies at Western Michigan University by Europe-based scholars. A volume recently edited for Routledge by Thomas Noble, *From Roman Provinces to Medieval Kingdoms*, likewise includes significantly more contributors who work outside than within the United States.[25]

There is no doubt that a high degree of internationalism characterizes early medieval studies. Conferences in the field, like the volumes of essays that may grow out of them, typically include scholars from both sides of the Atlantic. Specialists from Europe, North America, and elsewhere conduct research in the same European museums and archives and work side by side on European archaeological excavations. Within the last decade, the greater ease of communications through the Internet has augmented the possibilities of collaboration across the globe. Furthermore, early medievalists regularly move into and out of the United States for their teaching and research, as shown by the careers of the noted historians Walter Goffart, Julia M.H. Smith, and David Ganz. Goffart was born in Berlin in 1934, spent his early years in Europe and the Middle East, studied at Harvard, and then taught at the University of Toronto, before returning to the United States on his retirement.[26] Born in England and educated at Cambridge and Oxford Universities, Smith taught at Trinity College in Hartford, Connecticut, from 1986 to 1995; she then moved to St. Andrew's University and from there to the University of Glasgow, where she holds the Edwards Chair in Medieval History.[27] Ganz taught at the University of North Carolina (Chapel Hill) before becoming professor of Paleography at King's College, University of London.[28]

Partly as a consequence of this extensive scholarly interaction, one finds widespread agreement among early medievalists, no matter where they study or teach, on the important subjects and strategies of research. If one peruses the issues of *Early Medieval Europe* or volumes such as those in the American Early Medieval Studies series, it seems impossible to draw any one-to-one connection between the theme of an article and its author's place of origin or work. Yet from the perspective of American academia, one cannot help but wonder whether this blending of the international professional community is not a reason the energy of early medieval studies in the United States is at times overlooked. One purpose of this collection, therefore, is to encourage renewed attention to the field as it is currently practiced here.

Although our contributors all work in the United States, they are at differing stages of their careers, having completed graduate studies between the 1960s and the late 1990s. Their specific areas of expertise vary as well, and—as is inevitable with a small volume—there are some marked lacunae in the subject matter treated. None of the essays, for instance, deals in a significant manner with the eastern Mediterranean, the Middle East, or North Africa. Among the editors' further regrets is that there is little attention to religious practices or beliefs outside Christianity, and virtually no close treatment of the history of philosophy, theology, or music. Other gaps, too, will be noticed by our readers. Yet the scope of what is discussed remains wide. Geographically, the essays encompass the full expanse of "Europe," as early medievalists today generally conceptualize the region: from Scandinavia to the Italian peninsula, and from the Black Sea to Spain and the British Isles. Methodologically and thematically, the range is also considerable, with essays that draw on art history, archaeology, and varying modes of textual study to explore government administration, the economy, military strategy, religion, gender relations, art and architecture, and more.

The temporal boundaries of the collection deserve closer explanation. With the exception of one essay that critically examines the construct of medieval history as a whole, every essay concentrates on themes that fall within the span of ca. 400 to ca. 1100. The eleventh century is a commonly accepted endpoint for "early" medieval, even though the ninth to eleventh centuries are sometimes designated the central Middle Ages. Since the nineteenth century, scholars who have studied the seventh through eleventh centuries, such as MacKinney in his history of medicine, have often also researched the fourth through sixth centuries without seeing a need to clarify why that period, too, belongs in their domain of expertise.[29] Other publications by our own contributors examine both ends of this chronological spectrum.[30] Seen in this light, the idea that "early medieval" comprises the total length of time covered in our volume is in keeping with established historiographical conventions.

But even so, to include essays on fourth- to seventh-century topics may seem problematic to certain readers, because of associations with late antique studies. Inspired by the ground-breaking work of Peter Brown, in particular his 1971 book, *The World of Late Antiquity*, many scholars today understand the field of late antique studies to begin with the late Roman Empire of Constantine I, and to involve research on the transformation of cultural, social, political, and economic norms in the Empire, former Empire, and neighboring territories as far forward as the eighth century or even, for some, up until the "feudal mutation" of the eleventh century.[31] For certain scholars, then, the early Middle Ages have ceased to exist as an identifiable, discrete area of study. To be sure, the terms "late antique" and "early medieval" are still routinely used to imply chronologically ordered epochs. Yet as discussed in a few essays in this collection, in such cases scholarly views seem to differ about the dating and nature of the transition or transformations. Frequently, where authors evidently have in mind sequential periods of time, there is no analysis of just when antiquity stops and early medieval begins, which developments belong to which, or what political and military events, social forms, economic patterns, cultural tastes, or other traits may indicate the passage from the earlier to the later era.

These temporal ambiguities, which regularly overlap with questions about the geographic extent of both late antique and early medieval studies, are possibly an additional factor behind the impression of some that the latter field counts for little in the United States. The terms employed to denote historical periods in publications, descriptions of academic positions, conferences, and other arenas carry real weight, and in general, especially in the last two decades, one seems more likely to find references to the study and teaching of late antiquity in the United States than of the early Middle Ages. American departments of History regularly advertise positions in "Late Antiquity" but far more rarely seek "Early Medieval" specialists. Often, the inclusion—in books or other forms of communication—of scholarship on "early medieval" material is obscured by titles carrying other connotations. This is especially apparent if we consider, as well, studies of the earlier centuries classified as "Byzantine" or "Islamic." Two blockbuster exhibitions at the Metropolitan Museum in New York, "The Age of Spirituality" (1977–1978) and "The Glory of Byzantium" (1997), illustrate the point. The first show, curated by the

German-born art historian Kurt Weitzmann, whose studies of early medieval art shaped that field through the twentieth century, brought together Jewish, Christian, and "pagan" works of art produced throughout the Mediterranean in the third to seventh centuries.[32] The subtitle of the catalog for the second show, edited by its curator Helen C. Evans with William D. Wixom, describes the purview as *Art and Culture of the Middle Byzantine Era, AD 843–1261*; geographically, however, the exhibition reached well beyond the Greek empire into the Kievan Rus' state, western Europe, and the Islamic world. Both exhibitions incorporated, and presented research on, objects that in other circumstances would surely have been identified as "early medieval."[33]

We cannot in this introduction make a strong argument for a precise chronological demarcation between late antique and early medieval studies, nor is it evident that there would be merit in doing so. What we would like to suggest, instead, is that temporal boundaries may be less important in deciding what constitute early medieval studies today than are theoretical and methodological approaches. Despite the temporal overlap between the two fields, early medieval studies, we think, are distinguished by the tendency of specialists, first, to look back at the earlier centuries from the later centuries (in order, for example, to locate antecedents of later phenomena), and second, to adopt methods and approaches such as have been refined for study of the "barbarian" societies and cultures of the Roman Empire and its successor states. To a large degree, those methods and approaches have been informed by exceptionally difficult evidentiary conditions, a matter to which we will shortly return.

At least in part, the widely accepted *terminus ante quem* of the eleventh century for early medieval is also methodologically driven and linked to the field's evidentiary situation. From approximately 1000 CE, scholars of Europe and the Mediterranean benefit from a much greater quantity of sources. More things were produced and more things survive, including buildings, other large structures, smaller objects, and manuscripts, with many more written in vernacular languages. The extent to which this increase reflects changes in "realities" is a matter of debate. What is certain, though, is that to work with the extant material from after the end of the first millennium requires methods and approaches different from those to which early medievalists are accustomed.

From a methodological and theoretical viewpoint, our book demonstrates that early medieval studies remain important in American academics, despite those who might assert that the field has been swallowed up by late antique studies. Another important feature of the articles presented here is that they directly analyze some of its dominant research strategies. In the last two decades, scholars of late antiquity, Byzantium, early Islam, "early" and "later" medieval Europe, and the Mediterranean have all become more sensitive to problems with the heuristic structures and methods informing their work.[34] So far as we know, however, this is the first book, whether a monograph or a collection of essays, published in the United States or elsewhere, to examine theoretical and methodological issues specifically relating to early medieval studies.

As already suggested, a driving consideration behind the theoretical approaches and methods of this area of historical research is the need to wrestle with limited and often difficult evidence. Even for the Carolingian realm and empire, the sources are in general much fewer than from the later Middle Ages, and those that exist are often less accessible. Consider, first, the situation with texts. In the last few decades, a growing number of well-prepared critical editions involving careful study of the manuscripts of early medieval writings have been published. Their scholarly apparatuses clarify the textual transmission and the sources of this literature, thereby deepening our knowledge of its complex relation with older works. For many early medieval texts, though, the only printed editions are still those in the *Patrologia Latina* and *Patrologia Graeca* or in nineteenth-century volumes of the series, Monumenta Germaniae Historica (MGH). The *Patrologiae*, entirely produced in the nineteenth century, are compendiae of older, usually noncritical editions, many from the eighteenth century or earlier. Most specialists are aware of the problems generally presented by the *Patrologiae* and early volumes of the MGH, which can be error-ridden and misidentify authors, dates, and places of the texts' production; but the flaws in specific edited writings often remain unknown beyond a narrow circle.[35]

Furthermore, numerous writings from the early Middle Ages have never been edited, yet it is by no means certain that modern editing is suited to much of this literature. Unless a facsimile, the printed edition usually sets out what is supposedly a text's original version; but manuscript "copies" could vary widely in content and form, assuring individual early medieval readers quite different experiences of purportedly the same work. Interpolations, marginalia, decoration, and other features that might shed light on the conditions of production or broader context of a writing or manuscript can be imperceptible from a modern edition, even where a scholarly apparatus is included.[36] Countless manuscripts of known and unidentified works and portions of early medieval works, however, lie completely unexploited in scattered collections, mainly in Europe—in part due to ignorance of their existence, in part to difficulties of access. Overall, because of the often poor condition of early medieval manuscripts, libraries are more likely to restrict scholars' study of them than of later medieval codices. The problems seem to grow each year, as archives put yet greater restrictions on the availability of fragile codices and parchment fragments.[37]

The situation for nontextual sources is comparable. For architectural studies, considerably less survives above ground than from classical antiquity or later centuries. Outside Italy, only a few structures stand more or less intact; for the most part, early medieval architectural historians must rely on uncertain written references to buildings, excavated partial remains, remnants incorporated into later structures or removed from any architectural setting (e.g., placed in museums), and traces discerned through aerial photography. Other objects, as well, have taken longer to be located than for the later Middle Ages. Archaeological sites, especially funerary, have revealed a treasure trove of sources: sarcophagi, other types of burial settings, grave goods, and of course skeletons.[38] Yet early medievalists are conscious that much is still buried and thus, at least for the present, largely out of reach. One of the outstanding "technical" problems for early medieval archaeologists remains the difficulty of access to evidence beneath inhabited locations or in other sites for which excavation funds are lacking. Further, like many manuscripts, excavated objects are frequently in poor condition or lack clues as to the circumstances of their fabrication. Questions of date and place of origin, or other forms of "fact-seeking" questions about who, what, when, and where cannot be answered with any confidence.

The scarcity of sources for the early Middle Ages, written or nonwritten, with sometimes a near total absence of comparanda, means we often cannot use the methodologies for adjudicating among multiple materials that work well in some other fields of history, such as are described in the recent survey, *From Reliable Sources: An Introduction to Historical Methods*.[39] Although this excellent book contains numerous illustrations from medieval studies—one of its authors, Martha Howell, is a late medieval historian—it ignores many of the evidentiary difficulties for the early medieval centuries. Yet in spite of these problems, early medievalists labor under similar pressures as other historians to present orderly scenarios of continuity, change, and transformation. Like scholars of periods and regions with more abundant evidence, therefore, they often organize and interpret their sources to fit larger narrative frames, often provided by other secondary literature. Sometimes the master plots on which they rely, descriptions of political and military occurrences (history's "big" events), are traceable back to the nineteenth century. Or, where no such narrative previously exists, the evidence from disparate writings and artifacts may be linked together by stressing points of resemblance, downplaying differences, and hypothetically reconstructing "lost" sources in order to plot networks of development across time or space.

The temptation to write narrative history in this fashion is in certain respects fundamental to the historical profession as such.[40] But early medievalists face unusual perils when they undertake large-scale syntheses, because of the problematic quality of so much of the material they study. Simply the paucity of sources means such narratives have often taken much longer to construct than for later medieval centuries but, by the same token, can be less trustworthy.[41] A significant body of recent scholarship underscores the dangers. In the last twenty or so years, influenced by the impact of the linguistic turn on all areas of historical studies,[42] a number of early medievalists have pointed out the signs of rhetorical artifice in many written documents from the era, clues that their language may actually prevent more than assist efforts to gain insights into an externally existing "reality." Among the writings questioned are early medieval "historical" texts that, studied as if transparent windows onto a recoverable past, served as the principal sources for some of the older narrative frames just noted.[43] A growing concern among early medievalists is, consequently, the uncertainty of matters earlier thought to be settled; increasingly, we are compelled to admit that much of the scaffold on which knowledge of the period has been erected since the nineteenth century is dismayingly flimsy. Thus Gregory of Tours, an early medieval author long taken essentially at his word, whose "historical" writings are the sole source for many supposed political and religious developments in sixth-century Francia, has become the subject of a groundswell of skeptical analyses from both sides of the Atlantic.[44] Similarly, the controversial book *The Dangers of Ritual* by Philippe Buc, a French-born historian who teaches at Stanford, argues that an array of early medieval accounts of rituals and ceremonies formerly interpreted as straightforward reports may tell us almost nothing at all about the reality of such events.[45]

Postmodernist scholarship like Buc's work has engendered debate over how far this contesting of textual veracity should proceed;[46] but a more positive outcome is that it has also fueled efforts to find new paths around the various difficulties presented by the sources. Those efforts have in turn encouraged and informed discussions of other, related theoretical and methodological issues. Our volume exemplifies these developments. Broadly speaking, our contributors agree that in spite of the evidentiary problems, it is possible to build some knowledge of the early Middle Ages; but their essays reveal different, in some cases conflicting, opinions about the nature of the obstacles and how to surmount them. The divergences represent a deliberate choice on the editors' part: rather than seek essays that plumb a single thematic vein or take the same theoretical stance, we have tried to provide a representative cross-section of the field's theoretical and methodological spectrum. Some of the essays draw on traditional methods to critique established paradigms and propose alternatives to them; others suggest modifications to existing methods, and a few contend that older modes of inquiry should be altogether abandoned in favor of new ones. A collection of this size cannot be comprehensive, yet taken together, its essays attest the variety of questions that engage early medievalists today, in the United States and elsewhere.

Several of our contributors, while well aware of the sparcity of early medieval written sources and the many that remain unedited, offer new interpretative approaches to texts long available in printed editions. Bernard Bachrach argues that Carolingian military and political historians have wrongly ignored material in some of the major (edited) capitularies and other government documents extant from Charlemagne's administration. For Bachrach, these texts can still be read as realistic bureaucratic directives with critical information about early Carolingian fiscal management, the foundation of Charlemagne's military juggernaut. Charles Bowlus draws from edited Carolingian, papal, and Byzantine literature to elucidate competing military and diplomatic strategies in *Mitteleuropa* (central Europe), and thus to challenge the persistent influence of the divergent periodization schemes for the European Middle Ages that Henri Pirenne and Francis Dvornik put forward in the early and mid-twentieth century. For Bowlus, it was neither the rise of Islam in the seventh century (Pirenne's classic formulation) nor the migration of Avars and Slavs in the sixth century (as argued by Dvornik) that marked the transition from antique to medieval, but the Carolingian expansion into a region often treated as peripheral in medieval European historiography: the Carpathian Basin and the Balkans. Constance Bouchard shows how modern scholars erroneously assume that the royal and imperial family trees presented in well-known (edited) Carolingian historical writings are transparent records of dynastic connections. By probing beneath the surface of these texts, she uncovers important relatives, among them women, whom the eighth- and ninth-century authors "pruned" from the branches of descent to create a straight-line, male-dominated lineage. This discovery of new evidence for early medieval women's and gender history leads her to question the dominant scholarly theory that patrilineage first emerged as a family model only in the twelfth century.

Two other essays concentrate on the written contents of manuscripts. Felice Lifshitz demonstrates how a group of eighth- and ninth-century liturgical codices from the Mainz region undermines the widely held theory of baptism's development that sees the early Middle Ages as a way station in a long-term linear process, a paradigm largely based on historians' readings of only a few edited sources. The Carolingian-era manuscripts not only reveal the existence of locally differentiated belief and practice, but point the way to a new model for understanding the gendered aspects of early medieval baptism. Jason Glenn surveys changing interpretations of the autograph manuscript of the historical narrative by the tenth-century monk Richer of Reims, and the nationalist agenda that informed nineteenth- and early twentieth-century historians' approaches to his text. By insufficiently attending to Richer's manuscript, Glenn suggests, as opposed to its printed editions and translations, scholars have generally failed to appreciate that his work constitutes less a window on the political world it pretends to describe, than on Richer's own active intervention in his political sphere.

Nearly half the essays, though, delineate research strategies involving a focus on nontextual evidence. Due to the limited quantity and difficulties of the sources for early medieval studies, it is essential to bring together the methods of textual studies ("history") with those of art history and archaeology.[47] Michael Kulikowski discusses archaeological material in order to measure the transition from antique to medieval by the yardstick of Iberia, explicitly refusing to subordinate the history of the peninsula to the stories of Italy and Gaul. As he points out, some archaeologists in Spain still date this epochal shift by graphing excavated sites onto older narratives of the region's history, themselves derived largely from face-value readings of fifth-century literature, even though the writings and archaeological remains imply conflicting periodization schemes. The written and non-written sources should be given equal weight and read against each other, Kulikowski contends, in ways that respect their independence and potential disagreement. Celia Chazelle studies the portrait of Ezra in the Anglo-Saxon Codex Amiatinus to critique the long-lived paradigm according to which early medieval expressions of *romanitas*, both texts and works of art like this classicizing image, signify the continuous transmission of traditions from Mediterranean antiquity. Her reading of the Ezra miniature against older literature and contemporary writings by Bede underscores its disjunctions with Mediterranean conventions, and reveals the ability of early medieval cultural agents to create new imaginings of the Roman culture they often claimed to emulate.

Three of the essays presenting new approaches to non-written materials address modern conceptions of ethnicity and barbarianism. Genevra Kornbluth applies methods that she earlier honed in studies of Carolingian gems and crystals to a tiny fourth- or fifth-century sculpted crystal conch probably from the Black Sea region. Careful analysis of the crystal casts doubt on the value of paradigms of ethnogenesis for interpreting early medieval, nontextual artifacts. Such objects, she proposes, are better understood through a model of "situational identity" that may, in the future, assist historians to refine ethnogenesis theories. Florin Curta contests the value of notions of ethnicity to explain Baltic amber deposits found near the Black Sea. Although the amber possibly served to mark ethnic identity, for Curta the beads formed from this material were primarily indicators of elite status, especially female. Against economic historians such as Michael McCormick who view early medieval trade mainly through the lens of commerce, Curta asserts that we must consider other exchange phenomena such as gift giving.

Lawrence Nees offers a broad assault on the pervasive role of the ethnic paradigm in early medieval art history. Tracing conceptualizations of early medieval artifacts in terms of "Lombard fibulae, Frankish brooches, Anglo-Saxon jewelry, Celtic pins, and the like" back to the early twentieth century, he contends that they rest on a series of prejudices, chief among them orientalist-tinged views of "barbarian" versus "classical" styles, and the belief that a predilection for ornament is feminine and, as such, inherent to Irish culture whereas alien to other relevant populations such as inhabitants of Italy. An illustrated Orosius from Bobbio and the Anglo-Saxon Lindisfarne Gospels are his principal case studies; the art in these manuscripts, he asserts, is best classified and studied in terms not of ethnic paradigms but of the codices' geographic origins and contexts.

Finally, the essay by Lisa Bitel, on the periodization of medieval *per se*, offers perhaps the most thoroughgoing argument for change. Bitel rejects for pedagogical purposes the entire conventional edifice of medieval historical narrative for discussions of women in the later as well as earlier centuries. In her opinion, "the concept of time's movement and thus of history itself, whether traditionally male-exclusive, woman-focused, purportedly gender-neutral, or more inclusively gendered—undermines effective feminist inquiry into women's past." In place of a linear temporal scheme, she proposes one founded on "the kabbalistic concept of *tikkun olam* or ordering the world by gathering up fragments of dispersed divinity."

Like our contributors, most early medievalists today in North America, Europe, and other parts of the world are acutely conscious of the difficulties presented by the sources for their research and of the related problems outlined earlier; most of them would recognize the importance of the theoretical and methodological issues explored in these essays. That all our authors have pursued their careers primarily in the United States, though, makes it appropriate to ask whether the academic environment in this country has particular features that may encourage their interest in such matters.[48] Although we cannot fully respond to this question here, three facets of the American situation can be noted as possibly influential. One is the institutional isolation of many U.S.-based early medievalists, especially those working in smaller colleges and universities where they are routinely the only faculty who study or teach medieval topics at all. This situation may make it more likely for professional exchanges with colleagues in the same institutions to move away from detailed discussions of research subjects and toward more general, more likely shared, theoretical and methodological concerns. Second, it is perhaps telling that early medievalists in the United States are further removed geographically than their European colleagues from the majority of the sites where their sources are located. Though there are notable exceptions, they are less likely, for reasons simply of logistics, to undertake projects requiring access to multiple European collections of manuscripts, art, or artifacts or to participate in long-term archaeological excavations. This distance from most of their evidentiary base possibly again encourages interest in broad theoretical and methodological problems.

And third, we should consider a factor that may also help explain why our volume is appearing at this point in time: the impact of recent national and global events on the study of all humanities in the United States. As scholars in this country worry about the government's response to 9/11, the invasion of Iraq, Guantanamo Bay, Abu Ghraib, and threats to academic freedom from pressure groups such as Campus Watch, they have given new thought to their professional responsibilities in the public arena. In her October 2006 column in *Perspectives* (the newsletter of the American Historical Association), AHA president Linda K. Kerber remarked that the program of the organization's 2007 annual meeting reveals a new awareness among historians that "we are all historians of human rights." Sessions scheduled for the meeting consider, among other themes, "Interrogation, Imprisonment, and American Empire," "Warfare and Human Rights," and "Past Atrocities and Contemporary Debates: Historians, Human Rights, and Justice," to name only a few.[49] Most of the announced papers are by modernists and U.S. historians, but contemporary concerns are clearly influencing the work of premodern historians, as well. A recent article by Ralph Mathisen, on concepts of citizenship in the later Roman Empire, opens by linking his topic to the struggles over definitions of citizenship since the end of the Cold War, "in the context of the globalization of the economy, politics, and society."[50] Since 9/11, varied publications, conferences, and papers on medieval crusading and medieval thought about violence, war, and peace have drawn inspiration from the rhetoric of government and news pronouncements.[51]

Some of this scholarship offers new theoretical perspectives on how we periodize and conceptualize medieval versus modern, and on the sometimes attendant notions of the otherness and barbarity of medieval societies.[52] Only a few essays in our volume explicitly refer to present concerns, though there are obvious connections with their discussions of such topics as gender, ethnicity, and the impact of nationalism on modern historiography. Yet their authors' willingness to challenge basic theoretical approaches and methods, it seems probable, owes something, as well, to the destabilization of older modes of thought, including ideas about the past, that recent events have fostered.[53]

There is a flip side to this coin. While national and geopolitical developments may be influencing the research foci of American early medievalists (along with those of other humanists), early medieval studies can contribute to the efforts to address modern dilemmas. On the most general level, as MacKinney and Morey affirmed in the first part of the twentieth century, the better we understand the variety and complexity of past human thought and action, the richer will be our intellectual resources for assessing the viability of any solutions proposed to contemporary political, social, and cultural concerns. Study of the whole period of the Middle Ages is important in this respect. As Paul Hyams remarked a few years ago, referring to medieval Christendom, "the abundant written records of the medieval West, far outmatching those of most other premodern neighbors, enable us to map parts of its belief structure in detail nearly as fine as any but the best modern field study might provide." This culture, "en route to the modern West but still very different from it, offers insights into the differences between Western values and those of present-day non-western cultures that too often serve us as the various 'Others' of our world."[54] Research on early medieval Europe lacks the quantity of sources for later medieval Christianity; yet, where it is sensitive to new theoretical and methodological directions in the field, as are the essays in this volume, it too provides valuable examples and, more notably, counterexamples to weigh against modern experience. Although ties to our own world are apparent, early medieval studies have—more often than with many other fields of history—required that we confront episodes of seemingly stark alterity. The latest scholarship pushes us to interrogate the logical grounds for that perceived alterity, to resist the temptation to label the early medieval past "barbaric" or "primitive" simply because it is "other," and, accordingly, to reconsider its significance for how we understand "our" ("western") heritage. If we can continue to rethink "early medieval" in this profound sense, we may be able to rethink anything.

Notes

We wish to express our deep appreciation to Caroline Walker Bynum for her invitation to discuss an earlier draft of this essay with the Medieval Studies Colloquium at the Institute for Advanced Study. We are also very grateful to all the participants in the discussion for their many perceptive comments, which have guided us well in our revisions.

1. Loren C. MacKinney, *Early Medieval Medicine: With Special Reference to France and Chartres* (Baltimore: Johns Hopkins University Press, 1937).
2. Norman Foerster, "The Future of the Humanities in State Universities," in *A State University Surveys the Humanities*, ed. L.C. MacKinney, Nicholas B. Adams, and Harry K. Russell (Chapel Hill: University of North Carolina Press, 1945), p. 238 [205–62].
3. Charles Rufus Morey, "Medieval Art and America," *Journal of the Warburg and Courtauld Institutes* 7 (1944): 6 [1–6].
4. Karl Morrison, "Foreword," in *Religion, Culture and Society in the Early Middle Ages: Studies in Honor of Richard E. Sullivan*, ed. Thomas F.X. Noble and John J. Contreni (Kalamazoo: Western Michigan University, 1987), pages unnumbered. See Edgar Nathaniel Johnson, *The Secular Activities of the German Episcopate, 919–1024* (Lincoln: University of Nebraska Press, 1932) and Charles E. Odegaard, *Vassi and Fideles in the Carolingian Empire* (Cambridge, MA: Harvard University Press, 1945).
5. F.W. Buckler, *Harunu'l-Rashid and Charles the Great* (Cambridge, MA: Medieval Academy of America, 1931).
6. Charles Edward Russell, *Charlemagne, First of the Moderns* (Boston and New York: Houghton Mifflin, 1930). For biographical data on Russell, see Robert Miraldi, "Charles Edward Russell," in *American National Biography*, ed. John A. Garraty and Mark C. Carnes, 24 vols. (New York: Oxford University Press, 1999), 19: 89–91.
7. An important early work is Karl F. Morrison, *The Two Kingdoms: Ecclesiology in Carolingian Political Thought* (Princeton: Princeton University Press, 1964).
8. See *Opus Caroli regis contra synodum (Libri Carolini)*, MGH, *Concilia* II, *Supplementum* I, ed. Ann Freeman Unter Mitwirkung von Paul Meyvaert (Hannover: Hahn, 1998), with references to Freeman's earlier scholarship on this treatise.
9. Early works include A.R. Lewis, *The Development of Southern French and Catalan Society, 718–1050* (Austin: University of Texas Press, 1965), and idem., *The Northern Seas: Shipping and Commerce in Northern Europe, A.D. 300–1100* (Princeton: Princeton University Press, 1958).
10. An important early study is Bernard S. Bachrach, *Merovingian Military Organization, 481–751* (Minneapolis: University of Minnesota Press, 1972).
11. Works include *The Burgundian Code*, trans. (with introduction) Katherine Fischer Drew (Philadelphia: University of Pennsylvania Press, 1972), and

The Lombard Laws, trans. (with introduction) Katherine Fischer Drew (Philadelphia: University of Pennsylvania Press, 1973).

12. A major work is Ilene H. Forsyth, *The Throne of Wisdom: Wood Sculptures of the Madonna in Romanesque France* (Princeton: Princeton University Press, 1972).

13. For example, Richard L. Crocker, *The Early Medieval Sequence* (Berkeley: University of California Press, 1977).

14. See Patrick J. Geary, *The Myth of Nations: The Medieval Origins of Europe* (Princeton: Princeton University Press, 2002); Robert Morrissey, *Charlemagne and France: A Thousand Years of Mythology*, trans. Catherine Tihanyi (Notre Dame, IN: University of Notre Dame Press, 2003), and Jason Glenn, chapter 9 in this volume.

15. At the present, respectively, Janet Nelson, Rosamond McKitterick, Walter Pohl.

16. The imagined Norman ancestry of America(ns) is expressed most forcefully and poetically by Henry Adams, *Mont St. Michel and Chartres*, intro. and notes by Raymond Carney (New York: Penguin Books, 1986).

17. For an impression of early work in this area, see *Anniversary Essays in Mediaeval History, By Students of Charles Homer Haskins, Presented on his Completion of Forty Years of Teaching* ed. John La Monte (Boston and New York: Houghton Mifflin, 1929). Haskins taught at Harvard University. For a recent discussion of the tendency to prioritize the High Middle Ages over the "Dark Ages" in American contexts, see Bonnie Effros, "Art of the 'Dark Ages': Showing Merovingian Artefacts in North American Public and Private Collections," *Journal of the History of Collections* 17 (2005): 85–113.

18. The best example is Joseph R. Strayer, who was Professor of History and of International Affairs at Princeton University, and who served "as a consultant to the government of the United States": Gaines Post, "Foreword," in *Medieval Statecraft and the Perspectives of History: Essays by Joseph R. Strayer* (Princeton: Princeton University Press, 1971) p. xv.

19. Teofilo Ruiz, "Medieval Europe and the World: Why Medievalists should also Be World Historians," *History Compass* 4 (2006), <http://www.history-compass.com>.

20. MacKinney, *Early Medieval Medicine*, pp. 12, 21.

21. Rita Reif, "Antiques: Jewels that Shone in the Dark Ages," *New York Times*, November 3, 1985, remarked on how "jewelry enthusiasts today...admire primitive and highly expressive necklaces and earrings that are far closer in spirit to what was worn by the conquering hordes from the fifth century on than they are to the exquisitely refined classical adornments relished by the vanquished Romans." One editor of the present volume was recently contacted by KPI TV for advice (evidently unheeded) on the History Channel documentary.

22. See the contributors' biographies at the end of this volume.

23. One exception is the small volume, *Literacy, Politics and Artistic Innovation in the Early Medieval West*, ed. Celia M. Chazelle (Lanham, MD: University Press of America, 1992).

24. Catherine Karkov, "Introduction," in *Studies in Insular Arts and Archeology*, ed. Catherine Karkov and Robert Farrell, American Early Medieval Studies 1 (Oxford, OH: Miami University of Ohio, 1991), p. 1. Also see *Sutton Hoo: Fifty Years After*, ed. Robert Farrell and Carol Neuman de Vegvar, American Early Medieval Studies 2 (Oxford, OH: Miami University of Ohio, 1992), and *Spaces of the Living and the Dead*, ed. Catherine Karkov, Kelley M. Wickham-Crowley, and Bailey K. Young, American Early Medieval Studies 3 (Oxford, OH: Miami University of Ohio, 1999).

25. *From Roman Provinces to Medieval Kingdoms*, ed. Thomas F.X. Noble, Rewriting Histories (New York: Routledge, 2006). The American contributors are Patrick Geary, Bonnie Effros, Walter Goffart, and Michael McCormick; others are Herwig Wolfram, Ian Wood, Walter Pohl, Heinrich Härke, Guy Halsall, Peter Heather, Wolf Liebeschuetz, Stéphane Lebecq, and Alexander Callender Murray.

26. He is the author most recently of *Barbarian Tides: The Migration Age and the Later Roman Empire* (Philadelphia: University of Pennsylvania Press, 2006). See Alexander Callander Murray, "Introduction: Walter André Goffart," in *After Rome's Fall: Narrators and Sources of Early Medieval History, Essays Presented to Walter Goffart*, ed. Alexander Callander Murray (Toronto: University of Toronto Press, 1998), pp. 3–4.

27. She is the author most recently of *Europe after Rome: A New Cultural History, 500–1000* (Oxford: Oxford University Press, 2005).

28. Author of *Corbie in the Carolingian Renaissance* (Sigmaringen: Thorbecke, 1990).

29. For instance, the year after Bernard S. Bachrach published on the Merovingian military (see above, n10), he published a second monograph: *A History of the Alans in the West: From Their First Appearance in the Sources of Classical Antiquity through the Early Middle Ages* (Minneapolis: University of Minnesota Press, 1973). Walter Goffart followed up *The Le Man Forgeries: A Chapter from the History of Church Property in the Ninth Century* (Cambridge, MA: Harvard University Press, 1966) with *Caput and Colonate: Towards a History of Late Roman Taxation* (Toronto: University of Toronto Press, 1974). Chris Wickham first published in 1981 *Early Medieval Italy: Central Power and Local Society 400–1000* (Ann Arbor: University of Michigan Press, 1981), and in 2005 *Framing the Early Middle Ages: Europe and the Mediterranean, 400–800* (Oxford: Oxford University Press, 2005). Art historians, especially, have tended to range over the entire period; witness the surveys by Ernst Kitzinger, *Early Medieval Art with Illustrations from the British Museum Collection* (London: British Museum, 1941); Charles Rufus Morey, *Early Christian Art: An Outline of the Evolution of Style and Iconography in Sculpture and Painting from Antiquity to the Eighth Century* (Princeton: Princeton University Press, 1942); and

Lawrence Nees, *Early Medieval Art* (Oxford: Oxford University Press, 2002), all of which give extensive attention to the period before 500. Genevra Kornbluth, who has previously published *Engraved Gems of the Carolingian Empire* (University Park, PA: Penn State University Press, 1995), in this volume (chapter 2) turns her attention to a sculpted conch shell that she dates to the fourth or fifth century.

30. Just to take one randomly chosen, typical example, Felice Lifshitz published eight articles between 1998 and 2002. Of those, one concerned the eleventh century (in the journal *History and Memory*), one concerned the tenth century (in *Haskins Society Journal*), one concerned the ninth and tenth centuries (in *Annales de Normandie*), three concerned the eighth century (in *Early Medieval Europe* and in edited collections), one concerned the sixth century (in an edited collection), and one concerned the fourth and fifth centuries (in an edited collection).

31. Peter R.L. Brown, *The World of Late Antiquity, AD 150–750* (New York: Harcourt Brace Jovanovich, 1971); cf. idem., *The Rise of Western Christendom: Triumph and Diversity, A.D. 200–1000*, 2nd ed. (Oxford: Blackwell, 2003).

32. See Kurt Weitzmann, "Preface," in *Age of Spirituality: A Symposium*, ed. idem. (New York: Metropolitan Museum of Art, in association with Princeton University Press, 1980), pp. vii–viii.

33. *The Glory of Byzantium: Art and Culture of the Middle Byzantine Era, A.D. 843–1261*, ed. Helen C. Evans and William D. Wixom (New York: Metropolitan Museum of Art, 1997).

34. For a few general treatments of issues relating to medieval historical studies, see Laura Lee Downs, *Writing Gender History* (London: Arnold Press, 2004); Nancy Partner, *Writing Medieval History* (London: Arnold Press, 2004); Kathleen Biddick, *The Shock of Medievalism* (Durham: Duke University Press, 1998); Gabrielle Spiegel, *The Past as Text : The Theory and Practice of Medieval Historiography* (Baltimore: Johns Hopkins University Press, 1997).

35. One might compare the two editions, both in the Monumenta Germaniae Historica series, of the *Libri Carolini*, the second necessitated by long-disregarded flaws in the first: *Libri Carolini, sive, Caroli Magni Capitulare de Imaginibus*, MGH, Concilia II, Supplementum I, ed. Hubert Bastgen (Hannover: Hahnsche, 1924), replaced by *Opus Caroli regis contra synodum (Libri Carolini)* (see above, n8).

36. See John Lowden, *The Making of the Bibles Moralisées* (University Park, PA: Pennsylvania State University Press, 2000).

37. Rosamond McKitterick, in particular, has reminded us of the research potential of the manuscripts; see most recently her, *History and Memory in the Carolingian World* (Cambridge, UK: Cambridge University Press, 2004).

38. See, for example, Bonnie Effros, *Merovingian Mortuary Archaeology and the Making of the Early Middle Ages* (Berkeley: University of California Press, 2003).

39. Martha Howell and Walter Prevenier, *From Reliable Sources: An Introduction to Historical Methods* (Ithaca: Cornell University Press, 2001).
40. See Robert F. Berkhofer, *Beyond the Great Story: History as Text and Discourse* (Cambridge, MA: Harvard University Press, 1995).
41. See Celia Chazelle (chapter 5 in this volume) for a critique of this approach by early medievalists.
42. See Elizabeth A. Clark, *History, Theory, Text: Historians and the Linguistic Turn* (Cambridge, MA: Harvard University Press, 2004).
43. John Moreland, "What is Archaeology? An Essay on the Nature of Archaeological Research," *History and Theory* 30 (1991): 246–61.
44. See the articles in *The World of Gregory of Tours*, ed. Kathleen Mitchell and Ian Wood (Leiden: Brill, 2002).
45. Philippe Buc, *The Dangers of Ritual: Between Early Medieval Texts and Social Scientific Theory* (Princeton: Princeton University Press, 2001).
46. Geoffrey Koziol, "The Dangers of Polemic: Is Ritual Still an Interesting Topic of Historical Study?" *Early Medieval Europe* 11 (2002): 367–88.
47. See John Moreland, *Archaeology and Text* (London: Duckworth, 2001).
48. It is perhaps also telling that although the main journal in early medieval studies, *Early Medieval Europe*, is published in England, one of the most heated theoretical debates in recent years in the field, which took place partly in the pages of that journal, involved two scholars working in the San Francisco Bay area of California: Philippe Buc and Geoffrey Koziol (see above, notes 45, 46).
49. See Linda K. Kerber, "We Are All Historians of Human Rights," *Perspectives* October, 2006, <http://www.historians.org/Perspectives/issues/2006/0610/0610pre1.cfm>. The conference theme is "Unstable Subjects: Practicing History in Unsettled Times."
50. Ralph Mathisen, "*Peregrini, Barbari, and Cives Romani*: Concepts of Citizenship and the Legal Identity of Barbarians in the Later Roman Empire," *American Historical Review* 111 (2006): 1011 [1011–40].
51. For instance, the plenary address at the Twentieth Annual Barnard College Medieval and Renaissance Conference, on the theme of "War and Peace in the Middle Ages and Renaissance" (December 2, 2006) was delivered by Samuel Edgerton under the somewhat anachronistic title, "The Sacredness of Violence: Why Even Artists in the Middle Ages Supported the Death Penalty."
52. See, for example, Bruce Holsinger, *The Premodern Condition: Medievalism and the Making of Theory* (Chicago: University of Chicago Press, 2005).
53. Alluded to in the announced theme of the 2007 American Historical Association conference (Atlanta, January 2007); see above, n49.
54. Paul Hyams, *Rancor and Reconciliation in Medieval England* (Ithaca: Cornell University Press, 2003), p. xii.

PART I

PARADIGMS: *ROMANITAS*,
ETHNICITY, AND VISUAL CULTURE

CHAPTER 2

MATERIAL ETHNOGENESIS? A CRYSTAL CONCH OF THE "GOTHS"

Genevra Kornbluth

Analysis of a fourth- to fifth-century crystal conch challenging the ethnogenesis paradigm, and arguing that such nontextual objects are better understood in terms of situational identity.

Historians do least violence to our sources when we draw boundaries in the same places as the people we study. Ethnogenesis theory appears to offer art historians just that possibility. Certain early medieval groups, for example the Goths and Franks, are thought to have gradually developed a sense of "ethnic" identity[1] manifested in characteristic art forms. One can therefore speak of Gothic amulets or Frankish fibulae, label those objects medieval (rather than ancient), and map their formal changes over time, bringing order to a large body of chaos. But the theory is not without its own problems. We cannot be sure whether or in what ways textual terminology related to actual groups. How can we discuss Gothic development when we do not know whether people called Goths by outsiders thought of themselves that way, whether unrelated groups were given the same name, or whether the name is properly used for more than one generation? Archaeology is sometimes brought in to refine our definitions, but that, too, is fraught with peril. Surviving objects can fail to conform to the expected orderly progression.

Though the association between archaeological cultures and ethnicity has been and continues to be debated,[2] the discussion has not yet found its way into most art historical scholarship. Is the theory useful for art historians? Conversely, can our evidence help refine that theory? A short essay cannot address the conceptual validity of early medieval ethnicity as such.[3] The ethnogenesis paradigm, dealing only with the birth and earliest development of ethnic identity, is more manageable. I argue that the theoretical bases for that paradigm are inherently unsuited for classifying non-narrative material culture. Specific objects and their functions are better understood in terms of the construction of situational identity, whether tied to location, gender, or social status, without ethnic qualifiers. Art historical studies may help others to make a case for or against ethnic identity, but arguments about ethnicity are more likely to derail our own analysis than to help us.

A small conch shell executed in rock crystal (natural quartz stone), measuring about 2.5 × 2 × 1.5 cm. (figures 2.1 and 2.2),[4] can illustrate the problematic nature of both ethnic designation and the ethnogenesis model. Now in the British Museum, it lacks all provenance. I suggest that it dates from the fourth or fifth century, that it was used in the region to the north and west of the Black Sea, and that there is insufficient evidence to call it Gothic (much as we might like to be able to connect it to historically documented conflicts by doing so).[5]

The sculpted conch is damaged, but its extraordinary naturalism allows identification of its species as the Mediterranean murex brandaris. (This identification is critical, because among conchs only the brandaris had the unique functions discussed below.) Unlike the purpura haemostoma most commonly used for purple dye, it does not have a rounded, narrow profile; nor does it have the overall diamond shape, the sharply projecting spiral, or the gradually narrowing sides of the murex trunculus.[6] Instead its spiral projects less sharply, its profile narrows more quickly toward the shell opening, and it has projecting spines or knobs. The natural murex brandaris also has a long, narrow extension at the base, but this distinctive feature is easily broken off, so shells must often be identified by the shape of the upper part. The same fate has befallen this artificial brandaris, depriving us of the clearest evidence for its use. Fortunately, the shape of the surviving portion and its surface abrasion patterns are very revealing. Unlike the Roman game pieces (some shaped like shells) with which it has been confused,[7] this is neither flattened for stability nor worn on one side from moving around on a game board. Rather, abrasion is evenly distributed all around the stone. As on a gemstone scallop shell in Stuttgart that retains its apparently unrestored suspension loop (attached to a prong inserted into a hole in the top of the shell, where the two valves of a living scallop would join together),[8] this is the pattern of wear that results from use as a pendant.

Some natural murex brandaris shells were likewise worn as pendants. Each shell was pierced through the narrow end opposite the projecting

Figure 2.1 Conch shell, rock crystal, obverse. Length 2.57 cm. London, British Museum, Department of Greek and Roman Art, 1923/4-1/1180. Photo: author, courtesy of the British Museum.

spiral, normally just at the beginning of the long extension. A metal loop was threaded through the hole, and the pendant was worn with the spiral pointing down (figure 2.3).[9] If the gemstone conch was pierced as these natural versions were, the hole would have been bored just where we now find a broken edge. Indeed, the position of the break supports the

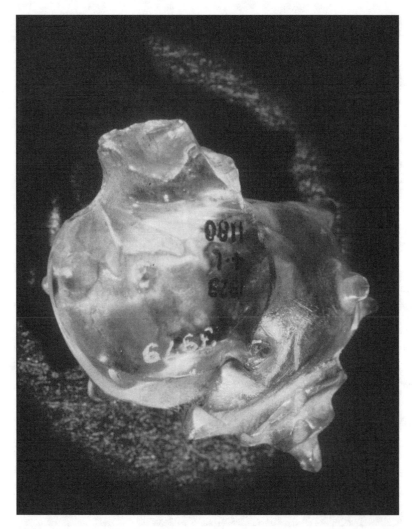

Figure 2.2   Conch shell, rock crystal, reverse. Length 2.57 cm. London, British Museum, Department of Greek and Roman Art, 1923/4-1/1180. Photo: author, courtesy of the British Museum.

idea that the stone was so pierced, since such a hole would have made it especially fragile at precisely this point. The crystal was apparently suspended in the same way as natural shells.

Natural brandaris pendants are not at all common in the historical record. On the Mediterranean shore, the shells were normally smashed to retrieve their meaty contents. The surviving murex brandaris shell

Figure 2.3   Natural conch shell from Basel-Gotterbarmweg grave 6, obverse. Length 4.68 cm. Basel, Historisches Museum, inv. no. 1915.75. Photo: A. Seiler, Historisches Museum Basel, by permission.

pendants have been cataloged and mapped by the archaeologist Mechthild Schulze-Dörrlamm.[10] Almost all have come from burials of the so-called Černjachov and Sântana-de-Mureş cultures, located in modern Romania, Moldova, and Ukraine. Like other archaeological "cultures," these are useful groupings of distribution patterns for the organizational purposes of modern scholars, and may or may not correspond to historical entities—in this case, possibly Goths or Slavs.[11] The Černjachov/Sântana-de-Mureş groupings are generally dated to the fourth or fifth century. Their distinguishing markers include cemeteries with both cremation and inhumation, handmade ceramics, and composite bone combs with rounded projections. Cemeteries from both cultures, including those at Černjachov and Sântana-de-Mureş themselves, have yielded a total of sixteen brandaris pendants.[12] Like the cowries and local snail shells more widely used, and like the Hercules clubs and other items found with them, these were probably apotropaic.[13] They were thought to protect their bearers from disease or injury, and promote strength or fertility, though the precise mechanisms by which they functioned are still unexplained. The London conch, though made from different materials, fits within local Sântana de Mureş-Černjachov usage. Since it fits virtually nowhere else, I propose that it was made for a patron within the population associated with those cultures. It could have been produced by one of the many artisans in Roman territory proficient in the technically complicated process of working with gemstone; but it could equally well have been locally made. A great many beads have been found in Ukrainian graves. Most are of glass. Many, however, are of rock crystal and carnelian (another equally hard stone).[14] These are cut into cubes with flattened corners, faceted beads with fourteen sides. Of course, such beads could easily have been imported. But the tools to make them are the same as those used to cut cold glass,[15] including the faceted glass "Kowalk" beakers associated with Černjachov sites; and we know that a workshop was active making such glass in Komarov, Ukraine, from the third to the fifth century.[16] Since such beakers were produced locally, gemstone beads were probably locally made, as well.[17] Creating a conch shell in rock crystal required great skill on the part of the sculptor, but the same tools as the production of crystal beads. Is this, then, a "Gothic" pendant?[18]

It is the distributional limit of natural brandaris amulets that makes possible association of the British Museum crystal with the archaeological cultures discussed here. But the chronological limit to that same distribution makes it impossible to use this material to discuss continuity over time. This is a problem in considering ethnogenesis.

Ethnologists and anthropologists have offered numerous general definitions of ethnicity. Primordialist understandings, asserting actual biological linkage within groups, have been discredited for several generations. Indeed, they were already out of favor when the historian Reinhard Wenskus published his seminal work, the basis for most modern scholarship on medieval ethnogenesis, in 1961.[19] Most definitions now given any credence describe ethnicity as subjective self-identification on the basis of real or perceived shared characteristics and/or common ancestry, identity asserted by individuals and accepted by others.[20] Shared characteristics can include language, religion, armament, dress, and of course amulets. Ethnogenesis theories present models for the historical development of ethnic identity.

Early medieval ethnogenesis, as defined by the text historian Walter Pohl, one of the most influential followers of Wenskus and exponents of the currently dominant paradigm, depends on belief in myths of common ancestry.[21] Other ethnic identifiers, even when mentioned in early texts, are seen as too problematic to be of real use. The developmental stemmata of languages do not necessarily correspond to specific peoples; arms, ways of fighting, and costume changed over time and were shared among many different groups of varying ethnicity; and hairstyles sometimes called group markers could in fact differ wildly. Only communal narratives that claimed common descent, narratives normally embodied in texts, carried groups through changing situations with their developing identities intact.[22] Ethnogenesis is, by definition, a narrative strategy for cultural continuity, focused on blood ties.

But the paradigm of ethnogenesis has been taken in a different direction by other scholars relying on the chronological framework of the historian Herwig Wolfram,[23] another important developer of Wenskus's ideas. These scholars are concerned with the linkage of textual and material evidence, and it is they who argue the association of the Černjachov/Sântana-de-Mureş cultures with the Goths. Volker Bierbrauer and Michel Kazanski, both archaeologists, document the correspondence between archaeological chronology and textual history. Thus one of Bierbrauer's key arguments is that an archaeological break precisely matches Gothic suffering in 375/376 at the hands of the Huns.[24] Michel Kazanski attributes greater importance to the assignment of Pannonia to Goths in 456/457, arguing that the Černjachov culture continued until that later breaking point.[25] For both historians, it is unimportant whether any particular marker continued from one phase of Gothic history to the next. Rather, both scholars catalog successive archaeological cultures and note the match between those cultures and ethnogenetic phases as defined by Wolfram. Correspondence trumps continuity.

The difference in approach between Pohl and Bierbrauer/Kazanski is inevitable, given their different disciplines. Archaeological cultures defined by their beginning and endpoints cannot demonstrate continuity over time. Insofar as analysis of the crystal conch in London is conditioned by archaeological context, as argued above, it too must be limited to a single moment, one defined by historical correspondence rather than by narrative continuity. But on a theoretical level, art history might be able to narrow the gap between the disciplines of text history and archaeology, and hence between the narrative and correspondence models, by constructing a historical narrative using non-narrative objects. In this study, it could do so by establishing that there were analogous traditions of gemstone usage in the Černjachov/Sântana-de-Mureş cultures and among the Goths.

The best-known gemstone work associated with the early Goths is the sapphire ring stone (2.1 × 1.7 cm) now in Vienna, inscribed with a frontal

Figure 2.4 Seal of Alaric, sapphire intaglio. Height 2.06 cm. Vienna, Kunsthistorisches Museum inv. no. VII B 23. Photo: author, courtesy of the Kunsthistorisches Museum.

figure and the reversed words ALARICUS REX GOTHORUM, "Alaric king of the Goths" (figure 2.4).[26] It must refer to either Alaric I (395–410) or Alaric II (484–507) of the Visigoths.[27] Most scholars choose the second king as the more likely to have employed the Roman-style title *rex Gothorum*.[28] In fact neither ruler is known to have used this formula. Alaric I never called himself king; and in his legal documents Alaric II styled himself simply *Alarici regis*, without the added ethnic identifier *Gothorum*.[29] It therefore seems unlikely that the seal was an official insigne of either leader. But even if unofficial, the stone was probably made in Goth-dominated territory. Its epigraphy, a combination of Square and Rustic Capitals using a distinctive "G" with a straight, horizontally ser-iffed hanging spur, is most closely paralleled by early sixth-century inscriptions from north Italy.[30] I argue elsewhere that the Ostrogothic king Theoderic (r. 493–526) may have commissioned the seal as a diplo-matic gift for Alaric II, his daughter's husband.[31] His engraver adapted a standard coin obverse type, the so-called three-quarter facing bust with the figure rotated to frontality, found on Byzantine and western solidi since the late fourth century (e.g., figure 2.5).[32] Unlike the coins, how-ever, the ring stone does not include a spear, shield, or helmet.[33] Its only martial element is Alaric's garb, probably a military breastplate.[34] The numismatic parallel is close enough to have reminded contemporary

Figure 2.5 Solidus of Emperor Zeno (r. 474–491), gold, obverse. Washington, D.C., Dumbarton Oaks Byzantine Collection. Photo courtesy of the Dumbarton Oaks Byzantine Collection.

viewers of militant imperial coinage, so the more pacific imagery on the stone would probably have been noted. Alaric's "ethnic" title would also have been striking: in itself highly unusual, it is visually emphasized by its compositional prominence. The king is presented as a recognized military leader ruling over Goths, as opposed to other peoples; but although a warrior, he is also a man of peace. In my opinion, this object was commissioned as part of an attempt by Theoderic to keep Alaric out of war with Clovis and the Franks, the conflict in which he was in fact killed in 507. Letters of 506/507 sent from Theoderic to Alaric, Clovis, and other rulers argue that a good king is self-restrained, preserving his people by his willingness to make and keep peace via kinship ties.[35] The seal stone in Vienna presented Alaric with an image of himself as a Goth (like Theoderic) and a guardian of peace. The medium itself helped convey a flattering message, since sapphire was associated with imperial power and was, indeed, reserved for imperial usage in a sumptuary law of Leo VI (457–474).[36] Use of a gem in this diplomatic effort would have been analogous to Theoderic's similar use of elaborate clocks documented in another series of letters.[37] The Alaric seal would then be a gemstone sculpture commissioned for a person of the highest status, used to make a political/social statement about that person by means of Roman linguistic and pictorial conventions.

The British Museum conch (figures 2.1 and 2.2) also made social statements for someone of very high status, activated by reference to Roman forms. Natural brandaris shell pendants (figure 2.3) have been found almost exclusively in female graves, indicating that they served as gender markers.[38] They also had clear economic-cum-political significance. The murex brandaris lives only in the Mediterranean and in the Atlantic between Portugal and Africa, not in the Black Sea. The brandaris in Černjachov/Sântana-de-Mureş burials were imports from the Empire, shipped as shells and not as living animals (usable for food or dye), since the mollusk could not survive long transport.[39] As imports they, like Byzantine silver,[40] must have been associated with the great Mediterranean power. Wearing a brandaris shell clearly stated that a woman had some connection, commercial or political, with the South. It was thus a way to define and reinforce social hierarchy. The geographically limited distribution of the shell amulets makes them also markers of locational identity. People within Roman borders, among others, employed different amulets. Worn *here* and not *there*, the shells created a spatial border between *us* and *them*. A brandaris pendant carried in one place and not another defined identity and alterity. At the same time that an imported shell marked connection with the Romans, it also proclaimed some measure of difference from them, allowing simultaneous claims of both linkage with and separation from the empire.[41]

A brandaris shell made out of rock crystal shared all these roles and introduced a new element of hierarchical differentiation. It is an extremely expensive version of a luxury import item. Among wealthy families in this one area, it set apart the very *very* rich. It could even have distinguished a ruling (or potentially ruling) family from the rest of the nobility, insofar as either of those categories existed in the fourth/fifth century—surely part of any elite group that would have had an interest in promoting ethnic coherence.[42] And for at least one brief historical moment, it is quite certain that a slightly lower-status object did not originate as merely the poor approximation of a richer one. The natural shell must have come first, since no one could have grown an animal to imitate the crystal version. There may have been a time when women of the second tier had adopted the custom of wearing natural brandaris shells from the richer or royal, who then raised the social bar another notch by commissioning gemstone conchs; but whatever came before, crystal represented a step up.[43] At least a small part of visual tradition moved upward, not downward.

The rock crystal shell was, then, also a gemstone sculpture commissioned for a person of the highest status, used to make a political/social statement about that person by pictorial means drawn from the Roman world. It is in many important ways similar to the seal of Alaric, which perhaps a century later proclaimed its subject Gothic. Is this similarity evidence of ethnic continuity from the Black Sea to the Ostrogothic and Visigothic kingdoms? It could be. Both objects speak to situationally constructed identity, and use similar means for similar purposes. Historians from Reinhard Wenskus to Peter Heather have argued that Gothic identity was established very early, and that although people were reshuffled into Ostrogoths and Visigoths in the fifth century, they still retained a sense of themselves as Goths.[44] Art historical investigation, tightly focused on some of the most sophisticated early medieval artifacts, could offer some hope for resolving questions about early ethnicity. If a continuous series of objects could be shown to symbolically construct identity in similar ways, and if some of those objects named groups to which we could link that identity, then we would have material evidence of what we might call ethnicity (if that term were used with full knowledge of its difference from the modern variety). But in fact we have very few artifacts that deploy the same group names as historical texts, and no series of linked objects has yet been found. The present study establishes only one point of similarity between the Černjachov/Sântana-de-Mureş cultures and Goths, not a full bridge. Perhaps both the shell and the seal are Gothic, but we cannot be sure that the conch is, and identifying it in that way does not increase our understanding of it. The paradigm of ethnic identity stretches the evidence in this study, though it does not do actual violence to it.

Ethnogenesis is another matter. The narrative model of ethnogenesis defined by Walter Pohl includes the belief in real or mythical common descent. An object that itself lacks even implicit narrative cannot tell us what a group of people thought about their ancestry. Without text history to suggest a linkage with the Goths, the British Museum conch could be just as easily paired with sixth-century crystal amulets from Frankish territory [45] as with the ring stone of Alaric. It is only the inscribed text on the sapphire seal that links it to Goths. The crystal shell has no such marker. There is certainly nothing about it that suggests a myth of common descent, or indeed common religion or language. Where the theoretical model is defined as a narrative strategy, the London conch does not, and cannot, give evidence of ethnogenesis. And correspondence with textual history, the ethnogenetic criterion used by Bierbrauer and Kazanski, is also unrecoverable in a single non-narrative object, no matter how complex.

In the current state of knowledge, the paradigm of ethnogenesis is not truly applicable to the material of art history. Neither the narrative nor the correspondence model can simply be taken over into our discipline. But as in the case of ethnicity itself, a series of objects art historically analyzed could offer a bridge between models. Art history can draw historical narrative out of an uninscribed object. For the moment there is no true model of material ethnogenesis. But though ethnogenesis theory cannot now help art historians, one day we may be able to help other scholars construct a more useful paradigm of early medieval identity.

Notes

1. On medieval ethnicity: Robert Bartlett, "Medieval and Modern Concepts of Race and Ethnicity," *The Journal of Medieval and Early Modern Studies* 31 (2001): 39–56. On the early medieval period: Patrick J. Geary, "Barbarians and Ethnicity," in *Interpreting Late Antiquity: Essays on the Postclassical World*, ed. G.W. Bowersock, Peter Brown, and Oleg Grabar (Cambridge, MA: Belknap Press of Harvard University Press, 2001), pp. 107–29; Walter Pohl, "Conceptions of Ethnicity in Early Medieval Studies," *Archaeologia Polona* 29 (1991): 39–49.

2. Briefly summarized by Siân Jones in "Historical Categories and the Praxis of Identity: The Interpretation of Ethnicity in Historical Archaeology," in *Historical Archaeology: Back from the Edge*, ed. Pedro Paulo A. Funari, Martin Hall, and Siân Jones (London: Routledge, 1999), pp. 219–32; at greater length, Siân Jones, *The Archaeology of Ethnicity: Constructing Identities in the Past and Present* (London: Routledge, 1997); see the review by Sebastian Brather in *Ethnographisch-Archäologische Zeitschrift* 39 (1998): 457–62.

3. See the article by Lawrence Nees in this volume. Against ethnicity as significant in early medieval societies, also Sebastian Brather, *Ethnische Interpretationen in der frühgeschichtlichen Archäologie: Geschichte, Grundlagen und Alternativen*, Ergänzungsbände zum Reallexikon der Germanischen Altertumskunde 42 (Berlin: Walter de Gruyter, 2004); abbreviated in Sebastian Brather, "Historische Fragestellungen in der Archäologie? Zur Rekonstruktion frühmittelalterlicher Identitäten," *Słowianie i ich sąsiedzi we wczesnym średniowieczu*, ed. Marek Dulinicz (Lublin-Warsaw: Uniwersytetu Marii Curie-Skłodowskiej, 2003), pp. 35–44.

4. From the tip of the spiral to the opposite broken end 2.57 cm., width 2.17 cm., thickness 1.56 cm.: H.B. Walters, *Catalogue of the Engraved Gems and Cameos, Greek, Etruscan and Roman in the British Museum*, rev. and enlarged ed. (London: British Museum, 1926), p. 372, no. 3979 (Department of Greek and Roman Art, 1923/4-1/1180). I am grateful to Drs. Dyfri Williams and Donald Bailey for allowing me to examine and photograph this object.

5. On such temptations, see the essay by Michael Kulikowski (chapter 10 in this volume).

6. Types and uses of conchs: Otto Keller, *Die Antike Tierwelt*, vol. 2, *Vögel, Reptilien, Fische, Insekten, Spinnentiere, Tausendfüssler, Krebstiere, Würmer, Weichtiere, Stachelhäuter, Schlauchtiere* (1913; repr. Hildesheim: Georg Olms, 1963), pp. 524–39.

7. As by Walters, *Catalogue of the Engraved Gems*, pp. 371–72. See Genevra Kornbluth, "Games (including Backgammon and Chess)," in *Late Antiquity: A Guide to the Postclassical World*, ed. Glen W. Bowersock, Peter Brown, and Oleg Grabar (Cambridge, MA: Harvard University Press, 1999), pp. 459–60. For shell-shaped game pieces, see Alexander Mlasowsky, *Die antiken Tesseren im Kestner-Museum Hannover* (Hannover: Kestner-Museum, 1991), no. 126; Berta Segall, *Katalog der Goldschmiede-Arbeiten* (Athens: Druckerei Pyrsos, 1938), no. 94.

8. Württembergisches Landesmuseum, Gundelsheim F58/18: height with fitting 3.52 cm. See Robert Roeren, "Ein frühalamannischer Grabfund von Gundelsheim (Kr. Heilbronn)," *Fundberichte aus Schwaben*, N.F. 15 (1959): 83–93; Rainer Christlein, *Die Alamannen: Archäologie eines lebendigen Volkes* (Stuttgart: Konrad Theiss, 1978), p. 115, pl. 35. I am grateful to Drs. Rotraut Wolf and Dieter Quast for permission to study this stone and for discussing it with me.

9. Examples with preserved suspension loops: V.P. Petrov, in *Materialy i Issledovaniia po Arkheologii SSSR* 116 (1964): 112–13 [53–117] (fig. 14 nos. 1, 6), from the Černjachov cemetery. I am grateful to Dr. Pia Kamber for permission to study the Basel example in figure 2.3.

10. Mechthild Schulze-Dörrlamm, "Gotische Amulette des 4. und 5. Jahrhunderts n. Chr.," *Archäologisches Korrespondenzblatt* 16 (1986): 347–55. I am grateful to Dr. Dieter Quast for this reference.

11. Stephen Shennan, "Introduction: Archaeological Approaches to Cultural Identity," in *Archaeological Approaches to Cultural Identity,* ed. Stephen Shennan (London: Unwin Hyman, 1989), esp. pp. 5–14 [1–32]; Florin Curta, "From Kossinna to Bromley: Ethnogenesis in Slavic Archaeology," in *On Barbarian Identity: Critical Approaches to Ethnicity in the Early Middle Ages,* ed. Andrew Gillett (Turnhout: Brepols, 2002), pp. 201–18; Florin Curta, *The Making of the Slavs: History and Archaeology of the Lower Danube Region, ca. 500–700* (Cambridge, UK: Cambridge University Press, 2001). For an introduction to these cultures: Mads Ravn, "A Survey of the Sîntana de Mures,-C(ernjachov Culture: A Social-Economic Perspective," in idem., *Death Ritual and Germanic Social Structure (c. AD 200–600),* BAR International Series 1164 (Oxford: British Archaeological Reports, 2003), pp. 53–64; Peter Heather and John Matthews, "The Sântana de Mureş-Černjachov Culture," in *The Goths of the Fourth Century,* ed. Peter Heather and John Matthews, Translated Texts for Historians 11 (Liverpool: Liverpool University Press, 1991), pp. 51–101; Peter Heather, *The Goths* (Oxford: Blackwell, 1996), pp. 18–19.

12. Schulze-Dörrlamm, "Gotische Amulette," nos. 1–12, some with multiple pendants; nos. 2 and 12 from the cemeteries mentioned. Three from a pair of graves in Basel (including figure 2.3) are coin-dated to the second quarter of the fifth century and the mid-fifth century: Rudolf Moosbrugger-Leu, *Die Schweiz zur Merowingerzeit: Die archäologische Hinterlassenschaft der Romanen, Burgunder und Alamannen,* 2 vols. (vols. A-B), Handbuch der Schweiz zur Römer- und Merowingerzeit (Bern: A. Francke, 1971), A: 58–59, 221. Other finds are either undatable or too fragmentary to allow assessment, and a few may be reused from older graves, for example, one now strung sideways in a strand of glass beads: Vilém Hrubý, *Uherské Hradiste-Sady, stredisko velkomoravské kultury a moci* (Brno: Maravské Muzeum, 1975), p. 17.

13. Joachim Werner, "Herkuleskeule und Donar-Amulett," *Jahrbuch des Römisch-Germanischen Zentralmuseums Mainz* 11 (1964): 176–97; Audrey L. Meaney, *Anglo-Saxon Amulets and Curing Stones* (Oxford: British Archaeological Reports, 1981). This usage will be explored in my forthcoming book, *Amulets, Power, and Identity in Early Medieval Europe* (Oxford: Oxford University Press).

14. Birgit Arrhenius, "Bergkristall," *Reallexikon der Germanischen Altertumskunde,* 2nd ed. (Berlin: Walter de Gruyter, 1976), 2: 267–69. For finds probably from this area, especially Crimea, Inciser Gürçay Damm, "Goldschmiedearbeiten der Völkerwanderungszeit aus dem nördlichen Schwarzmeergebiet: Katalog der Sammlung Diergardt 2," *Kölner Jahrbuch für Vor- und Frühgeschichte* 21 (1988): 65–210. I am grateful to the author for a copy of this work and discussing the objects with me. Fourteen-sided beads (restrung) of garnet and carnelian: Damm, "Goldschmiedearbeiten," no. 42; of crystal, nos. 47, 48. Carnelian: Bucur Mitrea and Constantin Preda, *Necropole din secolul al IV lea e.n. în Muntenia*

(Bucharest: Editura Academiei Republicii Socialiste România, 1966), p. 186. Examples from just one area, readily accessible in Mitrea and Preda, *Necropole*: from Spantov: Mitrea and Preda, *Necropole*, p. 20 and fig. 6 (grave 3 no. 3), p. 24 and fig. 31 (grave 16 no. 6), p. 38 and fig. 87 (grave 63 no. 15); p. 39 and fig. 91 (grave 65 no. 7); p. 40 and fig. 94 (grave 67 no. 7); from Independenta: Mitrea and Preda, *Necropole*, p. 48 and fig. 108 (grave 3 no. 17), p. 49 and fig. 117 (grave 7 no. 9), p. 54 and fig. 141 (grave 25 no. 9); from Olteni: Mitrea and Preda, *Necropole*, p. 63 and fig. 158 (grave 25 no. 3).

15. For Roman faceted glass, see Donald B. Harden et al., *Glass of the Caesars: The Corning Museum of Glass, Corning, the British Museum, London, Römisch-Germanisches Museum, Cologne* (Milan: Olivetti, 1987), pp. 179–88 and nos. 102–06.

16. Hermann Günter Rau, "Facettschliffgläser und die Chronologie der Spätkaiserzeit," *Archäologisches Korrespondenzblatt* 3 (1973): esp. n14 citing Russian literature [441–45].

17. See Arrhenius, "Bergkristall," p. 268.

18. See Heather, *Goths*, pp. 84–93 on what Gothic ethnicity may have meant in the fourth century.

19. Reinhard Wenskus, *Stammesbildung und Verfassung: Das Werden der frühmittelalterlichen Gentes* (Cologne: Böhlau, 1961); Alexander Callander Murray, "Reinhard Wenskus on 'Ethnogenesis', Ethnicity, and the Origin of the Franks," in Gillett, *On Barbarian Identity*, pp. 39–68.

20. For example, Jones, "Historical Categories," p. 224; Patrick Geary, "Ethnic Identity as a Situational Construct in the Early Middle Ages," *Mitteilungen der Anthropologischen Gesellschaft in Wien* 113 (1983): 15–26.

21. Walter Pohl, "Telling the Difference: Signs of Ethnic Identity," in *Strategies of Distinction: The Construction of Ethnic Communities, 300–800*, ed. Walter Pohl and Helmut Reimitz (Leiden: Brill, 1998), pp. 17–69.

22. Narrative definition accepted: Ian Wood, in Hans J. Hummer, "Franks and Alamanni: A Discontinuous Ethnogenesis," with discussion, in *Franks and Alamanni in the Merovingian Period: An Ethnographic Perspective*, ed. Ian Wood, Studies in Historical Archaeoethnology 3 (Woodbridge: Boydell Press, 1998), pp. 9–32, discussion p. 28; definition accepted but applicability questioned in Patrick Amory, *People and Identity in Ostrogothic Italy, 489–554* (Cambridge, UK: Cambridge University Press, 1997), p. 14 and passim.

23. Herwig Wolfram, *History of the Goths*, rev. ed., trans. Thomas J. Dunlap (Berkeley: University of California Press, 1988).

24. Wolfram, *History of the Goths*, pp. 64–75, 401 n116, and esp. 399 n78; Volker Bierbrauer, "Archäologie und Geschichte der Goten vom 1.-7. Jahrhundert. Versuch einer Bilanz," *Frühmittelalterliche Studien* 28 (1994): esp. 117–21, 133–34 [51–171].

25. Wolfram, *History of the Goths*, pp. 248–61, esp. 485 n51; Michel Kazanski, "Les Goths et les Huns: À propos des relations entre les barbares sédentaires

et les nomades," *Archéologie Médiévale* 22 (1992): 191–229; M. Kazanski
and R. Legoux, "Contribution à l'étude des témoignages archéologiques
des Goths en Europe orientale à l'époque des Grandes Migrations: la
chronologie de la culture Cerhjahov récente," *Archéologie Médiévale* 18
(1988): 7–53; Michael Kazanski, "Contribution à l'étude des migrations
des Goths à la fin du IVe siècle et au Ve siècle: le témoignage de
l'archéologie," in *Gallo-Romains, Wisigoths et Francs en Aquitaine, Septimanie
et Espagne: Actes des VIIe Journées internationales d'archéologie mérovingienne,
Toulouse, 1985,* ed. Patrick Périn (Rouen: Association française
d'Archéologie mérovingienne, 1991), esp. p. 11 [11–25].
26. Kunsthistorisches Museum Inv. VII B 23: 2.06 x 1.67 cm. Erika Zwierlein-
Diehl, *Die Antiken Gemmen des kunsthistorischen Museums in Wien,* 3 vols.
(München: Prestel, 1991), 3.1732:73–74. I am grateful to Dr. A. Bernhard
for permission to study and photograph the stone. The following argument is a condensation of my "The Seal of Alaric, *rex Gothorum,*" *Early
Medieval Europe,* forthcoming.
27. J.R. Martindale, *The Prosopography of the Later Roman Empire,* Vol. 2, *A.D.
395–527* (Cambridge, UK: Cambridge University Press, 1980), pp. 43–48.
28. Zwierlein-Diehl, *Antiken Gemmen,* pp. 73–74 with bibliography; and esp.
Percy Ernst Schramm, "Brustbilder von Königen auf Siegelringen der
Völkerwanderungszeit," in P.E. Schramm, *Herrschaftszeichen und
Staatssymbolik: Beiträge zu ihrer Geschichte vom dritten bis zum sechzehnten
Jahrhundert,* 3 vols. (Stuttgart: Hiersemann, 1954–1956), 1 (1954): 213–22;
also Herwig Wolfram, *Intitulatio I: Lateinische Königs- und Fürstentitel bis
zum Ende des 8. Jahrhunderts* (Graz: Hermann Böhlaus, 1967), pp. 77–79.
On *Rex* as a Roman title, Steven Fanning, "Emperors and Empires in
Fifth-Century Gaul," in *Fifth-Century Gaul: A Crisis of Identity?,* ed. John
Drinkwater and Hugh Elton (Cambridge, UK: Cambridge University
Press, 1992), pp. 288–97.
29. Andrew Gillett, "Was Ethnicity Politicized in the Earliest Medieval
Kingdoms?" in *On Barbarian Identity,* esp. pp. 92, 108–09 [85–121].
30. 541 epitaph of Seda, eunuch in the service of Theodoric (d. 526),
inscribed on an earlier sarcophagus: *"Corpus" della scultura paleocristiana
bizantina ed altomedioevale di Ravenna,* ed. Giuseppe Bovini, 3 vols.
(Rome: De Luca, 1968–1969), Vol. 2, Giselda Valenti Zucchini and
Mileda Bucci, *I sarcofagi a figure e a carattere simbolico* (1968), no. 42. Epitaph
of Agate from Milan, dated 512: Angelo Silvagni, *Monumenta Epigraphica
Christiana saeculo XIII antiquiora quae in Italiae finibus adhuc extant,* Vol. 2
fasc. 1, *Mediolanum* (Vatican: Pontificium Institutum Archaeologiae
Christianae, 1943), pl. 4 no. 6.
31. Stefan Krautschick, "Die Familie der Könige in Spätantike und
Frühmittelalter," in *Das Reich und die Barbaren,* ed. Evangelos K. Chrysos
and Andreas Schwarcz, Veröffentlichungen des Instituts für Österreichische
Geschichtsforschung 29 (Vienna: Böhlau, 1989), pp. 109–42. I am grateful to Jonathan Conant for this reference.

32. Philip Grierson and Melinda Mays, *Catalogue of Late Roman Coins in the Dumbarton Oaks Collection and in the Whittemore Collection: From Arcadius and Honorius to the Accession of Anastasius* (Washington, DC: Dumbarton Oaks, 1992), p. 74. I am grateful to Dr. Gudrun Bühl for permission to study the Dumbarton Oaks coins.

33. I here propose a more differentiated view of the missing items than other scholars, not simply insignia, but also military equipment. Compare, for example, Gerd G. Koenig, "Archäologische Zeugnisse westgotischer Präsenz im 5. Jahrhundert," *Madrider Mitteilungen* 21 (1980): esp. p. 223 [220–47 and pls. 59–67].

34. Compare a medallion of Theoderic, mounted as a brooch (Rome, 500?): Phillip Grierson, "The Date of Theoderic's Gold Medallion," *Hikuin* 11 (1985): 19–26.

35. Cassiodorus, *Variae* 3.1–4, ed. A.J. Fridh, CCSL 96 (Turnhout: Brepols, 1973), pp. 96–100; *The Variae of Magnus Aurelius Cassiodorus Senator*, trans. Samuel J.B. Barnish, Translated Texts for Historians (Liverpool: Liverpool University Press, 1992), pp. 45–49.

36. *Codex Justinianus* 11, title 12 (11), in *Corpus Iuris Civilis*, ed. Paul Krueger (Berlin: Weidmann, 1929), 1:433; trans. as title 11 in, "The Code of Justinian," *The Civil Law*, trans. S.P. Scott, 17 vols. in 7 (Cincinnati: The Central Trust Company, 1932), 15: 177–78.

37. Cassiodorus, *Variae* 1.45–46, pp. 49–52; *Variae*, trans. Barnish, pp. 20–24. See Danuta Shanzer, "Two Clocks and a Wedding: Theodoric's Diplomatic Relations with the Burgundians," *Romanobarbarica* 14 (1996–1997): 225–58.

38. This will be discussed in greater detail in my *Amulets, Power, and Identity* (see above, n13).

39. On shells as imports, Moosbrugger-Leu, *Schweiz zur Merowingerzeit*, A:224 (see above, n12). On trade with the empire, E.A. Thompson, *The Visigoths in the Time of Ulfila* (Oxford: Clarendon Press, 1966), pp. 34–43. See also the essay by Florin Curta in this volume, on inter-elite gift exchange.

40. Marlia Mundell Mango, "Silver Plate among the Romans and among the Barbarians," in *La Noblesse romaine et les chefs barbares du IIIe au VIIe siècle*, ed. Françoise Vallet and Michel Kazanski, Mémoires publiées par l'Association Française d'Archéologie Mérovingienne 9 ([Rouen]: Association Française d'Archéologie Mérovingienne and Musée des Antiquités Nationales, 1995), pp. 77–88.

41. Kevin Greene, "Gothic Material Culture," in *Archaeology as Long-Term History*, ed. Ian Hodder (Cambridge, UK: Cambridge University Press, 1987), esp. p. 125 [117–31]. Also see Gisela Ripoll López, "Symbolic Life and Signs of Identity in Visigothic Times," in *The Visigoths from the Migration Period to the Seventh Century: An Ethnographic Perspective*, ed. Peter Heather, Studies in Historical Archaeoethnology 4 (Woodbridge: Boydell Press, 1999), esp. p. 412 [401–46].

42. On a member of a "noble" family, existing from the third/fourth century, with discussion, Peter Heather, "The Creation of the Visigoths," in *Visigoths from the Migration Period*, esp. pp. 59, 73 [41–92]. I am also evoking here the idea of the *Traditionskern* from Wenskus and Wolfram, a relatively small group that set the program for the artificial development of unifying characteristics of identification. Heather argues for a wider definition of such an elite: *Goths*, pp. 300–03 (see above, n11).

43. Compare, with discussion, Frank Siegmund, "Social Structure and Relations," in *Franks and Alamanni in the Merovingian Period*, pp. 177–212 (see above, n22).

44. For example, Heather, "Creation of the Visigoths," p. 55; Heather, *Goths*, pp. 52, 130–65.

45. For example, Hermann Hinz, "Am langen Band getragene Bergkristallanhänger der Merowingerzeit," *Jahrbuch des Römisch-Germanischen Zentralmuseums Mainz* 13 (1966): 212–30 (a group to be discussed at greater length in my *Amulets, Power, and Identity*).

CHAPTER 3

ETHNIC AND PRIMITIVE PARADIGMS IN THE STUDY OF EARLY MEDIEVAL ART

Lawrence Nees

Discussion of the detrimental effect in early medieval art history of the "ethnic paradigm," which has fostered primitivist interpretations of artistic conventions and distorted ideas about their transmission.

Thomas Kuhn has much to say about stubborn adherence to an under-lying paradigm, a tendency apparently embedded deep in human psychology. In his classic discussion of the issue, Kuhn quotes one study in which people persisted in identifying playing cards as "normal" even when shown cards that were obviously impossible, such as a red six of spades or a black four of hearts.[1] Scholars tend to be conservative; expertise is often associated with conviction,[2] and paradigms are resistant to change partly because they are literally taken for granted. So one should probably view as a hopeful sign of the growing recognition that a paradigm shift is needed in the study of early medieval art that, in 1992, Per Jonas Nordhagen, referring (to me, ironically) to Kuhn's theoretical presentation, criticized Ernst Kitzinger for proposing we substitute a new paradigm of "stylistic modes" for the older one of "local schools." This older paradigm was codified in 1924, in a famous diagram by Charles Rufus Morey that Nordhagen thought still fundamentally valid.[3] On its face, the local schools concept seems geographical, contrasting traditions primarily associated with different cities; but Morey revealed he was thinking in terms of ethnic distinctions when he described one of his major trends as "neo-Attic" and another as "Asiatic," evoking a dichotomy that goes back to Aeschylus.[4]

The ethnic paradigm has had remarkable staying power, especially in art historical discourses concerning the early medieval period. In these it has often been linked with concepts of primitivism, contrasting allegedly pure, autochthonous, ethnically linked barbarian artistic traditions with the civilized art of the classical Greco-Roman world. Two widely used recent college textbooks on medieval art begin the story with the Christian Roman Empire of Constantine and his successors, followed by summary treatment of Byzantine art, before turning to the emergence of a distinctive new tradition in northern and northwestern Europe. In 1986, Marilyn Stokstad opened her chapter, "Barbarian Art" with, "barbarian tribes [who were]...nomadic bands of brutal warriors," and began the discussion of artistic material with prehistoric, Celtic La Tène style metalwork said to represent a combination of Mediterranean motifs "with their native geometric decoration."[5] The nomadic barbarians were said to have migrated into the Roman world; but in Stokstad's formulation, "even after they accepted Christianity, the barbarian artists did not forget their ancestors' worship of the forces of nature and creation," especially various forms of animals "once employed as tribal totems."[6] In 1989, James Snyder began the story of medieval as opposed to early Christian and Byzantine art with a chapter titled, "The North." This opened with Bede's famous comparison between the life of man and a sparrow taking refuge from a winter storm in a great royal hall. Snyder linked the new artistic tradition to the northern climate and geography of "cold, icy crags and fearsome mountains" that sound rather more like Tolkien stories than the actual geography of northern Europe, whose mountains do not, after all, begin to compare in height with those of Spain and Italy; most of the area of northern Germany and southern Scandinavia widely conceived as the "homeland" of the barbarians is, in fact, exceptionally flat. "Terrifying elemental forces were always at hand...fierce monsters, both seen and imagined." The "arts of these wandering peoples" and "nomadic tribes" were derived from the ancient art of the steppes reaching as far as China.[7] These passages introduce various critical terms laden with programmatic connotations, to some of which I shall return: tribal, ancestors, wandering, animals, decoration, totem. Together they construct the art of the early medieval as quintessentially "primitive" and evoke a constellation of associated concepts: anonymity and ethnic group identity as opposed to individuality, traditionalism and copying as opposed to invention or originality, abstraction as opposed to naturalism.

It is not only important textbooks that cling to the ethnic or primitive conception of early medieval art, linking it with supposedly "tribal" and ethnic origins and significance. Most museums known to me still exhibit their collections and publish catalogs of material according to (allegedly) ethnic categories: Lombard fibulae, Frankish brooches, Anglo-Saxon jewelry, Celtic pins, and the like. The collections and catalogs are themselves variously termed "the Dark Ages" or, following German academic tradition, die *Völkerwanderungszeit*, "the Age of Migrations."[8] The approach has connections to archaeology, but little beyond scholarly custom ever supported this terminology; for the most part, it is geography masquerading as demographics. Recently, Bonnie Effros reviewed this archaeological tradition, effectively pointing out that plausible interpretations of the material evidence taking into account personal selection, gift-exchange, and so on have been, and in some cases still are, ignored in favor of ethnic readings.[9] More scientifically defensible would be to catalog these objects simply from their find spots as Italian, French, Spanish, or English; though obviously anachronistic, such terms are merely (if confusingly) geographic. Why continue to use the ethnic terminology? What does it tell us that we do not already know or believe? The answer rests on two fundamental and related but distinct bases: our sources, and ourselves.

★   ★   ★

Modern scholarly acceptance of ethnic terminology stems at least in part from our sources. Snyder's opening words about early medieval art in "the North" explicitly invoke Bede, and his focus on the frosty weather is at least indirectly inspired by the opening of Paul the Deacon's *History of the Lombards*.[10] Behind our medieval sources stand the ancient sources that helped shape them; Eleanor Duckett's designation of Bede's great history as an English *Aeneid* acknowledges the strong classical tradition Bede follows.[11] Vergil's story of the arrival from disparate homelands and mingling of separate Trojan, Latin, and Arcadian peoples to make the new race of Romans evidently underlies the tropes to explain the origins of barbarian "peoples" deployed by other early authors such as Jordanes.[12] The division of humanity into groups regarded as "tribes," and the notion that history is made by the migration of those tribes to new places are as old as the historical discipline, a potent traditional view strengthened by frequent repetition as well as an appealing way of spinning a yarn. Thucydides began his story of the Peloponnesian War with its deep background, a Hellas of old inhabited by migrating tribes, except in the case of his own city of Athens.[13] Aristotle, and following him Roman historians such as Tacitus, listed the special characteristics of different peoples.[14] Perhaps the most widely known text, in the minds of medieval as of modern readers, for this conception of ethnic or national character is Vergil's summing up of the destiny of

Romans: "For other peoples will, I do not doubt, still cast their bronze to breathe with softer features, or draw out of the marble living lines, plead causes better…but your will be the rulership of nations [*populos*], remember, Roman, these will be your arts."[15]

In its current avatar, this idea only emerged at the end of the nineteenth and, especially, first half of the twentieth century. In his introduction to the 1889 publication of essays by S.R. Maitland, for example, titled *The Dark Ages*, Frederick Stokes followed Maitland in concentrating on issues of religion, not only as the object of study in a medieval "age of faith" but as the issue dominating contemporary discourse on the Middle Ages, and he distinguished the historical views of Protestant from Catholic historians.[16] Arnold Angenendt has also discussed the importance of this confessional divide in modern historical writings on the early medieval period.[17] This alternative paradigm did not remain significant, however, but was replaced in the twentieth century with ethnicity as a framework of thought whose history and implications need to be recognized and unpacked, and in my view largely rejected. In this brief essay I should like to offer, as an exemplum, some remarks on modern treatments of the origins of medieval book illumination in the seventh and eighth centuries. A convenient focus will be two pages given over entirely to ornament. One, prefacing the Gospel of Mark in the Lindisfarne Gospels, counts among the most famous works of the period (figure 3.1);[18] the other is among the earliest—if not the earliest—surviving examples of such a composition, in a manuscript of Orosius from Bobbio now in Milan (figure 3.2).[19]

To my knowledge, no one has tried to compare the two designs or noticed that the inner frame around the central medallion of the Lindisfarne page has an implicit eight-petal rosette formed by the changing colors of the interlace; the blue-grey, cardinal points, and yellow make an x-shaped pattern that may be related to the large eight-petal forming the center of the Orosius page's composition. Both pages also have framed medallions in the four corners around the central medallion, creating a quincunx pattern, and the whole composition is set within a broad ornamented frame. The ornament *per se* is different of course, as are the materials, colors, and finesse of execution. But the general theme, syntax, and function make for what seems to me a far better comparison than any of the jewels from Sutton Hoo, with which the Lindisfarne design has been commonly linked and from which it is often supposed to be derived. Although Françoise Henry noted the chronological priority of the Bobbio page as a purely ornamental composition (she calls it a "page-tapis"), she saw the Irish as very much the leaders within the shared development; Bobbio's early decorated manuscripts seemed to her isolated

Figure 3.1 London, British Library Cotton MS Nero D. IV, fol. 94v, Lindisfarne Gospels, ornamental page before the Gospel of Mark. Photo: London, British Library, by permission.

both in their script and in their decoration within the Italian context. That the ornamental patterns of the Orosius page are all simple variations on common Mediterranean patterns, and that the overall quincunx composition could be paralleled within earlier Italian manuscripts like the

Figure 3.2 Milan, Biblioteca Ambrosiana, cod. D. 23 sup., fol. 1v, Orosius manuscript from Bobbio, ornamental page as headpiece, (redrawing, after T.D. Kendrick et al., *Evangeliorum quattuor Codex Lindisfarnensis* [Olten and Lausanne: Urs Graf Verlag, 1960], pl. 20). Photo by kind persmission of Urs Graf Verlag.

probably sixth-century Ambrose manuscript in St. Paul im Lavanthal,[20] did not dissuade her from deriving the Bobbio decoration from Irish exemplars later in date. Henry shared with other scholars of her generation a general preference for the view that the ornament of early Insular books descended from "primitive" Celtic and/or Germanic traditions,[21] especially after the discovery of the Sutton Hoo ship burial in 1939. Janet Backhouse and George Henderson are just two among a great many who have made this comparison,[22] implicitly deriving the book art from the metalwork; the latter was itself constructed as part of an ancient inherited and ethnically marked tradition, although works from Sutton Hoo that themselves seemed to be far from pure and, indeed, appeared to reflect prototypes in the form of book art or textiles were almost totally ignored.[23] The Orosius page in Milan (figure 3.2) was universally recognized as the earliest page completely devoted to ornament;[24] but because its ornament was manifestly based on Mediterranean traditions of rosettes and twist patterns, it could not be seen as developmentally early, or primitive, or a point from which the Lindisfarne page could be developed. Recognizing the chronological problem, E.A. Lowe provided a striking instance of trying to make the evidence fit the paradigm rather than challenging the validity of the paradigm when he suggested, in spite of the total lack of supporting physical evidence, that "the decoration [of the Orosius page] is perhaps a later addition" because "it is not at all typically Insular." [25]

I agree with Jonathan Alexander that the new art we call manuscript illumination has among its "fundamental principles...an alternation and counterpoint of forms which stresses always the ambiguity of relationships."[26] My difference of opinion with him is that I find such principles very much at play in the Orosius from Bobbio, and even more so in some manuscripts associated with Luxeuil, such as the splendid copy of Gregory the Great's commentary on Ezechiel in St. Petersburg, codex Z.v.I.13.[27] The degree of difference between such works and the Lindisfarne Gospels is in my view quantitative, rather than qualitative, and I have little faith that, given the highly fragmentary nature of our surviving evidence, we can really ascribe priority to one area or center within what is fundamentally a shared tradition. We should probably give greater scope to travel by artists as well as books, to the memory of artists and patrons. I shall argue in detail elsewhere that the decoration of continental books such as the Bobbio Orosius and the Luxeuil St. Gregory deploys a sophisticated and extensive vocabulary and, especially, syntax of decoration yet evinces no trace of any specifically Insular theme or ornament, and no direct relationship to metalwork. Although fundamentally distinct, it emerges from later Roman and early Christian art and book decoration; even without the issue of chronological priority, it is unlikely to have been adapted from an imported model such as the Book of Durrow or Lindisfarne Gospels and translated back into a more traditional, late antique ornamental vocabulary. Why then insist on Insular priority? It is just here that a consideration of the historiographical tradition reveals the central role of the ethnic and primitive paradigms.

In a well-known 1977 book, in which this ornamental page from the Lindisfarne Gospels serves as one illustration,[28] Carl Nordenfalk presented the new style of book decoration emerging between the sixth and eighth centuries in a Hegelian manner, as a synthesis between the "historic civilization" of the Roman world transmitted through Christianity, and the "prehistoric character" of the British Isles.[29] The association of the Irish with nature as opposed to law, or what Lowe described as the tendency of the Irish scribe to "whim and fancy" rather than ordered discipline (which pertained to "the English genius"), [30] conceived as a criticism as early as the work of David Hume,[31] helped establish the dramatically un-Roman quality of the new kind of manuscript illumination associated with the British Isles. When Romanticism revalued the place of nature and imagination in developing works of art, the primitive then became linked with the creative, the original, the Other. In her stimulating recent study of Arthur Kingsley Porter's 1931 book, *The Crosses and Culture of Ireland*, Carol Neuman de Vegvar develops the theme of the supposedly autochthonous character of early medieval art in Ireland in relationship to the personal and political context in which Porter was thinking and writing.[32] The title of an influential paper by Kenneth Jackson exemplifies this trend of scholarship and culture with an often cited metaphor, "The Oldest Irish Tradition: A Window on the Iron Age."[33] In recent years, the older views espoused by Porter and many others of Irish "primitivism" and isolation have been castigated as nativism and subjected to trenchant criticism,[34] including strong empirical challenges to the assumption that the purportedly "ancient, pagan" Irish heroic poems upon which Porter believed cross iconography to draw were ancient at all, rather than works of the Christian period.[35] As long ago as 1985, Patrick Sims-Williams contributed an important, and humorous, warning about the special construction of the "Visionary Celt" in the modern period.[36] The conception is one aspect of the master narrative of modern western European and American historiography: the development of the uniquely "modern" west is sketched against varying Others, whose art and history are themselves construed within a western historiographical perspective and western assumptions that such Others are primitive and tribal, and their art anonymous, even when we have abundant sources showing that such is not the case.[37]

Nordenfalk's 1977 book should be seen in connection with this broader historiographical tradition, which was already sketched in 1916 in Ernst Heinrich Zimmermann's still fundamental, four-volume corpus. Zimmermann treated, first, books produced on the continent and, second, those produced in the British Isles and on the continent in what he considered Insular style; style construed in ethnic categories took precedence over geography. The continental books, including those from the Frankish monasteries of Luxeuil and Corbie, the former founded by the Irish missionary Columbanus and the latter three quarters of a century later by monks from Luxeuil, were recognized as stemming from a late Roman Mediterranean tradition of ornament and layout; but for Zimmermann the Insular and Insular-style books were completely different ["ganz anders"], representative of a different point of departure and an entirely independent development.[38] This is scarcely the place to reassess the Irish contribution to early medieval art and culture, a rich subject in which many scholars have tried to steer between an Iromaniac Scylla and an Irophobic Charybdis.[39] In recent years, eminent scholars have taken positive and negative views,[40] and these will continue to be productively debated. The convenient term "Insular" was coined by Ludwig Traube for the script ["insulare Schrift"][41] precisely because it is so difficult to distinguish between manuscripts written in Irish, Welsh, or Anglo-Saxon centers on paleographical grounds. Scholars such as Ludwig Bieler who used the term "Insular" on some occasions nonetheless could continue to suggest that "Irish script" was an acceptable substitute, given the alleged leading role of the Irish in its development.[42]

Nordenfalk combined the tradition of Insular and especially Irish alterity with another distinctive element. Referring to the impact of Christianity upon primitive Irish culture, he wrote, "the very process of writing changed from a simple means of communication to something almost talismanic, by being combined with ornament."[43] The script, he stated already in a groundbreaking article of 1947, was no longer "taboo" to the painter.[44] The language of magic is important and revealing here, identifying the new book decoration as pertaining to the critical category of "primitive" then, and to a remarkable degree still, associated with non-western peoples and cultures.[45] In 1947, Nordenfalk saw the decisive moment of origin for Insular book illumination in the late seventh century and its place of origin in Northumbria, where it "makes contact with the great culture streams, the Nordic-Germanic and the Roman-Oriental." The new style is associated not so much with a cultural context as with "peoples"; in keeping with the chosen title of his 1977 book, *Celtic and Anglo-Saxon Painting*, the subject is identified not by political dynasty, location, or style, but by categories presumed to describe the ethnicity of its makers.

The long debate about the respective roles of Irish and Anglo-Saxons in the development of Insular art tells us a good deal more about the agendas and prejudices of modern scholars than of early medieval monks and artists, for whom these ethnic categories are inappropriate on many levels.[46] Further, it obscures a more fundamental issue invoking the essentialist paradigm, according to which differing artistic traditions are associated with "ethnic" groups conceived as if stable breeding and cultural populations. All sides, in other words, seem explicitly or implicitly to have accepted that a new artistic phenomenon for which we have scanty documentary evidence should be understood as the product of "new peoples," in this context "the barbarians." Such attempts to solve the mystery of a work of art's origin by identifying its ethnic character have been commonplace. To give but one example, in his discussion of the *Edictus Rothari* fragments scattered among St. Gallen and several other libraries, Alban Dold concluded that the manuscript must be attributed to Bobbio, on "Lombard ground," and seen as free of influence from Luxeuil or Ireland because of its "'nationalem germanischem Gut' [national Germanic assets] exemplified by the frequent use of animal heads in the initials."[47] Bobbio is as much "Lombard" (Germanic) to Dold as it was "Irish" to Henry, and with as little evidence. Such a view recognizably rests on the same underlying paradigm and assumptions as a remark by Meyer Schapiro that, "you cannot read James Joyce's *Finnegan's Wake* without thinking often of the Book of Kells; and modern Irish literature abounds in poetic details that remind one of features of the old manuscript."[48] Schapiro went on to suggest that, in combination—to be sure—with other factors, he was thus "inclined to believe" that the manuscript was written either in Ireland or, if produced in England or Scotland as some scholars had argued, by "migrant Irish monks." Schapiro was a brilliant scholar; his lectures of 1968, published posthumously only in 2005, from which I quoted, are still worth reading and an important contribution to the field, full of fresh ideas and insights. I hope, however, that such commonality of thought among scholars as diverse as Dold, Henry, and Schapiro makes clear that this ethnic paradigm is not national (German, Franco-Irish, American), political (right- or left-wing), or confessional (Catholic, Protestant, Jewish), but simply modernist, a view shared widely for much of the twentieth century. We should contest this reasoning not because of its historical associations (though it would be unwise to ignore the lurking dragons), nor in order to defend the whimsicality of the English or the rationalism of the Irish, but because it is a blunt scholarly tool—circular reasoning based on prejudicial assumptions.

The ethnic designation is almost always impossible to verify in a meaningful way, and even if we could do so it would not tell us anything useful. It is, therefore, a dead end for historical investigation.

The designation of early medieval art as "primitive" or "barbaric" is partly achieved, of course, by imposing the classical bias that an artistic tradition whose focus is not the human figure rendered in an (apparently) more-or-less naturalistic mode falls beyond the pale of the "civilized." Ernst Kitzinger's wonderful 1940 essay *Early Medieval Art* relates how, despite the impact of Christian missions and the emulation of Mediterranean models in "the North," "the barbaric spirit soon gained the upper hand again."[49] He illustrates this point with the production of "pages covered entirely with ornament, a thing unheard of in the book illumination of the South," to whose miniaturists "a leaf bearing nothing but ornament would have appeared meaningless." Kitzinger then proceeds to link this essentially ornamental art with Coptic and other "oriental influence." [50] In fact, his description of the Mark ornamental page in the Lindisfarne Gospels (figure 3.1) as covered with "carpet-like patterns" is the earliest example I have yet found, at least in English, of the "carpet" analogy, which any survey of more recent literature, including general books, shows to have become ubiquitous.[51] It is an index of the changing scholarly language and interpretation that in the 1940 edition of Kitzinger's book the caption to the illustration of this leaf identifies it as an "ornamental page," but the caption to the same illustration in the slightly revised 1983 edition identifies it as a " 'Carpet-page,' " setting the term in quotation marks.[52]

The "orientalist" interpretation of the beginnings of medieval book illumination in northwestern Europe seems primarily a phenomenon of the twentieth century, especially its later decades, rather than a heritage from the nineteenth century. For example, writing in 1921 about the same Lindisfarne Gospels that struck Kitzinger as reminiscent of carpets and redolent of oriental influence, Gerard Baldwin Brown was at pains to argue that although "the pages of pure ornament... are not classical in the sense that they were directly derived from antique models... [they] *are* [his emphasis] classical in that sense that they are based on fundamental principles of design that are in evidence in classical work but not in oriental, the latter characterized by an 'all-over' rather than a balanced and focused pattern."[53] In describing the same feature in his 1843–1845 *Art of Illuminated Manuscripts*, J.O. Westwood illustrated no entirely ornamental pages from the Lindisfarne or any other manuscript. A mere two sentences were devoted to a feature described as a "page completely covered with colored tessellated patterns of the utmost intricacy, generally disposed so as to form a cruciform design in the center of the page"; this attribute, he says, is "entirely peculiar to manuscripts executed in Ireland, or by the Irish scholars."[54] In his 1935 textbook written with J.J. Garrison, David Robb referred to the barbarism of the "decorative abstract patterns" in Insular manuscripts,[55] whereas his general book on manuscript illumination of 1971 refers to the "so-called carpet page of almost purely ornamental design."[56] The widespread use of the term "carpet page" and related formulations, more significant, in my view, than its moment of first use, seems to be during and in the decades following World War II. In 1954 Robert Branner referred to "monumental pages-tapis," a term he restricted to Insular manuscripts, not the Luxeuil manuscripts that were his subject; for in his opinion, "the Luxeuil style has no inner rhythm or organization."[57]

The term "carpet page" does not seem to be a heritage from the nineteenth-century heyday of "orientalist" painting and literature, although it surely reflects that tradition obliquely. Kitzinger was perhaps drawing upon his important earlier works on Anglo-Saxon vine-scroll ornament, Coptic sculpture, and the imported Sutton Hoo silver.[58] In this context, the epithet seems natural and innocent enough, and useful, although the connotations and associations, which Christopher De Hamel has rightly labeled "evocative,"[59] came, I believe, to enhance its appeal and help validate an "orientalist" interpretation. Words matter! Joined with Henri Pirenne's pivotal *Mahomet et Charlemagne*, published in 1937 and translated into English in 1939,[60] which argued for Mediterranean continuity and an extensive east–west trade through the seventh century ruptured only by the Islamic conquests, Kitzinger's studies created a strong hypothetical case for Coptic and other "oriental influence" upon the art of the early medieval west. Within the same historiographical tradition, a brief article by Harry Bober and the many studies by his student, Martin Werner, have been widely received as authoritative especially by non-specialists in the area.[61] In 1968, Nordenfalk proposed that a surviving sixteenth-century Persian manuscript of Tatian's *Diatessaron* served as evidence that the Book of Durrow in particular, and by extension Insular book illumination in general, rested upon the impact of an early import from the Christian Orient. Schapiro thoroughly and effectively rebutted this hypothesis only five years later, and Nordenfalk himself withdrew much of it,[62] yet some writers continue to accept Nordenfalk's 1968 article; a widely read book by William Dalrymple is one instructive example.[63] This reception history points toward scholars' predisposition in favor of this manner of looking at the history of art. It is the story our culture wants to hear told.

The growing use of the term "carpet page" with its orientalist connotations, and the increasing disposition to see early medieval manuscript illumination as derived from Coptic or other eastern sources, dates from the second quarter of the twentieth century: the period of crusading high Modernism, the triumph of the avant-garde. It is instructive to consider briefly the contemporary discourse around Modernist art and architecture in relation to that about medieval art and architecture. Publications associated with early stages of the International Style of architecture presented in a great MOMA exhibition of 1932 linked the taste for ornament with primitive peoples, lower cultures, women, and racial differences. In that year George Howe, architect of the first Modernist skyscraper in the United States, the PSFS Building in Philadelphia, published an article that compared two power plants. One was shown in a still taken from Fritz Lang's film, "Metropolis" representing a horror-world of smoke, darkness, and Victorian style; the other was an alternative future power plant, clean and uncluttered by ornament, with a caption telling the reader that "functional design" can establish order and "achieve architecture by an intense expression of the racial ideal."[64] Writing in 1931 about "this New Architecture" of the not-yet named International Style, the architect Norman Rice manages a breathtakingly condensed dismissal of ornament or decoration of all sorts as the preference of anyone not an upper-class white male in the western tradition. "Decoration," he states, "is of a sensorial order and belongs, primarily, to simple races, peasants and savages. Harmony and proportion incite the intellectual faculties and arrest the man of culture. Decoration is the essential overplus, the quantum of the peasant; proportion is the essential overplus, the quantum of the cultured man."[65] In a remarkably revealing illustration to his paper (whose other reproductions showed, as one might expect, buildings), Rice presented a pair of images of women: one, a nearly naked African woman adorned with scarifications, the other an elaborately garbed and coiffed upper-class western woman of Victorian taste if not date. The caption maligned "decoration, the essential overplus of the uncultured"[66] and the antithesis of the "new architecture" and new culture of the 1930s.

In Modernist twentieth-century discourses, ornament *per se* is constructed as primitive, barbaric, uncultured, female.[67] This conception passed at the time for "the latest in scientific evidence." Naomi Schor quotes Jean Larnac's 1929 history of French literature by women writers as making a distinction between women's preference for "the decorative, the concrete, the individual," where "men prefer what is most distant, the constructive, the general and the abstract."[68] Associating ornament with women is hardly new in the twentieth century; it has been traced as far back as ancient Greek and Roman sources.[69] In the eighteenth century, Lord Kames, writing about garden architecture and criticizing the overuse of "embellishments," linked this defect with a "woman who has not taste, [and] is apt to overcharge every part of her dress with ornament."[70] Kames's term "overcharge" is eerily reminiscent of Rice's strange usage "overplus"; one must also sadly note, however, that whereas for Kames such over-decoration was deemed characteristic only of women lacking in taste, by the twentieth century the criticism was reduced and essentialized to women in general. Cultures whose artistic traditions grant a very large role to ornament, such as the arts of Islam,[71] are in this scheme gendered as female, and also amalgamated with the primitive. In this light, it is interesting to note that in a very popular and widely distributed series of lectures presented in the late nineteenth century, published in 1902, John L. Stoddard wrote of Ireland that it was one of the "countries [that] are essentially feminine in character," and hence lovable. Thus Ireland is to be distinguished from those [here unnamed] "nations which are distinctively masculine in the aggressiveness, indomitable energy, and indefatigable pursuit of the practical at the expense of the ideal," nations more likely feared than loved.[72] Stoddard even published a photograph of cattle grazing by a stream with the caption, "a feminine landscape."[73] In such popular scholarly contexts, making the development of early Insular art, characterized then and often still as concentrated upon ornament, begin in the eternally barbarous context of Ireland or in a mythical ancient Germany made powerful sense.

It is by no means my intention to denigrate the achievements of Insular artists, nor to deny that during the eighth century the grandest achievements were produced in the Insular world. It is certainly noteworthy that Luxeuil and Bobbio were founded by an Irishman from northern Ireland, Columbanus. The "ethnic" constitution of such monasteries is unknown, unknowable, and not worth knowing. Names are a poor guide to ethnicity,[74] but Columbanus's successor at Bobbio was Atalanus, not an evidently Irish name, and his name occurs in one other important, early decorated book from Bobbio in the new style.[75] These extraordinary new books were created by individuals in a particular historical context; concerning both makers and context something can be known and knowledge increased. Reducing either to generic types, ethnic or otherwise, is the heritage of a viciously circular and reductive early modern categorialism,[76] and not a promising way forward.

Notes

1. Thomas S. Kuhn, *The Structure of Scientific Revolutions*, 3rd ed. (Chicago: University of Chicago Press, 1996), pp. 62–63.
2. For the rewards of being more a hedgehog than a fox see, Philip E. Tetlock, *Expert Political Judgment, How Good Is It? How Can We Know?* (Princeton: Princeton University Press, 2005).

3. Per Jonas Nordhagen, "C. R. Morey and His Theory on the Development of Early Medieval Art," *Konsthistorisk Tidsskrift* 61 (1992): 1–7, referring to Charles Rufus Morey, "The Sources of Medieval Style," *Art Bulletin* 7 (1924): 50 [35–50], cited and discussed in Lawrence Nees, "The Originality of Early Medieval Artists," in *Literacy, Politics, and Artistic Innovation in the Early Medieval West*, ed. Celia Chazelle (Lanham MD: University Press of America, 1992), p. 80 [77–109], fig. 1.

4. *Aeschylus I, Oresteia*, ed. and trans. Richmond Lattimore (Chicago: University of Chicago Press, 1953), p. 63, l. 919.

5. Marilyn Stokstad, *Medieval Art* (New York: Westview Press, 1986), p. 78.

6. Stokstad, *Medieval Art*, p. 82.

7. James Snyder, *Medieval Art: Painting–Sculpture–Architecture, 4th–14th Century* (Englewood Cliffs, NJ: Prentice Hall, 1989), p. 175.

8. *From Attila to Charlemagne: Arts of the Early Medieval Period in The Metropolitan Museum of Art*, ed. Katharine Reynolds Brown, Dafydd Kidd, and Charles T. Little (New York: Metropolitan Museum of Art, 2000). *Merowingerzeit: Die Altertümer im Museum für Vor- und Frühgeschichte*, ed. Marion Bertram (Berlin: Staatliche Museen and Mainz: Philipp von Zabern, 1995) often uses ethnic categories in the text, for example, "Fränkische Bügelfibeln" (p. 28, pls. 1–3), "Langobardische Bügelfibel" (p. 38 and pl. 10), "Westgotische Bügelfibelpaar," (p. 52, pl. 26); but the captions to the illustrations only use geographical terms (Frankreich, Italien, Spanien) that denote find spots or presumed origins without distinguishing between the two.

9. Bonnie Effros, "Dressing Conservatively: Women's Brooches as Markers of Ethnic Identity?," in *Gender in the Early Medieval World: East and West, 300-900*, ed. Leslie Brubaker and Julia M.H. Smith (Cambridge, UK: Cambridge University Press, 2004), p. 179 [165–84].

10. Paul the Deacon, *History of the Lombards*, 1.1, trans. William Dudley Foulke (Philadelphia: University of Pennsylvania Press, 1907, repr. 1974), p. 1.

11. Eleanor Duckett, *Anglo-Saxon Saints and Scholars* (New York: Macmillan, 1947), p. 320, as noted in Walter Goffart, *The Narrators of Barbarian History (A.D. 550–800): Jordanes, Gregory of Tours, Bede, and Paul the Deacon* (Princeton: Princeton University Press, 1988), p. 235.

12. See Goffart, *Narrators*, p. 89 and n. 331.

13. See *Thucydides*, trans. Charles Forster Smith, 4 vols. (Cambridge, MA: Harvard University Press, 1969), 1:3–5.

14. Aristotle, *Politics* 7.7.1327b, noted by Thomas Grane, "Roman Sources for the Geography and Ethnography of *Germania*," in *The Spoils of Victory: The North in the Shadow of the Roman Empire*, ed. Lars Jørgensen, Birger Storgaard, and Lone Gebauer Thomson (Copenhagen: Nationalmuseet, 2003), p. 127 [126–47].

15. *Aeneid* 6.847–51, in *P. Vergili Maronis Opera*, ed. R.A.B. Mynors (Oxford: Clarendon Press, 1969), p. 254; *The Aeneid of Virgil*, trans. Allen Mandelbaum (Berkeley: University of California Press:, 1971), p. 160. Augustine quotes these verses in *De civitate Dei* 5.12.

16. Frederick Stokes, "Introduction," in Samuel R. Maitland, *The Dark Ages: Essays Illustrating the State of Religion and Literature in the Ninth, Tenth, Eleventh, and Twelfth Centuries* (1889; repr. Port Washington, NY: J. Hodges, 1969), p. v.

17. Arnold Angenendt, *Das Frühmittelalter: Die abendländische Christenheit von 400 bis 900* (Stuttgart: Kohlhammer, 1990), pp. 27–29.

18. London, British Library, Cotton MS Nero D. IV, fol. 94v. Fundamental now is Michelle P. Brown, *The Lindisfarne Gospels: Society, Spirituality and the Scribe* (London: British Library, 2003), with earlier literature.

19. Milan, Biblioteca Ambrosiana, cod. D. 23 sup., fol. 1v. See Jonathan J.G. Alexander, *Insular Manuscripts, 6th to the 9th Century* (London: Harvey Miller, 1978), no. 3, figs. 6–7, with earlier literature.

20. MS 1, fol. 72v; see Robert Eisler, *Die illuminierten Handschriften in Kärnten* (Leipzig: Hiersemann, 1907), no. 53.

21. Françoise Henry, "Les Débuts de la miniature irlandaise," *Gazette des Beaux-Arts* 37 (1950): 24–26 [5–34]; Françoise Henry, *Irish Art in the Early Christian Period (to 800 A.D.)* (Ithaca: Cornell University Press, 1965), pp. 168–71, referring to the "primitive audacity . . . of an art . . . still at the stage of discovery and invention."

22. Janet Backhouse, *The Lindisfarne Gospels* (Oxford: Phaidon, 1981), pp. 74–75, pls. pp. 76–77; George Henderson, *From Durrow to Kells: The Insular Gospel-books, 650–800* ((London: Thames and Hudson, 1987), p. 32.

23. I address this issue in "Weaving Garnets: Thoughts about Two 'Excessively Rare' Belt Mounts from Sutton Hoo," in *Making and Meaning: Proceedings of the Fifth International Conference on Insular Art*, ed. Rachel Moss (Dublin: Four Courts Press, 2006), pp. 1–17.

24. Alexander, *Insular Manuscripts*, no. 3, with earlier literature.

25. *CLA* 3.328:17.

26. Alexander, *Insular Manuscripts*, p. 10.

27. *CLA* 11.1617, with description and bibliography. For a convenient color reproduction and brief discussion see Lawrence Nees, *Early Medieval Art* (Oxford: Oxford University Press, 2002), pp. 159–63 and pl. 91.

28. Carl Nordenfalk, *Celtic and Anglo-Saxon Painting* (New York: Braziller, 1977), pl. 20.

29. Nordenfalk, *Celtic and Anglo-Saxon Painting*, p. 7.

30. *CLA* 2:xvi; cited by Marco Mostert, "Celtic, Anglo-Saxon or Insular? Some Considerations on 'Irish' Manuscript Production and their Implications for Insular Latin Culture, c. AD 500–800," in *Cultural Identity and Cultural Integration: Ireland and Europe in the Early Middle Ages*, ed. Doris Edel (Dublin: Four Courts Press, 1995), pp. 92–115. See also Dáibhí Ó Cróinín, "Bischoff's *Wendepunkte* Fifty Years On," *Revue bénédictine* 110 (2000): 236–37 [204–37].

31. Discussed by Nancy Netzer, "The *Book of Durrow*: The Northumbrian Connection," in *Northumbria's Golden Age*, ed. Jane Hawkes and Susan Mills (Newcastle-upon-Tyne: Sutton Publishing, 1999), pp. 315–26.

32. Carol Neuman de Vegvar, "In the Shadow of the Sidhe: Arthur Kingsley Porter's Vision of an Exotic Ireland," *Irish Arts Review Yearbook* 17 (2001): 48–60. Porter's nativism was coupled with his orientalism, which prompted him to claim Coptic sources for certain iconographic motifs not found by him in Irish secular literature; see Neuman de Vegvar, loc. cit., 57, with references.

33. *The Oldest Irish Tradition: A Window on the Iron Age*, Rede Lectures (Cambridge, UK: Cambridge University Press, 1964).

34. Kim McCone, *Pagan Past and Christian Present in Early Irish Literature* (Maynooth: An Sagart, 1991) is perhaps the most vivid and comprehensive anti-nativist work.

35. N.B. Aitchison, "The Ulster Cycle: Heroic Image and Historical Reality," *Journal of Medieval History* 13 (1987): 87–116.

36. Patrick Sims-Williams, "The Visionary Celt: The Construction of an Ethnic Preconception," *Cambridge Medieval Celtic Studies* 11 (1986): 70–96.

37. Ikem Stanley Okoye, "Architecture, History and the Debate on Identity in Ethiopia, Ghana, Nigeria and South Africa," *Journal of the Society of Architectural Historians* 61 (2002): 381–96; Ikem Stanley Okoye, "Tribe and Art History," *Art Bulletin* 78 (1996): 610–15.

38. Ernst Heinrich Zimmermann, *Vorkarolingische Miniaturen, Textband* (Berlin: Deutscher Verein für Kunstwissenschaft, 1916), p. 20.

39. Compare, for example, Thomas Cahill, *How the Irish Saved Civilization* (New York: Doubleday, 1996); Johannes Duft, "Iromanie–Irophobie. Fragen um die frühmittelalterliche Irenmission, exemplifiziert an St. Gallen und Allemannien," *Zeitschrift für schweizerische Kirchengeshichte* 50 (1956): 241–62.

40. For strong claims against and for, respectively, Michael Gorman, "The Myth of Hiberno-Latin Exegesis," *Revue bénédictine* 110 (2000): esp. 55–59 [42–85], and Dáibhí Ó Cróinín, "The Irish as Mediators of Antique Culture on the Continent," in *Science in Western and Eastern Civilization in Carolingian Times*, ed. Paul Leo Putzer and Dietrich Lohrmann (Basel: Birkhauser, 1993), pp. 41–52.

41. Ludwig Traube, "*Perrona Scottorum*, ein Beitrag zur Überlieferungsgeschichte und zur Paläographie des Mittelalters," *Sitzungsberichte der philosophische-philologische and historische Classe der Königliche Bayerische Akademie der Wissenschaften* (1900), pp. 469–537, repr. in Ludwig Traube, *Kleine Schriften*, ed. Samuel Brandt (Munich: C.H. Beck, 1920, repr. 1965), pp. 95–119.

42. See Marco Mostert, "Celtic, Anglo-Saxon or Insular?"(see above, n30).

43. Nordenfalk, *Celtic and Anglo-Saxon Painting*, pp. 7–8.

44. Carl Nordenfalk, "Before the Book of Durrow," *Acta Archaeologica* 18 (1947): 141–74.

45. For early-twentieth-century discussions of Primitivism, taking sharply divergent approaches, see *"Primitivism" in 20th-Century Art: Affinity of the*

Tribal and the Modern, ed. William Rubin, 2 vols (New York: Museum of Modern Art, 1984); and Mark Antliff and Patricia Leighten, "Primitive," in *Critical Terms for Art History*, ed. Robert S. Nelson and Richard Shiff (Chicago: University of Chicago Press, 1996), pp. 170–84, with bibliography. For two among many recent treatments of this important and fascinating theme, see *Primitivism and Twentieth-Century Art: A Documentary History*, ed. Jack Flam with Miriam Deutch (Berkeley: University of California Press, 2003); and Ernst H. Gombrich, *The Preference for the Primitive: Episodes in the History of Western Taste and Art* (London: Phaidon, 2002).

46. Mostert, "Celtic, Anglo-Saxon or Insular?" (see above, n30), pp. 94–98.

47. Alban Dold, *Zur ältesten Handschrift des Edictus Rothari* (Stuttgart: Kohlhammer, 1955), referring to his fundamental earlier treatment: Alban Dold, "Zur Langobardengesetz," *Deutsches Archiv für Erforschung des Mittelalters* 4 (1940): 1–52. The main portion of the manuscript is St. Gallen, Stiftsbibliothek, cod. 730, for which see *Eremus und Insula: St. Gallen und die Reichenau im Mittelalter*, ed. Ernst Trempf, Karl Schmucki, and Theres Flury (St. Gallen: Am Klosterhof, 2002), pp. 115–17.

48. Meyer Schapiro, *The Language of Forms: Lectures on Insular Manuscript Art* (New York: Pierpont Morgan Library, 2005), pp. 176–77.

49. Ernst Kitzinger, *Early Medieval Art with Illustrations from the British Museum Collection* (London: British Museum, 1941), pp. 37–38.

50. Kitzinger, *Early Medieval Art*, p. 39.

51. Kitzinger, *Early Medieval Art*, p. 39, pl. 16. To take only a few, nearly randomly chosen examples: Stokstad, *Medieval Art*, p. 99; George Henderson, *Vision and Image in Early Christian England* (Cambridge, UK: Cambridge University Press, 1999), p. 42 (among many other instances); Christopher De Hamel, *A History of Illuminated Manuscripts* (London: Phaidon, 1986), p. 21; Otto Pächt, *Book Illumination in the Middle Ages: An Introduction*, translated by Kay Davenport from the 1984 German edition (London: Harvey Miller, 1986), p. 175; Robert Calkins, *Illuminated Books of the Middle Ages* (Ithaca: Cornell University Press, 1983), p. 36. Françoise Henry, *The Book of Kells* (London: Thames and Hudson, 1974), p. 182, uses the term "carpet-page" to refer to a completely reversible pattern of pure ornament, which "has almost probably [*sic*] an Oriental and more specifically a Coptic origin."

52. Ernst Kitzinger, *Early Medieval Art with Illustrations from the British Museum and British Library collections*, rev. ed. David Buckton (London: British Museum, 1983), pl. 5.

53. Gerard Baldwin Brown, *The Arts in Early England*, Vol. 5 (New York: E.P. Dutton, 1921), p. 332. See now, Robert Stevick, *The Earliest Irish and English Bookarts: Visual and Poetic Forms before A.D. 1000* (Philadelphia: University of Pennsylvania Press, 1994), which argues vigorously for the generation of such ornamental compositions using classical geometrical methods, yet sees their application as distinctively Insular.

54. J.O. Westwood, *The Art of Illuminated Manuscripts* (London: Bracken, 1988, repr. of *Palaeografia Sacra Pictoria*, London: William Smith, 1843–1845), s.v. Anglo-Saxon Gospels [no. 45], p. 3.

55. David Robb and J.J. Garrison, *Art in the Western World* (New York: Harper, 1935), pp. 460–61.

56. David Robb, *The Art of the Illuminated Manuscript* (Philadelphia: Philadelphia Art Alliance, 1971), p. 86.

57. Robert Branner, "The Art of the Scriptorium at Luxeuil," *Speculum* 29 (1954): 688 [678–90].

58. Ernst Kitzinger, "Anglo-Saxon Vinescroll Ornament," *Antiquity* 10 (1936): 61–71; Ernst Kitzinger, "The Sutton Hoo Finds: The Silver," *Antiquity* 14 (1940): 40–63.

59. De Hamel, *History*, p. 21 (see above, n51).

60. Henri Pirenne, *Mahomet et Charlemagne* (Paris: F. Alcan, 1937); Henri Pirenne, *Mohammed and Charlemagne*, trans. Bernard Miall (New York: Norton, 1939).

61. Harry Bober, "On the Illumination of the Glazier Codex: A Contribution to Early Coptic Art and Its Relation to Hiberno-Saxon Interlace," in *Homage to a Bookman: Essays on Manuscripts, Books and Printing Written for Hans P. Kraus on His Sixtieth Birthday*, ed. Hellmut Lehmann-Haupt (Berlin: Mann, 1967), 31–49; by Martin Werner (e.g.), "The Cross-Carpet Page in the Book of Durrow: The Cult of the True Cross, Adomnán and Iona," *Art Bulletin* 72 (1990): 174–223, with earlier literature.

62. Carl Nordenfalk, "An Illustrated Diatessaron," *Art Bulletin* 50 (1968): 119–40; Meyer Schapiro and Seminar, "The Miniatures of the Florence Diatessaron (Laurentian MS. Or. 81): Their Place in Late Medieval Art and Supposed Connection with Early Christian and Insular Art," *Art Bulletin* 55 (1973): 494–533; Carl Nordenfalk, "The Persian Diatessaron Once More," *Art Bulletin* 55 (1973): 534–46.

63. William Dalrymple, *From the Holy Mountain: A Journey among the Christians of the Middle East* (London: Harper Collins, 1997), pp. 108–11.

64. George Howe, "Functional Aesthetics and the Social Ideal," *Pencil Points* 13 (1932): 215–18. I am very grateful to David Brody for this reference.

65. Norman N. Rice, "This New Architecture," *T-Square Club Journal* 1 (1931): 33 [14–19, 31–33].

66. Rice, "This New Architecture," p. 19.

67. For a historiographical overview, see James Trilling, *The Language of Ornament* (London: Thames and Hudson, 2001).

68. Naomi Schor, *Reading in Detail: Aesthetics and the Feminine* (New York: Methuen, 1987), p. 17, quoting Jean Larnac, *Histoire de la littérature féminine en France* (Paris: Editions Kra, 1929), pp. 267–68. The quotation reproduced here is Schor's translation. I am grateful to Melody Deusner for this reference.

69. Schor, *Reading in Detail*, p. 19.

70. Cited in Schor, *Reading in Detail*, pp. 19–20; the quotation is attributed to a 1967 New York reprint edition of Kames's *Elements of Criticism*.

71. See Terry Allen, "The Arabesque," in his, *Five Essays on Islamic Art* (Manchester, MI: Solipsist Press, 1988), pp. 1–15; Eva Baer, *Islamic Ornament* (New York: New York University Press, 1998); Oleg Grabar, *The Mediation of Ornament* (Princeton: Princeton University Press, 1992).

72. *John L. Stoddard's Lectures: Supplementary Volume: Ireland (Two Lectures), Denmark, Sweden* (Boston: Balch, 1902), pp. 9–10.

73. *Stoddard's Lectures*, p. 9.

74. See bibliography in *Europe after Rome. A New Cultural History, 500-1000*, ed. Julia M. H. Smith (Oxford: Oxford University Press, 2005), pp. 323-24.

75. Milan, Biblioteca Ambrosiana, cod. S. 45sup, p. 2; Alexander, *Insular Manuscripts*, no. 2, pp. 27-28, fig. 8, with bibliography.

76. Harriet Ritvo, *The Platypus and the Mermaid and Other Figments of the Classifying Imagination* (Cambridge, MA: Harvard University Press, 1997).

CHAPTER 4

THE AMBER TRAIL IN EARLY MEDIEVAL EASTERN EUROPE

Florin Curta

> *Critique of the model of commercial transaction, with gift exchange proposed instead to explain the flow of Baltic amber into Black Sea regions as markers of elite status.*

Prestige goods of Scandinavian origin have often been excavated along the northern frontier of the early Byzantine Empire. For instance, several dress accessories (brooches and buckles) and bracteates found in sixth-century burial assemblages in Hungary display ornamental patterns that are most typical for the so-called Animal Style I, a tradition characteristic of the ornamental arts of early medieval Scandinavia.[1] Conversely, eagle-headed buckles produced in the region of present-day Hungary have been found on sites in Mazuria (northeastern Poland) that have been dated to the 500s.[2] Artifacts from the Middle Danube region have also been found in rich warrior burials in the Baltic lands, such as Taurapilis in Lithuania and Warnikam in the Kaliningrad *oblast'* of Russia.[3] The focus here is on a different type of prestige goods: amber beads. Against commercial conceptions of an Amber Trail, this essay argues that Baltic amber reached eastern Europe as a status marker acquired through inter-elite gift exchange.

The standard method employed in characterization studies of amber, namely infrared spectrography, can discriminate roughly between Baltic amber and amber from other European sources (Sicily, Germany, or Romania), although it cannot pinpoint the exact place of origin, nor can it distinguish artifacts made of drift amber from those of mined amber.[4]

The distribution of amber beads in eastern European sites shows two clear clusters; one is along the left bank of the Middle Tisza River, not far from the present-day border between Hungary and Romania, and the other—with an even larger quantity of beads—is in Crimea, where the sixth- to seventh-century cemetery in Suuk Su produced over 1,200 specimens (map 4.1).[5] Amber beads were also found in great quantity on sixth-century sites in the Caucasus region, especially in large cemeteries.[6] In general, more amber beads have been found with female than with

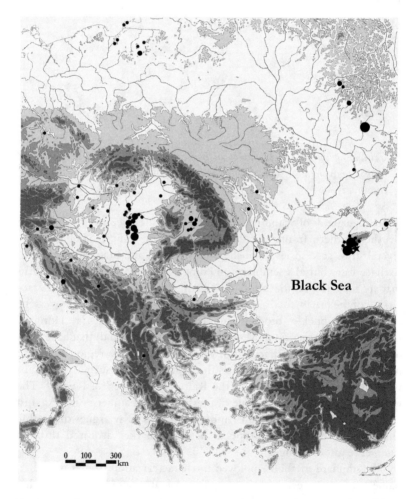

Map 4.1 Distribution of amber beads in late fifth- and sixth-century burial and hoard assemblages in eastern Europe. Smallest circle up to 5, thereafter up to 20, 50, 100, and 300 specimens. Star: over 1,000 beads.

male burials.[7] Only a few characterization studies have been conducted, but Emma Sprincz has sampled 105 beads from third- to sixth-century cemeteries in Hungary and found that all specimens were made of Baltic amber.[8]

The most common beads in Hungary are disc- or barrel-shaped, cylindrical, spherical, or elongated, and, in virtually all cases, handmade (rather than lathed). Most beads found on fifth- to sixth-century sites in Lithuania are also handmade, irregularly shaped, and often unpolished.[9] A pile of amber consisting both of manufactured beads and raw amber, found in the grave of an eighteen-year-old woman in Hódmezővásárhely-Kishomok (Hungary), suggests that at least some amber reached the Middle Danube region from the Baltic in raw form and that beads were then manufactured locally (although no sixth-century amber workshop has so far been identified in Eastern Europe). In other cases, amber may have been hand-processed in the Baltic region and sent to the Danube region in bead form. Whatever the efforts locally invested in the processing of raw amber, the distribution of beads shows that few specimens were redistributed into neighboring regions. The clusters of finds in the Middle Tisza and Crimea strongly point to the existence of limited areas of consumption, if not also production. Access to amber beads seems to have been restricted to specific groups in specific areas. Indeed, amber beads used as female dress accessories may have served as markers of group identity.[10]

How did amber reach the territories of present-day Hungary and Crimea, two regions in which it seems to have been in high demand in the mid-sixth century? During the first three centuries CE, amber traveled along the trade route linking the Baltic coast to the Roman provinces in central Europe and to the Adriatic coast.[11] That route remained in use in the mid-fifth century, as indicated by amber deposits found along the river Vistula.[12] But by 500, although amber still appears in central and southeastern Europe, the most conspicuous feature of its distribution is a general fall-off in quantity from the Baltic zone, particularly in those areas closest to the Baltic amber sources, as shown in table 4.1. Table 4.1 tabulates amber finds based on published archaeological reports. Because it is impossible to pinpoint the exact source of the amber, the distances are calculated as straight-line map measurements from the find spots to the nearest point on the southeastern Baltic coast. Furthermore, only amber beads identified as such in both the texts and the illustrations of the archaeological reports have been taken into account, which excluded from analysis amber beads appearing in an indistinguishable mass together with glass or carnelian beads. The numbers given in table 4.1 are thus to be viewed as minimal, and bear no implications for the overall volume of amber in circulation.

Table 4.1 Quantity of sixth- and seventh-century amber in eastern Europe in relation to the distance from source

Distance in km. from the nearest point on the southeastern coast of the Baltic Sea	Number of beads
0–250	23
251–500	0
501–750	9
751–1,000	318
1,001–1,250	189
1,251–1,500	1,692
1,501–1,750	6
1,751–2,000	1
2,001–2,250	16
	Total: 2,254

Table 4.1 reveals that almost all sixth- and seventh-century amber beads known from archaeological assemblages in eastern Europe have been found within a distance of 750–1,500 kilometers from the Baltic coast. Between ca. 500 and ca. 700, amber reached present-day Hungary and Crimea in far greater quantities than before, and the boundary of its distribution extended further south to the Black Sea shore in Crimea and to the Caucasus region. The quantity of amber, however, decreased markedly in those regions of eastern Europe closest to the Baltic coast. There were now greater quantities of amber farther away from the source than there were close to it, with a vast region in central and eastern Europe completely devoid of amber finds. This finding nicely dovetails with another pattern of distribution that has been established for the territory of present-day Lithuania. During the fifth and sixth centuries, funerary amber appears in Lithuania more frequently within a range of 75–100 kilometers away from the coastline, than it does on sites located either on the coast or much farther away (100–200 km.).[13]

The spotty pattern of distribution of amber beads revealed in table 4.1 cannot be fully explained through the paradigm of commercial exchange that currently dominates thinking on relations between southeastern Europe and the north, and which has been articulated by Nils Åberg, Joachim Werner, and Michael McCormick (among others). Åberg suggests that Scandinavian finds in Hungary indicate a commercial network in existence in the sixth century between Gotland and Italy, in which the territory of present-day Hungary played a major role.[14] Werner interprets the presence of so-called Slavic fibulae in mortuary assemblages in northeastern Poland as evidence for the continuation, after 600, of trade relations along an Amber Trail established in the 500s between the Danube region and the amber-rich region of Mazuria, although he simultaneously blames Avars and Slavs for interrupting, shortly after 600, regular trade relations between the Danube region and the Baltic coast.[15] In his book about long-distance trade as a major factor in the growth of the European economy, McCormick maintains that (at some point after 700) a new network of trade routes emerged between the Mediterranean and the upper and middle Danube following the southern segment of the ancient Amber Trail.[16] Following two centuries of apparent disruption caused by Lombards and Avars, Charlemagne's destruction of the Avar "kingdom" in the late eighth century brought back to life the ancient trade route.[17] Trade along an Amber Trail is even invoked to explain the presence of artifacts presumably of Lithuanian origin on sixth- and seventh-century sites in Belarus and the neighboring regions.[18]

The distribution of sixth-century finds, though, in relation to sources on the Baltic coast (as shown in table 4.1) suggests an exchange system very different from the down-the-line trade postulated for this period by Åberg, Werner, and McCormick. The presence of amber in sixth-century burial assemblages in central and southeastern Europe cannot be interpreted as trade, but must be accounted for otherwise.[19] Here I would like to pursue an explanation based on noncommercial models that have been advanced to illuminate exchange systems in traditional societies.[20] In the last few years the study of early medieval trade has played a major role in the search for a "post-Pirenne paradigm" as an overarching model to explain the transition from the classical to the medieval world.[21] The basis of this revival of interest has been the theoretical and methodological introduction of archaeology to the field of economic history. Karl Polanyi's classical distinction between reciprocity, redistribution, and market exchange has been adopted and much elaborated to assess the significance of "Dark Age economics."[22] Philip Grierson's equally influential critique of traditional approaches to commerce in the Dark Ages has received comparatively less attention from archaeologists.[23] To be sure, Grierson's thesis that during the early Middle Ages gift giving prevailed over "true" monetary commerce has been contradicted by extensive research on trade centers such as Birka, Hedeby (Haithabu), and Dorestad, all of which emerged ca. 700 as points of exchange for commodities such as precious metals and gems, tableware and glass, wine, textiles, and weapons.[24] But Grierson's conceptual distinction is fundamental for understanding some of the archaeologically observable phenomena. Following Marcel Mauss, he understood gift giving as a special form of transaction in which goods were transferred from donor to receiver, with the consent of the former, for social prestige rather than for material or tangible profit. The logic of gift giving is thus fundamentally different from that of trade, for the only "profit" one can hope to gain from making a present is to place the receiver in one's debt.

Despite the great potential this idea has for understanding the role of "exotic" artifacts in the representation of social status and power, the archaeology of early medieval gift giving is in its infancy. Old Roman coins or brooches deposited in sixth-century graves of the so-called *Reihengräberkreis* cemeteries and usually found in purses attached at the waist may have been small presents of apotropaic value, much like the contorniates Late Roman aristocrats were exchanging in Rome and Ravenna on various ceremonial occasions such as the New Year, birthdays, or weddings.[25] It is indeed ceremonial gifts that appear most prominently in written sources, but archaeologists have so far not explored all the possibilities offered by ceremonial contexts, despite the growing interest in material symbols, meaning, and practice.[26] Gifts, and not commodities, may provide a new avenue of research for scholars interested in such diverse phenomena as mortuary rituals, the representation of power, or matrimonial alliances. Despite the existence of some exploratory essays, much more work is needed before we can understand the complex articulation of noncommercial practices and trade in early medieval economics and politics.[27]

To build an alternative explanation for the particular distribution of amber finds in sixth- to seventh-century eastern Europe, one must first consider the relationship between the circulation of amber and its deposition. There are theoretically two possibilities: either the circulation coincided in space with the deposition, or it was an expansion of the practice of depositing amber in areas where it had been circulating from an early date. A careful examination of the archaeological record shows that the latter possibility cannot be easily dismissed. In Hungary, there is evidence of reuse of prehistoric amber pendants during the Avar period (ca. 570–ca. 700).[28] Elsewhere, the evidence of recycled amber is even more compelling. All amber beads found in the sixth- to seventh-century Shoinaiag cemetery, as well as on the contemporary cult sites at Borganǎel and Iuvakaiag in the Vychegda River region of northeastern Russia, although undoubtedly of Baltic origin, cannot be dated later than ca. 300, and must thus be viewed as recycled material.[29] The lathed beads found in a sixth-century burial in Miętkie (northeastern Poland) had been in circulation for at least fifty years before their deposition.[30] Finally, the amber bead carved in the shape of an African head found in a sixth-century female burial in Hódmezővásárhely (Hungary) is clearly of early Roman origin.[31]

In all other cases, however, the archaeological record suggests that amber artifacts were deposited with individuals on burial. This is particularly true for handmade, irregularly shaped beads, which appear in much greater quantities than lathed beads and have no analogies in earlier periods. No analogies are known in the lands by the Baltic Sea for the disc- and barrel-shaped beads, or for the elongated beads, found in burial assemblages in Hungary or Crimea, often in more than two specimens per burial.[32] Such beads were most likely produced locally and within the confines of the household, as suggested by their occasional association with pieces of raw amber. It appears likely that, in regions located at a considerable distance from the source, the deposition of amber was in direct relation to the amount in circulation. Conversely, where no archaeologically visible deposition of amber occurs during that same period, the conclusion can only be that amber was not circulating at all.

We have seen that sixth-century amber is found in particularly great quantities in Hungary and Crimea. Both regions are known for large cemeteries, in which members of the elite were buried together with other members of the community, and accompanied by considerable wealth in the form of silverwork and lavishly produced goods, often of foreign origin. Contacts between elites in these two regions at a great distance from each other have long been documented, and newly published materials indicate that, throughout the sixth century, each area maintained relations with the more northerly regions near the sources of amber.[33] But between the sources of amber on the Baltic Sea coast, on one hand, and the Middle Danube region and Crimea, on the other, there is a vast corridor completely devoid of amber finds. To be sure, parts of that region may have been only sparsely inhabited during the first half of the sixth century. However, amber is remarkably absent from sites in central and eastern Poland as well as western Ukraine, which have otherwise produced abundant material dated to the sixth century.[34] There is no amber on any of the many sites of the so-called Tushemlia or Kolochin cultures of the upper reaches of the Dvina and Dnieper Rivers, respectively.[35] Only one amber bead is known from the remarkably rich cemetery in Proosa (Estonia), which has been dated to the sixth and early seventh century.[36] No specimens are known from the many contemporary sites excavated in northwestern Russia and in Finland, and amber is absent from settlement sites of the so-called Pen'kovka culture of the forest-steppe belt of southern Ukraine.[37] By contrast, Baltic amber is conspicuously present on sites further to the east in the region of the Middle Volga and Kama Rivers and at the foot of the Ural Mountains.[38]

The distribution of the sixth-century amber finds in eastern Europe shows that amber was in high demand in some regions and of no use in others. A commercial network for the distribution of amber south- and eastward from the Baltic Sea shore would have produced a much more dispersed distribution, not unlike that of the early Roman period. The concentration of finds in Hungary and Crimea may have something to do with local conditions. By the sixth century, the Middle Danube region and Crimea were characterized by forms of society in which valuables of any kind, amber or otherwise, played a major role in defining social hierarchies.

Relatively large cemeteries in the Middle Danube region abound in artifacts used as status markers, many of which appear more often in women's than in men's graves. Among the most important were silver eagle-headed buckles, lavishly decorated with niello and cabochons, and equally luxurious silver or gilded brooches of the Aquileia and Gurzuf classes.[39] Both artifact categories also occur in contemporary funeral assemblages in Crimea, where the standard aristocratic female dress consisted of a large eagle-headed buckle at the waist and two silver brooches on the shoulders, in addition to several necklaces of amber, carnelian, rock crystal, and glass beads.[40] Most female skeletons found in such rich burial assemblages display clear signs of artificial skull deformation, a practice introduced in the early 400s and maintained as a status marker during the 500s.[41]

An explosion of conspicuous displays of exotic goods is associated with the "emblemic styles" that often appear at critical junctures in a region's political economy, when changing social relations impel displays of group identity.[42] This was clearly the case of the Middle Danube region that witnessed a continuous conflict between Lombards and Gepids throughout the first two thirds of the sixth century.[43] Ethnoarchaeological studies have demonstrated that material culture distinctions are in part maintained in order to justify between-group competition and negative reciprocity. On the other hand, between-group differentiation and hostility is often linked to the internal differentiation of age and gender categories.[44] While eagle-headed buckles, brooches of the Aquileia or Gurzuf class, as well as amber beads may have been used to mark ethnic boundaries, they were all at the same time employed to mark the status of aristocratic (married) women within one and the same group. During the sixth century, the maintenance of social hierarchies and of group boundaries in the Middle Danube region was thus closely tied to the consumption of prestige valuables, which in turn gave great social significance to contacts with elite groups elsewhere. Extensive contacts with distant groups served to deliver rare and foreign objects that became fundamental components of status display, as elites now strove to legitimize and "naturalize" the inherent inequality of the emerging system of social relations.

It thus appears that the exchange of amber was directed toward areas with particularly marked social differentiation. A number of areas had similar social systems that depended on the supply and consumption of prestige goods that were only available through contact with elites elsewhere, and an exchange network to serve elite needs must have been put in place. This can only have been a network of inter-elite gift exchange, not of trade. The association of amber with elites is amply confirmed by excavations in Crimea and the Caucasus region, where amber is restricted to a few, high-status sites. Out of some 1,400 amber beads known from Crimea, over 1,200 were found in Suuk Su alone, and most amber beads of Kovalevskaia's class 38 found in the Caucasus region come from the large cemetery excavated in Diurso.[45] In both Crimea and the Caucasus region, amber beads often appear in rich graves in association with such precious grave goods as silver or gold earrings, buckles, earrings, bracelets, and brooches, glass beakers, or Roman *solidi*.

Amber traveled in the sixth century from the Baltic coast to the Middle Danube and Crimea as part of a gift exchange system between elite groups, not as commodity, for no evidence exists of trade between these regions. The piece of evidence most often cited in support of the idea that the ancient Amber Trail was still in use in the early 500s is a letter of Theoderic the Great preserved in Cassiodorus's *Variae*. In this letter, the king of the Ostrogoths acknowledges the receipt of a shipment of amber, which had arrived with envoys from the Aesti, "who have pressed through many strange nations" to seek his friendship.[46] The last paragraph of the letter makes it clear that the envoys did not reach Ravenna along the well-trodden path of the Amber Trail, but "opened up" a road of their own on which more embassies from the Aesti were now expected to arrive. More important for the argument of this essay, the letter was written in response to a gift of amber, and was meant to accompany Theoderic's return gifts for the Aesti.[47] Similarly, the eagle-headed buckles found in burial assemblages in Mazuria, or the artifacts produced in the Middle Danube region that have been uncovered in warrior burials in Lithuania and the Kaliningrad *oblast'* of Russia, may also have been counter-gifts for shipments of amber to the territory of present-day Hungary.

As long as elites maintained their local basis of power, the exchange system continued to serve their needs. Although the number of amber artifacts from Lithuanian sites peters out after 600, amber beads appear with some frequency in burials of the Early (ca. 570–650/60) and especially the Middle Avar periods (650/60–700; map 4.2).[48] Toward the end of the Early Avar period, most amber beads appear singly in extraordinarily rich male burials, in association with amazing quantities of gold, such as in Kunbábony.[49] A little later, during the second half of the seventh

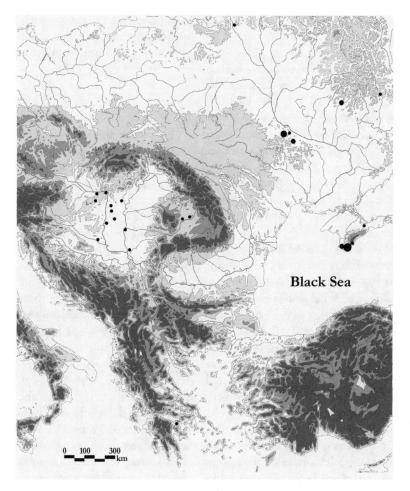

Map 4.2 Distribution of amber beads in seventh-century burial and hoard assemblages in eastern Europe. Smallest circle up to 5, thereafter up to 20, 50, 100, and 300 specimens.

century, amber beads appear in larger numbers in female burials, often accompanied by rich grave goods, such as silver earrings or glass beakers and drinking horns.[50] There is ample evidence of contacts between Mazuria and the Avar elites in the Middle Danube region.[51] After 600, amber probably traveled southward in the same way as before, namely through gift exchange, and a few artifacts and ornamental styles moved northward from the territory of present-day Hungary. That burial assemblages excavated in Hungary and dated after 650/660 contain a larger quantity of amber beads than those dated to the Early Avar period strongly suggests that such exchange continued well into the 600s, in spite of the possibility that some amber beads in circulation in Hungary were by then fifty to one hundred years old. The gift amber may have been offered in raw form, only to be processed locally and redistributed among members of the regional elite.

During the seventh century, amber beads continued to appear in Crimean cemeteries, but also in hoards of bronze in Right and Left Bank Ukraine.[52] As in the earlier period, amber beads were used as markers of social status. Baltic amber also reached the Caucasus, either along the Dnieper River or along the Volga and the Don Rivers. In fact, the largest number of amber beads have been found in that region in burial assemblages dated after ca. 600, leading some scholars to argue that, by 600, the Amber Trail had shifted eastward from the Lower Vistula to the Biebrza and Narew Rivers, and to stress the increasing importance of the Mazurian Lake region of northeastern Poland in seventh-century long-distance exchange linking the Baltic Sea to Crimea and the Caucasus region.[53] Yet, exchanges along this route were unidirectional, with few, if any, counter-gifts moving from south to north. For instance, no "Slavic" bow fibulae of Werner's class II C (probably first produced in Crimea) have so far been found in Mazuria.[54]

The disappearance of amber from archaeological assemblages in the Middle Danube region cannot be dated earlier than ca. 700 and must be understood as an interruption of contacts with elites on the Baltic Sea coast. This coincides in time with the abrupt break in amber deposition in Crimea, a phenomenon that may equally be interpreted in the light of the interruption of contacts with the north, because of the rise of the Khazars in the Lower Dnieper steppe.[55] By that time, burial had also ceased on most, if not all, cemetery sites in the Mazurian Lake region. Dramatic changes were meanwhile taking place in Lithuania. All inhumation cemeteries in the region of the Courland Lagoon on both sides of the present-day border between Lithuania and the Kaliningrad *oblast'* of Russia were abandoned after 600. Shortly thereafter, new cremation cemeteries appeared at completely different locations and with completely different grave goods.[56] Contacts with the south broke down as social and economic changes brought about the demise of the elites in the region of the Baltic Sea coast. Although contacts between the Middle Danube region and southern Poland continued after 700,[57] amber no longer moved southward. The demise of the Avar elites around 800, following the military defeat inflicted by the Frankish armies, had no effect on the revival of the Amber Trail. Whatever the effects of the Carolingian conquest on the regions of present-day Poland, when the distribution of amber began to expand again, the Middle Danube region was not part of that expansion. No Amber Trail linked the Frankish eastern borderlands to the rising ports-of-trade on the southern and eastern Baltic coasts. The East European "dirham zone" never extended into the Lower and Middle Danube region, and only a few isolated dinars have been found in Late or post-Avar assemblages.[58]

In early medieval eastern Europe, amber helped define unique social hierarchies, and the breakdown of long-established exchange networks was the consequence, not the cause, of the demise of competitive elites that had been responsible for its widespread consumption in the sixth and seventh centuries. Insights such as this can help lead the study of early medieval exchange in eastern Europe out of the impasse in which it has long been stuck. Much debate has been sparked by the recent search for a "post-Pirenne paradigm" as a model to explain the transition from the classical to the medieval world. The revival of interest in early medieval trade, however, has obscured other forms of exchange, the understanding of which cannot be based on either the Pirenne or the post-Pirenne paradigm. Most of these debates have not introduced new thinking on such exchange phenomena as gift giving, nor have they drawn on important recent work by sociologists and anthropologists. Instead, they have simply stressed the centrality of commercial exchanges. In contrast, I have drawn on recent developments in the study of medieval gifts to offer a new paradigm for approaching the topic of exchange in eastern Europe.[59]

Notes

1. Dezső Csallány, *Archäologische Denkmäler der Gepiden im Mitteldonaubecken* (Budapest: Akadémiai kiadó, 1961), pp. 59–62 and pls. 39/5 and 42/1 (Szentes-Nagyhegy), p. 113 and pl. 192/2 (Gyula); István Bóna, "Die Langobarden in Ungarn: Die Gräberfelder von Várpalota und Bezenye," *Acta Archaeologica Academiae Scientiarium Hungaricae* 7 (1956): 192 [183–242] and pl. 44/1-2 (Bezenye); István Bóna and Margit Nagy, *Gepidische Gräberfelder am Theissgebiet*, 1 (Budapest: Magyar Nemzeti Múzeum, 2002), pp. 211–12, 312 pl. 38/73.3 (Szolnok-Szanda). See also Morten Axboe, "Ein C-Brakteat aus Ungarn," *Acta Archaeologica* 49 (1978): 198–202; Günther Haseloff, *Die germanische Tierornamentik der Völkerwanderungszeit: Studien zu Salin's Stil I* (Berlin/New York: Walter de Gruyter, 1981), pp. 187–88, 702.

2. Vladimir I. Kulakov, "Mogil'niki zapadnoi chasti Mazurskogo Poozer'ia kontsa V-nachala VIII vv. (po materialom raskopok 1878–1938 gg.)," *Barbaricum* 1 (1989): 183 [148–276] and fig. 20. For eagle-headed buckles,

see Margit Nagy, "A gepida sasfejes csatok és kapcsolataik," *Móra Ferenc Múzeum Évkönyve* 8 (2002): 209–43.

3. Joachim Werner, "Der Grabfund von Taurapilis, Rayon Utna (Litauen) und die Verbindung der Balten zum Reich Theoderichs," in *Archäologische Beiträge zur Chronologie der Völkerwanderungszeit*, ed. Georg Kossack and Joachim Reichstein (Bonn: Rudolf Habelt, 1977), pp. 87–92; Vladimir I. Kulakov, "Gräber pruzzischer Stammesführer aus Warnikam," *Eurasia antiqua* 3 (1997): 598 [595–628].

4. C.W. Beck, E. Wilbur, S. Meret, D. Kossove, and K. Kermani, "The Infrared Spectra of Amber and the Identification of Baltic Amber," *Archaeometry* 8 (1965): 96–109.

5. Csallány, *Archäologische Denkmäler*, pp. 45–64 (Szentes-Nagyhegy and Szentes-Kökényzug); 74–94 (Berekhát); 154–66 (Szőreg); 173–93 (Kiszombor).

6. For Suuk Su, see N. Repnikov, "Nekotorye mogil'niki oblasti krymskikh gotov," *Izvestiia imperatorskoi arkheologicheskoi kommissii* 19 (1906): 1–80; N. Repnikov, "Nekotorye mogil'niki oblasti krymskikh gotov," *Zapiski Odesskogo obshchestva istorii i drevnostei* 27 (1907): 101–48. For the Caucasus region, see Vera B. Kovalevskaia, *Khronologiia vostochno-evropeiskikh drevnostei V-IX vekov: Kammenye busy Kavkaza i Kryma* (Moscow: Institut Arkheologii RAN, 1998), pp. 28–32.

7. Audronė Bliujienė, "Lithuanian Amber Artifacts in the Middle of the First Millennium and Their Provenance within the Limits of the Eastern Baltic Region," in *Proceedings of the International Interdisciplinary Conference: Baltic Amber in Natural Sciences, Archaeology, and Applied Arts*, ed. Adomas Butrimas (Vilnius: Vilniaus Dailes Akademijos Leidykla, 2001), p. 175 [171–86].

8. Emma Sprincz, "Amber Artifacts of Hungary from the Middle Bronze Age to the Hungarian Conquest (from 1600 BC to 896 AD)," in *Amber in Archaeology: Proceedings of the Fourth International Conference on Amber in Archaeology, Talsi 2001*, ed. Curt W. Beck, Ilze B. Loze, and Joan M. Todd (Riga: Institute of the History of Latvia, 2003), p. 203 [203–12].

9. Audronė Bliujienė, "Lithuanian Amber Artifacts from the Roman Iron Age to Early Medieval Times," in *Amber in Archaeology*, pp. 59–61 [47–71].

10. Florin Curta, *The Making of the Slavs: History and Archaeology of the Lower Danube Region, c. 500–700* (Cambridge, UK: Cambridge University Press, 2001), p. 196.

11. Jerzy Wielowiejski, "Bernsteinstrasse und Bernsteinweg während der römischen Kaiserzeit im Lichte der neueren Forschung," *Münstersche Beiträge zur antiken Handelsgeschichte* 3.2 (1984): 69–87; Annalisa Giovannini, "Le ambre di Aquileia: connotazioni generali e correlazioni culturali," in *Roma sul Danubio: Da Aquileia a Carnuntum lungo la via dell'ambra*, ed. Maurizio Buora and Werner Jobst (Udine: "L'Erma" di Bretschneider, 2002), pp. 159–64.

12. Jerzy Wielowiejski, "Depositi dell'ambra sul territorio tra la parte media del Danubio e il mar Baltico dal I secolo a.c. al V secolo d.c.," *Archaeologia Polona* 25–26 (1987): 75–84.

13. Raimundas V. Sidrys, "Vakarų baltų gintaro įkapės geležies amžiuje," in *Klaipėdos miesto ir regiono archeologijos ir istorijos problemos*, ed. Alvydas Nikžentaitis and Vladas Žulkus (Klaipeda: Klaipedos Universiteto, 1994), p. 63 [59–87]; Bliujienė, "Lithuanian Amber Artifacts from the Roman Iron Age," p. 58.

14. Nils Åberg, *Den historiska relationen mellan folkvandringstid och Vendeltid* (Stockholm: Wahlström & Widstrand, 1953), pp. 90, 100–01. This is repeated by John Hines, *The Scandinavian Character of Anglian England in the Pre-Viking Period*, British Archaeological Reports, British Series 124 (Oxford: British Archaeological Reports, 1984), p. 277.

15. Joachim Werner, "Slawische Bügelfibeln des 7. Jahrhunderts," in *Reinecke Festschrift zum 75. Geburtstag von Paul Reinecke am 25. September 1947*, ed. Gustav Behrens and Joachim Werner (Mainz: E. Schneider, 1950), p. 167 [150–72]; Joachim Werner, "Zu den Bügelfibeln aus den völkerwanderungszeitlichen Brandgräberfeldern Masuriens," *Germania* 62.1 (1984): 74–77.

16. Michael McCormick, *Origins of the European Economy: Communications and Commerce, A.D. 300–900* (Cambridge, UK: Cambridge University Press, 2001), p. 693.

17. McCormick, *Origins*, pp. 78, 370.

18. Jerzy Okulicz, *Pradzieje ziem pruskich od póznego paleolitu do VII w. n. e.* (Wrocław/Warsaw/Gdańsk/Cracow: Ossolineum, 1973), p. 565; Ia. G. Zverugo, "Slaviano-litovskie kontakty v srednevekov'e (po materialam belorusskogo-litovskogo pogranich'ia)," in *Problemy etnogeneza i etnicheskoi istorii baltov: Tezisy dokladov, mart, 1981*, ed. Regina Volkaitė-Kulikauskienė (Vilnius: Institut Istorii, 1981), p. 26 [24–27].

19. Paul M. Barford interprets one aspect of the distribution as a deliberate rejection of neighboring cultural models, in "Identity and Material Culture: Did the Early Slavs Follow the Rules or Did They Make Up Their Own?" *East Central Europe* 31.1 (2004): 99–123.

20. Colin Renfrew, "Alternative Models for Exchange and Spatial Distribution," in *Exchange Systems in Prehistory*, ed. Timothy K. Earle and Jonathan E. Ericson (New York: Academic Press, 1977), pp. 71–90. See also Stephen Shennan, "Exchange and Ranking: The Role of Amber in the Earlier Bronze Age of Europe," in *Ranking, Resource, and Exchange: Aspects of the Archaeology of Early European Society*, ed. Colin Renfrew and Stephen Shennan (Cambridge, UK: Cambridge University Press, 1982), pp. 33–45.

21. Richard Hodges, "Henri Pirenne and the Question of Demand in the Sixth Century," in *The Sixth Century: Production, Distribution, and Demand*, ed. Richard Hodges and William Bowden (Leiden: Brill, 1998), pp. 3–14.

22. Karl Polanyi, "The Economy as Instituted Process," in *Trade and Market in the Early Empires: Economies in History and Theory*, ed. Karl Polanyi, Conrad M. Arensberg, and Harry W. Pearson (Glencoe: Free Press, 1957),

pp. 243–70; Richard Hodges, *Dark Age Economics: The Origins of Towns and Trade, A.D. 600–1000* (London: St. Martin's Press, 1982).

23. Philip Grierson, "Commerce in the Dark Ages: A Critique of the Evidence," *Transactions of the Royal Historical Society* 5 (1959): 123–40.

24. Richard Hodges, *Towns and Trade in the Age of Charlemagne* (London: Duckworth, 2000).

25. Peter Franz Mittag, *Alte Köpfe in neuen Händen: Urheber und Funktionen der Kontorniaten,* Abhandlungen zur Vor- und Frühgeschichte, zur klassischen und provinzial-römischen Archäologie und zur Geschichte des Altertums 38 (Bonn: Rudolf Habelt, 1999), pp. 207, 210, 214. For old Roman coins in *Reihengräberkreis* burial assemblages, see Guido Krause, "Zur Münzbeigaben in merowingerzeitlichen Reihengräbern," in *Regio archaeologica: Archäologie und Geschichte an Ober- und Hochrhein: Festschrift für Gerhard Fingerlin zum 65. Geburtstag,* ed. Christel Bücker, Michael Hoeper, Niklot Krohn, and Jürgen Trumm, Studia honoraria 18 (Rahden: Leidorf, 2002), pp. 290–91.

26. For example, *Rituals of Power: From Late Antiquity to the Early Middle Ages,* ed. Frans Theuws and Janet L. Nelson, The Transformation of the Roman World 8 (Leiden: Brill, 2000).

27. See the exemplary study of Lotte Hedeager, "Warrior Economy and Trading Economy in Viking-Age Scandinavia," *Journal of European Archaeology* 2 (1994): 130–48.

28. Péter Somogyi, "A cikói temető," in *Tolna megyei avar temetök,* ed. Gábor Kiss and Péter Somogyi (Budapest: Akadémiai kiadó, 1984), p. 207 [205–46] and pl. 5/55.1.

29. K.S. Korolev, A.M. Murygin, and E.A. Savel'eva, "Vanvizdinskaia kul'tura (VI–IX vv.)," in *Arkheologiia Respubliki Komi,* Vol. 6 , ed. E.A. Savel'eva et al. (Moscow: DiK, 1997), p. 456 [400–77]. The amber beads found on sites in the Vychegda region may not even have arrived there from the Baltic region, but from the south, along the fur trade route. See Thomas S. Noonan, "The Fur trade Road and the Silk Road: The Relations between Central Asia and Northern Russia in the Early Middle Ages," in *Kontakte zwischen Iran, Byzanz und der Steppe im 6.-7. Jahrhundert,* ed. Csanád Bálint (Budapest: Akadémiai kiadó, 2000), pp. 285–302.

30. Kulakov, "Mogil'niki," pp. 183, 233 fig. 17/3.

31. Bóna and Nagy, *Gepidische Gräberfelder,* pp. 63–64, 119 fig. 58/37.

32. For example, grave 32 in Berekhát, with six specimens, found together with glass beads (Csallány, *Archäologische Denkmäler,* p. 74 and pl. LXII/1, 3, 5–7, 9); grave 41 at Dravlje (near Ljubljana, Slovenia), with at least eight specimens, found together with glass beads; Marijan Slabe, *Dravlje: Grobišče iz časov preseljevanja ljudstev* (Ljubljana: Narodni Muzej, 1975), p. 103 and pls. 15/20-4, 27-9); or skeleton 1 in the burial chamber 442 in Luchistoe (Crimea), with four elongated specimens, found together with glass beads: A.I. Aibabin, "Kompleksy s bolshymi dvuplastinchatymi fibulami iz Luchistogo," *Materialy po arkheologii, istorii i etnografii Tavrii* 4 (1994): 137–38, 165 fig. 20/12, 166 fig. 21/6-8 [132–72].

33. A.K. Ambroz, "Dunaiskie elementy v srednevekov'e kul'tury Kryma (VI–VII vv.)," *Kratkie soobshcheniia Instituta Arkheologii Akademii Nauk SSSR* 113 (1968): 14, 17 [10–23]; A.I. Aibabin, "Khronologiia mogil'nikov Kryma pozdnerimskogo i rannesrednevekovogo vremeni," *Materialy po arkheologii, istori i etnografii Tavrii* 1 (1990): 32–35 [5–68]; A.K. Ambroz, "Iuzhnye khudozhestvennye sviazi naselenie verkhnego Podneprov'ia v VI v.," in *Drevnie slaviani i ikh sosedi,* ed. I.V. Kukharenko, Materialy i issledovaniia po arkheologii SSSR 176 (Moscow: Nauka, 1970), pp. 70–74.

34. Wojciech Szymańki, *Szeligi pod Płockiem nad początku wczesnośredniowiecza. Zespół osadniczy z VI–VII w.* (Wrocław: Ossolineum, 1967); Zbigniew Kobyliński and Zdisław Hensel, "Imports or Local Products? Trace Elements Analysis of Copper-Alloy Artefacts from Haćki, Białystok Province, Poland," *Archaeologia Polona* 31 (1993): 129–40; V.V. Aulikh, *Zymnivs'ke horodishche—slov'ians'ka pam'iatka VI–VII st. n.e.* (Kiev: Naukova dumka, 1972).

35. E.A. Shmidt, "Problemy khronologii tushemlinskoi kul'tury v verkhov'iakh Dnepra," in *Arkhealogyia i starazhytnaia gystoryia Magyleushchyny y sumezhnykh terytoryi (Materyialy kanferencyi 22 krasavyka 1993 g.),* ed. A.A. Sedin (Magileu: Magileusky ablasny kraiaznauchy muzei, 1994), pp. 104–13; Valentin V. Sedov, "Osnovnye voprosy izucheniia tushemlinskoi kul'tury," in *Kraje słowiańskie w wiekach średnich: Profanum i sacrum,* ed. Hanna Kočka-Krenz and Władysław Losiński (Poznań: Wydawnictwo Poznańskiego Towarzystwo Przyjaciół Nauk, 1998), pp. 50–59; R.V. Terpilovskii, "Kolochinskaia kul'tura," in *Etnokul'turnaia karta territorii Ukrainskoi v I tys. n .e.,* eds. V.D. Baran, R.V. Terpilovskii, and E.V. Maksimov (Kiev: Naukova dumka, 1985), pp. 93–98.

36. K. Deemant, "Das Steingräberfeld von Proosa bei Tallinn," *Eesti NSV Teaduste Akadeemia Toimetised: Ühiskonnateaduste seeria* 24 (1975): 79 [78–80].

37. G.F. Korzukhina, "Klady i sluchainye nakhodki veshchei kruga 'drevnostei antov' v srednem Podneprov'e," *Materialy po istorii, arkheologii i etnografii Tavrii* 5 (1996): 397–402, 403–05 [352–435]; I.O. Gavritukhin and A.M. Oblomskii, *Gaponovskii klad i ego kul'turno-istoricheskii kontekst* (St. Petersburg: Institut Arkheologii RAN, 1996), pp. 45–46; V.S. Aksenov and L.I. Babenko, "Pogrebenie VI–VII vv. n.e. u sela Mokhnach," *Rossiiskaia arkheologiia* 3 (1998): 111–18; Rasho Rashev, *Prabălgarite prez V–VII vek* (Sofia: Faber, 2000), pp. 17, 118 fig. 12/2; Oleg M. Prikhodniuk, *Pen'kovskaia kul'tura: kul'turno-khronologicheskii aspekt issledovaniia* (Voronezh: Izdatel'stvo Voronezhskogo universiteta, 1998).

38. G.I. Matveeva, "Issledovaniia na Samarskoi luke v 1992 godu," in *Arkheologicheskie otkrytiia Urala i Povolzh'ia: Sbornik statei,* ed. V.V. Nikitin (Ioshkar-Ola: Mariiskii gosudarstvenyi universitet, 1994), p. 89 [89–90]; M.R. Polesskikh, "Armievskii mogil'nik," in *Arkheologicheskie pamiatniki*

mordvy Itysiacheletiia n.e., ed. G.A. Fedorov-Davydov (Saransk: Mordovskoe knizhnoe izdatel'stvo, 1979), p. 25 [5–56]; V.F. Gening, "Pamiatnik u s. Kushnarenkovo na r. Beloi (VI–VII vv. n.e.)," in *Issledovaniia po arkheologii Iuzhnogo Urala*, ed. R.G. Kuzeev (Ufa: Izdatel'stvo Bashkirskogo filiala AN SSSR, 1976), pp. 90–136; R.D. Goldina, O.P. Koroleva, L.D. Makarov, "Agafonovskii mogil'nik I—pamiatnik lomovatovskoi kul'tury na severe Permskoi oblasti," in *Pamiatniki epokhi srednevekov'ia v Verkhnem Prikam'e: Sbornik statei*, ed. V.F. Gening (Izhevsk: Udmurtskii gosudarstvenyi universitet,1980), pp. 3–66, 137–85.

39. Herbert Kühn, *Die germanischen Bügelfibeln der Völkerwanderungszeit in der Rheinprovinz* (Graz: Akademische Druck- und Verlagsanstalt, 1965), pp. 95–101; Herbert Kühn, *Die germanischen Bügelfibeln der Völkerwanderungszeit in Süddeutschland* (Graz: Akademische Druck- u. Verlagsanstalt, 1974), pp. 728–42. Also see above n2.

40. Elzara A. Khairedinova, "Zhenskii kostium s iuzhnokrymskimi orlinogolovymi priazhkami," *Materialy po arkheologii, istorii i etnografii Tavrii* 7 (2000): 91–133.

41. János Cseh, "Adatok az V.–VII. századi Gepida emlékanyag egységéhez," *A Szolnok Megyei Múzeumok Évkönyve* 7 (1984–1988): 60 [29–80]; K.F. Sokolova, "Antropologichni materiali mogil'nikov Inkermans'koi dolini," *Arkheologichni pam'iatki URSR* 13 (1963): 124–59; Živko Mikić, "Antropološki osvrt na veštački deformisane lobanje iz perioda velike seobe naroda," *Zbornik narodnog muzeja* 15 (1994): 133–38.

42. Curta, *Making of the Slavs*, pp. 203–04; also see D.L. Talis, "Nekotorye problemy istorii rannesrednevekovoi Tavriki i literatura poslednikh let," *Vizantiiskii vremennik* 19 (1961): 240–61.

43. Frank E. Wozniak, "Byzantine Diplomacy and the Lombard-Gepidic Wars," *Balkan Studies* 20 (1979): 139–58; Walter Pohl, "The Empire and the Lombards: Treaties and Negotiations in the Sixth Century," in *Kingdoms of the Empire: The Integration of Barbarians in Late Antiquity*, ed. Walter Pohl (Leiden: Brill, 1997), pp. 75–133.

44. Ian Hodder, *Symbols in Action: Ethnoarchaeological Studies of Material Culture* (Cambridge, UK: Cambridge University Press, 1982); Roy Larick, "Age Grading and Ethnicity in the Style of Loikop (Samburu) Spears," *World Archaeology* 18 (1986): 269–83.

45. V.B. Deopik, "Klassifikatsiia bus Iugo-Vostochnoi Evropy VI–IX vv.," *Sovetskaia Arkheologiia* 3 (1961): 214 [209–32] with table 1; Kovalevskaia, *Khronologiia vostochno-evropeiskikh drevnostei*, p. 30.

46. Cassiodorus, *Varia* 5.2, ed. A.J. Fridh, CCSL 96 (Turnhout: Brepols, 1973), p. 183: "Amate iam cognitum, quem requisistis ambienter ignotum, nam inter tot gentes viam praesumere non est aliquid facile concupisse." English translation from *The Letters of Cassiodorus*, trans. Thomas Hodgkin (London: H. Frowde, 1886), p. 265.

47. Danuta Shanzer, "Two Clocks and a Wedding: Theodoric's Diplomatic Relations with the Burgundians," *Romanobarbarica* 14 (1996–1997): 225–28.

48. Elvira H. Tóth and Attila Horváth, *Kunbábony: Das Grab eines Awarenkhagans* (Kécskemét: Museumdirektion der Selbstverwaltung des Komitats Bács-Kiskún, 1992), pp. 205–06; Sprincz, "Amber Artifacts," p. 210; Éva Garam, "Der awarische Fundstoff im Karpatenbecken und seine zeitliche Gliederung," in *Die Völker Südosteuropas im 6. bis 8. Jahrhundert,* ed. Bernhard Hänsel (Berlin: Südosteuropa-Gesellschaft, 1987), 191–202.

49. Attila Kiss, "A Kunbábonyi 1., kora-avar vezéri sír leleteinek belsö összefüggései. A leletanyag csoportosítása," *Communicationes Archaeologicae Hungaricae* (1994–1995): 267–84.

50. Attila Kiss, *Das awarenzeitlich-gepidische Gräberfeld von Kölked-Feketekapu A* (Innsbruck: Universitätsverlag Wagner, 1996), p. 142; Éva Garam, *Das awarenzeitliche Gräberfeld von Kisköre* (Budapest: Akadémiai kiadó, 1979), p. 17.

51. Przemysław Urbańczyk, "Geneza wczesnośredniowiecznej metalowych pochew broni białej ze stanowisk kultury pruskiej," *Przegląd Archeologiczne* 25 (1977): 107–45; Jerzy Kowalski, "Z badań nad chronologia okresu wedrówek ludów na ziemiach zachodniobałtyskich (faza E)," in *Archeologia bałtyska: Materiały z konferencij, Olsztyn, 24-25 kwietnia 1988 roku,* ed. Jerzy Okulicz (Olsztyn: Ośrodek badań naukowych im. Wojciecha Kętrzyńskiego, 1991), pp. 71, 81 [67–85].

52. M.I. Braichevskii, "Pastirs'kiy skarb 1949 r.," *Arkheolohiia* 7 (1952): 161–73; Korzukhina, "Klady i sluchainye nakhodki," pp. 372–73 (Khatski), 395–97 (Nova Odessa), 408–12 (Koloskovo).

53. Vladimir I. Kulakov, *Prussy, V-XIII vv.* (Moscow: Geoeko, 1994), p. 118.

54. Curta, *Making of the Slavs,* p. 267.

55. Svetalana A. Pletneva, *Ocherki khazarskoi arkheologii* (Moscow: Mosty kul'tury and Jerusalem: Gesharim, 1999), pp. 151–76.

56. Valentin V. Sedov, *Slaviane v drevnosti* (Moscow: Institut Arkheologii RAN, 1994), p. 76.

57. Helena Zoll-Adamikowa, "Zur Chronologie der awarenzeitlichen Funde aus Polen," in *Probleme der absoluten und relativen Chronologie ab Latènezeit bis zum Frühmittelalter: Materialen des III. Internationalen Symposiums: Grundprobleme der frühgeschichtlichen Entwicklung im nördlichen Mitteldonaugebiet: Kraków-Karniowice, 3-7 Dezember 1990,* ed. Kazimierz Godłowski and Renata Madyda-Legutko (Cracow: Secesja, 1992), pp. 297–315; Wojciech Szymański, "Stan więdzy o zabytkach awarskich obszarów położonych o połnóc od terytorium kaganatu," *Archeologia Polski* 40 (1995): 125–45.

58. Sebastian Brather, "Frühmittelalterliche Dirham-Schatzfunde in Europa: Probleme ihrer wirschaftsgeschichtlichen Interpretation aus archäologischer Perspektive," *Zeitschrift für Archäologie des Mittelalters* 23–24 (1995–1996): 73–153; Nebojša Stanojević, "Naselja VIII–IX veka u Vojvodini," *Rad Vojvodanskih Muzeja* 30 (1987): 130–31.

59. *The Question of the Gift: Essays across Disciplines,* ed. Mark Osteen, Routledge Studies in Anthropology 2 (London: Routledge, 2002);

Negotiating the Gift: Pre-Modern Figurations of Exchange, ed. Gadi Algazi, Valentin Groebner, and Bernhard Jussen, Veröffentlichungen des Max-Planck-Instituts für Geschichte 188 (Göttingen: Vandenhoeck & Ruprecht, 2003); Florin Curta, "Merovingian and Carolingian Gift-Giving," *Speculum* 81 (2006): 671–99.

CHAPTER 5

"ROMANNESS" IN EARLY
MEDIEVAL CULTURE

Celia Chazelle

Analysis of an eighth-century miniature reconceptualizing early medieval romanitas as a local re-imagining of Roman culture, rather than as reception of antique Mediterranean conventions.

Most historians of the early medieval West are aware of the significant problems posed by their sources: the scarcity of texts and objects extant from the era, relative to later centuries; their frequently far from perfect condition; the isolated states in which they are often found, with no indication of place or time of production and no comparanda. Partly because of the difficulties, scholars of culture and thought in this era have become adept at piecing together scattered fragments of evidence, squeezing it for information through a range of analytical techniques, and reconstructing lost writings and artifacts from limited surviving vestiges. Such methods have made it possible to locate relationships and continuities among seemingly disparate sources, and thus map the transmission and evolution of artistic, literary, and other cultural conventions across regions and considerable periods of time.[1]

A persistent interpretative paradigm indebted to these approaches concerns the cultural legacy of Antiquity and the Mediterranean—the heritage of "Rome," broadly defined. Perceived similarities between ancient or Mediterranean and early medieval texts and objects, together with hypothetical reconstructions of lost artifacts and writings, have long supported theories about the continuous dissemination of ideas and cultural forms from the ancient Roman Empire and postclassical Mediterranean to other parts of Europe, and through the Middle Ages.[2]

The channels of cultural transmission are generally thought to have intensified or weakened depending on the period and region; some places and times were more open to the influence of Roman culture than others. The Carolingian epoch is commonly viewed as a watershed, a century or so of heightened romanness (*romanitas*) paving the way for a yet more intense interest in this heritage in the eleventh and later centuries.[3]

Two additional factors may be noted that strengthen this paradigm. One is the tendency of many early medieval historians, still today in spite of the "linguistic turn," to take at face value the claims of early medieval writers to have borrowed from particular antique or Mediterranean sources: the church fathers, imperial law codes, Roman liturgical texts, and others. The potential for rhetorical artifice in these texts is underestimated; too often, they are treated as transparent windows on a past reality confirming the general picture of early medieval culture just outlined.[4] The second factor is the continued force of a periodization scheme, albeit rarely acknowledged, that goes back to the nineteenth century and treats the fifth through tenth centuries as the cultural bridge, or for some historians the barrier, between Antiquity and the so-called High Middle Ages. Until about thirty years ago, this scheme typically coincided with a view that romanizing attributes in early medieval writings or objects derived from a culture—of Antiquity and the Mediterranean— fundamentally more sophisticated than that of the early medieval producers. Whether, therefore, the authors and craftsmen were of Roman or barbarian ancestry and lived within or outside regions formerly controlled by the empire, it was assumed that their aim was to follow their exemplars as carefully as possible. Any divergences were held to be inadvertent, testimony to their limited skills or sources' defective condition. Some historians argued that the resulting early medieval productions were so inferior to their prototypes, and so distorted the legacy they were meant to imitate, that they impeded its reception in later centuries. For other scholars, despite the flaws, they were valuable for having preserved at least some elements of Roman culture, passing them on to later generations better able to build on this inheritance.

Such interpretations that stress decline or the passive emulation of antique and Mediterranean culture in the early medieval West still occasionally surface, especially in textbooks based on older scholarly literature.[5] Since the 1970s, though, historians have been more willing to recognize the creativity of early medieval producers. Greater emphasis is placed on the many signs that they made deliberate choices from varied source materials, amended those borrowings, and mingled them with ones from other sources and their own inventions. Yet even with this shift in scholarly outlook, early medieval *romanitas* remains, for the most part, at least implicitly identified with the quasi-linear, continuous transmission of texts, objects, and ideas from Antiquity and the Mediterranean that intersected and clashed with currents from the "non-Roman" world. The key issue in evaluating the romanizing early medieval text or object is thus seen as the degree of its adherence to versus deviation from such older, "Roman" prototypes.[6]

Studies of early medieval culture from these angles have taught us a great deal, and there is no doubt that the flow of ideas and forms from Antiquity and the Mediterranean had a profound affect throughout the early medieval West. In the last two decades, however, scholars have become increasingly sensitive to the difficulties for mapping the continuous diffusion of romanizing traditions, in this period, caused by the scarcity of surviving writings and artifacts, particularly from the eighth and earlier centuries, and their enormous variety: the disparities among supposedly romanizing artistic, architectural, and literary forms and styles; the variants, interpolations, and marginalia in manuscript "copies" of supposedly the same texts; divergent religious teachings and practices that contemporaries asserted were Roman and orthodox; and so on. As awareness of these conditions has grown, long-standing assumptions about *romanitas* in the era have become harder to sustain.

It is true that early medieval authors and craftsmen repeatedly claimed inspiration from ancient and Mediterranean productions. Indeed, they did so more often than modern historians at times appear aware. But what is often lacking is sufficient respect for their works' localized character. Antecedents and parallels are assumed to have existed where in fact we have no concrete evidence of this, where disjunctions—from other early medieval productions and from any traceable Roman legacy—actually appear to outweigh connections. Rather than trying so hard to link early medieval cultural developments across regions and over time, which often depends on problematic reconstructions of lost sources, we should pay more attention to the diversity of what survives. If there is any aspect of early medieval culture that might seem rightly identified with continuities, it is *romanitas*. Yet it seems to me that we should not think only in terms of encounters with actual sources and ideas from Antiquity or the Mediterranean; as Jennifer O'Reilly and Mayke De Jong have recently suggested, romanness in this era was also a mental or spiritual state.[7] Individual producers and centers, in different times and places, drew from diverse resources to conjure up new ideas of Roman culture—new romanizing traditions.[8] Their productions reflect their disparate *imaginings* of Rome—inspired partly, it is true, by Antiquity and the Mediterranean, but also by local conditions, non-Roman works, sources they decided were romanizing but have little actual connection with that heritage, and independent, creative thought.[9]

In the following pages, I present a single case study that I think illustrates well the continued importance of the scholarly tendencies described at the beginning of this essay and the distorting influence they can still exert on how we understand early medieval romanness. My focus is the portrait of the prophet Ezra in the Codex Amiatinus (figure 5.1), a biblical pandect, that is Bible containing the Old and New Testaments in one volume, produced at the Northumbrian monastery of Wearmouth-Jarrow.[10] According to two near-contemporary writings, the anonymous *Vita Ceolfridi* and Bede's *Historia abbatum*, three pandects were made at Wearmouth-Jarrow sometime during the abbacy of Ceolfrid over both houses (689-716). Two pandects were placed in the churches of Wearmouth and Jarrow, and in June 716 the third Bible, Amiatinus—the only one to survive with apparently all its leaves—was taken to St. Peter's shrine in Rome.[11] I try to show that if we investigate, more closely than have most earlier scholars, the disjunctions as well as continuities with antique Mediterranean culture so apparent in the Ezra miniature, we can shed clearer light on both its innovativeness and its ties to its own northern European place of production.

I have chosen a work of art—rather than, say, of literature—as a case study for two reasons. One is the particular strength of the older approaches that I noted above in art history, largely thanks to the scholarship of Kurt Weitzmann. Weitzmann put a premium on searching for the archetypes of early Christian and medieval art, and on plotting the paths along which forms were transmitted. Whether extant or lost and reconstructed from later evidence, the archetypes were valued as "purer" and hence more interesting than their medieval descendants.[12] Although much challenged in the last two decades,[13] Weitzmann's methods remain dominant in research on certain early medieval monuments, in particular ones thought to be romanizing. One painting almost exclusively examined through a Weitzmannian prism is Amiatinus's Ezra miniature.

Additionally, I hope to underscore the problems still caused, for early medieval cultural studies, by the boundaries between academic disciplines. Textual historians still too often fail to give sufficient thought to non-written sources, whereas scholars whose expertise lies with nontextual materials—art historians, architectural historians, archaeologists—show the reverse tendency. In dealing with a period from which sources of all kinds are so scarce, we must be able to investigate adequately the full range of evidence. This requires that we develop the skills to read both written and non-written works with equal care, for insights they may independently provide and ways those insights may intersect or, as often

Figure 5.1   Florence, Biblioteca Medicea Laurenziana, Cod. Amiatino 1, fol. 4/V recto: Portrait of the Prophet Ezra. Photo: Florence, Biblioteca Medicea Laurenziana, by permission.

happens, conflict.[14] In this regard, too, analysis of Amiatinus's Ezra portrait offers a useful guide.

The Ezra Miniature

The painting's subject is identified in its verse caption, which Paul Meyvaert demonstrated was probably composed by Bede: "When the sacred codices were incinerated in the enemy devastation, Ezra, burning with God, renewed this work" (figure 5.1).[15] Wearing the vestments of a Jewish high priest as described in Exodus 28, with gold trappings and nimbus,[16] Ezra sits in a simply furnished room writing in a book with a gold pen. The text he inscribes is visible, but the script cannot be linked to any known writing system. Behind him stands an armarium holding scribal tools and nine volumes labeled along their spines with the abbreviated titles of sections of the Old and New Testaments. An inkwell is on a table before him, and a book and writing implements lie on the floor.

Since the nineteenth century, the dominant issue in discussions of this painting has been the nature of its antique source.[17] A few features of Amiatinus can be tied to a lost biblical pandect containing an Old Latin translation, the Codex Grandior, made under Cassiodorus at Vivarium, Calabria, in the sixth century. Grandior was almost certainly the Bible that the *Historia abbatum* reports Ceolfrid to have acquired in Rome in 678. Amiatinus's first quire has a prologue in Cassiodorian prose style, likely copied from Grandior; a painting of the desert Tabernacle probably inspired by a picture in the Italian codex, briefly described by Cassiodorus; and three diagrams of scripture that, in their lists of biblical books, correspond to diagrams in some copies of Cassiodorus's treatise, the *Institutions*. The same lists, Cassiodorus notes there, were inserted in Grandior. Because of these ties between Amiatinus and Grandior, and because the Ezra portrait clearly shows the influence of antique Mediterranean art, many scholars have contended that it, too, must have been inspired by a picture in the Vivarium manuscript, though in this case there is no supporting written evidence. That is, since some leaves in Amiatinus seem to draw inspiration from pages in Grandior, the burden of proof has fallen on those scholars who would argue that other sources or original artistic creation underlie any of the folios.[18] Except where there is strong evidence to the contrary, Cassiodorus's Bible—an antique "Roman" source available at Wearmouth-Jarrow—is presumed the model by default. The most widespread opinions regarding the Ezra portrait are that it was copied from a picture of Ezra in Grandior, or it was adapted from a representation there of Cassiodorus.[19]

To the extent that the Amiatinus miniature can be said to have had a single pictorial model, there is no question this was an antique Mediterranean portrait. Furthermore, although I cannot discuss this here, the theory that the model was in Grandior and depicted Cassiodorus is plausible, despite the lack of written evidence.[20] Yet a major problem with such discussions of the painting is the underlying assumption that it is, in essence, a copy—whether of an image of Cassiodorus or another subject, in Grandior or another manuscript. Analysis rarely moves outside the parameters of this concept. The concern for the continuities with antique Mediterranean culture via Grandior, which the *Historia abbatum* seems to corroborate, overrides respect for the significant visual and textual evidence of disjunctures.[21]

First, so far as I can determine, no earlier image survives from the Mediterranean or western Europe representing any Jewish priest as a seated, writing scribe.[22] Second, although the poor survival rate of antique and early medieval artwork might explain this lacuna, no single Mediterranean or northern artwork or text from before the eighth century accounts for the combined presence of three other details in the Amiatinus miniature: Ezra's portrayal specifically as a high priest (Vulgate *pontifex*; the Vulgate I and II Esdras describe him as a scribe and priest, *sacerdos*); his unusual script; and the caption alluding to his restoration of burned scriptures. Each of these details can be related to an Old Latin or noncanonical scripture or to patristic literature, but they are not fused in these sources, and it is unlikely they were joined in any biblical or patristic manuscript at Wearmouth-Jarrow.[23]

The earliest extant writing to link Ezra with the office of high priest, a new script, *and* the recopying of burned biblical books is Bede's reply to Question 7 in his *Thirty Questions on the Book of Kings*, completed ca. 715. The passage explains why certain Old Testament scriptures have been lost:

> For when the Chaldeans destroyed Judea and the enemy fire consumed the library that, along with other treasures of the province, had been collected in ancient times, a few books from [the library] now contained in holy scripture were subsequently restored by the industry of Ezra, high priest [*pontifex*] and prophet. Whence it is written about him, 'Ezra went up from Babylon, and he was a ready scribe in the law of Moses' [I Esdras 7:6], namely ready (nimble) since he discovered more speedily written forms of letters than those the Hebrews had at the time.[24]

By the time Bede finished *Thirty Questions*, he had formulated a conception of Ezra not traceable to any single earlier writing, one combining distinct ideas that previously circulated independently. Yes, the Amiatinus miniature has ties to older artistic and textual traditions; its artist, doubtless guided by Bede, found inspiration in diverse materials. Yet we are seriously in danger of losing sight of the forest for the trees if we fail to stress that this is a Wearmouth-Jarrow invention. The critical ideas almost certainly came from Bede, not an earlier image or text, and the picture's creativity should be our chief concern.

The thoughts I offer here as to why this image was invented—not copied from a Mediterranean exemplar—for one of the Wearmouth-Jarrow

Bibles build on and revise the argument in my 2003 article on the miniature.[25] Careful consideration of the picture's signification and purpose can set the stage for a clearer understanding of the role that independent thought played, more generally, in the distinctive *romanitas* of this Northumbrian center. As I noted in my earlier article, another destination than Rome may have been initially envisaged for Wearmouth-Jarrow's third pandect. But once the decision was made to send it to Rome, this objective must have influenced the monks' perception of its contents. As in the passage just quoted, Bede regularly refers to Old Testament high priests with the Latin *pontifex* or the adjective *pontificalis*, terms he also employs for the archiepiscopal and papal offices.[26] Placed opposite the poem dedicating Amiatinus to St. Peter, the first Christian *pontifex* after Christ, the image of the Jewish *pontifex* Ezra is a powerful expression of pontifical prestige. The appropriateness of this picture in a volume given to Rome cannot have gone unnoticed at Wearmouth-Jarrow. The monks surely anticipated that the painting would be understood, at least in part, as a mirror of the papal office.

In order to assess the ideas about that office they might have hoped the miniature would convey, we need to be mindful of its caption's ambiguity: the enemy who burned the books and the place where this happened are unnamed, and, it seems to me, a certain disconnect exists between the burned codices and the *opus* (singular) renewed by Ezra. I suspect the ambiguity was deliberate, reflecting a multivalent interpretation along the lines of the levels of scriptural exegesis. The painting and caption commemorate Ezra's rewriting of lost scriptures, but educated viewers would have remembered, too, the different tasks attributed to him in the Vulgate I Esdras, where the copying of burned books is not mentioned: in particular, his role restoring the Temple in Jerusalem. We see Ezra, scribe and biblical scholar, dressed as a Jewish high priest, before an armarium containing the Old and New Testaments, recopying Christian scripture—the books behind him indicate—in new letters that Bede believed better, for this purpose, than the older Hebrew script. On one level, as Bede teaches in his later commentary on Ezra, the prophet thus foreshadows Christ, the Bible's source, who joined the old law to the new.[27] Ezra can perhaps be seen, as well, as the forerunner of scholars of scripture who follow Christ's model: among them Jerome, the author of the improved translation of the Vulgate that surpassed the earlier Old Latin versions; and the Wearmouth-Jarrow monks, who drew from different biblical codices to create the revised (hence improved) Vulgate copied in Amiatinus. But beyond this, Ezra's rewriting of scripture may be understood as a figure, in Christian terms, of the Temple's restoration, since for Bede and other exegetes, the ancient

Temple was the type of the Christian Bible as well as the Church of Rome and the heavenly Jerusalem.[28] Ezra's writing of scripture is indirectly the means by which he helps restore Christ's Temple. And yet, the artist has portrayed him in an interior that might have been familiar to the monks, not surrounded by the Temple's rich décor. The Amiatinus Ezra is a *pontifex*, but the picture confirms that his primary tasks are scribal work and biblical study. His restoration of the Temple—the Bible—occurs through these activities.

Interpreted in this manner, the painting recalls Bede's teachings on the virtues of bishops and other clerical leaders of the Church of Rome, including the pope. As Alan Thacker has shown, Bede's thinking about episcopal virtue was shaped by the thought of Pope Gregory I.[29] For Bede as for Gregory, bishops should combine pastoral activity with an ascetic monastic way of life, allotting sufficient time to scripture study to assure the quality of their preaching and teaching. The life of Gregory in Bede's *Ecclesiastical History* reflects this line of thought. Like the anonymous life written at Whitby (704–714), which Bede may have known, it recalls Gregory's deep knowledge of scripture.[30] Bede stresses the connection between Gregory's biblical studies and his monastic life even as pope, and he contrasts Gregory's scholarship, asceticism, and charity with the behavior of those Roman pontiffs who "strove to build churches and decorate them with gold and silver."[31]

It is possible that the election of new Pope Gregory (II) in 715 had some bearing on the decision to send a Bible to Rome. The Wearmouth-Jarrow scriptorium may not have been able to produce an entire pandect only a year before Amiatinus left the monastery; but the volume's first quire containing the Ezra miniature could have been finished in this time, perhaps with some pages designed earlier. So precise a date cannot be proven, yet it is worth investigating one tentative clue that the portrait, at least, postdates 709, since this may help clarify further how it should be read.

Another text by Bede is of interest here: his dedication letter to Bishop Acca of Hexham for the first part of his Genesis commentary, in which Bede comments on why he must interrupt work on that treatise:

> And I have carried through the work up to the point where Adam, having been ejected from the paradise of pleasure, entered the exile of the temporal life. I intend to write [*scripturus*] some things also about subsequent events of the sacred narrative, God willing, with the accompanying help of your intercession, after I have first examined [*perscrutatus fuero*] for a while the book of the holy prophet and priest [*sacerdos*] Ezra in which, as both prophet and historian, he wrote about [*conscripsit*] the sacred meanings of Christ

and the Church under the allegorical figure of the release from the long
captivity, the restoration of the Temple, the rebuilding of the city, the
return to Jerusalem of the vessels which had been taken away, the rewriting
of the law of God which had been burned, the purification of the people
from their foreign wives, and the people's conversion with one heart and
soul to the service of God; and after, with God's help, I have rendered [*reddidero*] some of these sacred meanings which I have mentioned clearer to
those desirous of learning [*studiosi*].[32]

Meyvaert has suggested the letter was written soon after Acca became
bishop in 709 and that this passage is evidence Bede wrote his commentary on Ezra and Nehemiah between 711 and 715. We should give thought
to these dates, since they may have a bearing on how we interpret the
miniature's relation to the letter and consequently the conception of
romanness the picture was meant to convey. Although Meyvaert's dating
of the letter itself is plausible, though it cannot be proven (Acca remained
bishop until 732), Scott DeGregorio's arguments for assigning the Ezra
commentary to the 720s strike me as persuasive. One consideration, as
DeGregorio has remarked, is that the letter does not clearly state that
Bede planned to write a commentary on Ezra.[33] Although he employs
verbs of writing (*scripturus, conscripsit*) to describe his work on Genesis and
Ezra's work as scribe, he does not use them for his study of the prophet.
Here the main verbs are *perscrutatus fuero* and *reddidero*, which do not necessarily indicate a plan for a treatise; they could refer to the preparation of
sermons or lectures for students and perhaps, in conjunction, the laying
of the groundwork for the painting. Moreover, it may be significant that
one of these verbs, *reddere*, occurs in I Esdras 6:5, where Cyrus commands
the restoration (*reddantur*) of the Temple's vessels, which Ezra oversaw;[34]
and that in I Esdras 7:17 Ezra is told to act *studiose* in spending the gold
and silver for the sacrifices.[35] Conceivably, Bede had these verses in mind
when he wrote to Acca: in the new task of studying Ezra, the letter may
imply, Bede and the *studiosi*, a group that obviously included Acca, emulate the prophet. Once it was decided to send Amiatinus to Rome, Bede
and his brothers may have hoped the picture of Ezra, who restores the
Temple by restoring scripture, would similarly suggest to Gregory II that
through his humility and devotion to the Bible he, too, imitates the
prophet, thus renewing Christ's Temple of the Church of Rome.

These analogies between the painting and letter support the view that
Bede's initial study of Ezra was partly motivated by plans for the miniature.
Another feature of the letter may harmonize with this view. The text
indicates familiarity with one of the traditions linking Ezra to the rewriting of burned scriptures, which Bede could have found in the noncanonical

IV Ezra or a few church fathers. But the letter does not mention two other non-Vulgate details alluded to in the painting and *Thirty Questions*: Ezra's new script and office of *pontifex*. The former detail was likely found at the time only in IV Ezra; the latter came from the Old Latin Ezra A'.[36] Arguments from silence are problematic, and Bede doubtless thought some things about Ezra well before writing them down. Nonetheless, the lack of reference in the letter *may* be a clue that at the time he had yet to put all these ideas together. He did not yet envisage Ezra as a *pontifex* and inventor of a new script. The picture, then, would have been prepared after the letter and closer to completion of *Thirty Questions*, ca. 715.

If the Ezra painting can be dated to approximately 710–716, what do we know about Wearmouth-Jarrow in those years that might cast additional light on its design? Let me note here just one possibly relevant circumstance, since it points to the differences in romanizing values that could exist even within so circumscribed a time and place as early eighth-century Northumbria. This is the promotion of the cult of Wilfrid, Acca's predecessor, following Wilfrid's death in 709. The *Historia ecclesiastica* and the *Vita Wilfridi* by Stephen of Ripon, probably written in the decade after 709, depict the late bishop as an energetic proponent of Roman traditions, and the *vita* makes clear Wilfrid's taste for material wealth.[37] Stephen relates how Wilfrid worked hard to provide for the cathedral of York, his first see, and his monasteries at Ripon and Hexham. New lands were acquired, churches renovated, and new constructions built with romanizing architecture and furnishings in gold, silver, and purple cloth.[38] One of Wilfrid's most magnificent commissions, according to Stephen, was a gospel book kept in the church at Ripon, written in gold on purple pages, stored in a gold and gemmed case.[39] In 708 as bishop of Hexham, Stephen reports, Wilfrid divided the Ripon treasure of gold, silver, and jewels into four parts. One portion was sent to Rome. The others were distributed among the poor, his followers, and the abbots of Ripon and Hexham, to provide—it is said—for gifts to kings and bishops.[40]

For Stephen, such actions were compatible with Roman episcopal virtue. There are similarities between the accounts of Wilfrid and his foundations, by Bede as well as Stephen, and those of Wearmouth-Jarrow. The *Ecclesiastical History* notes the embellishment of churches undertaken by both Acca and Wilfrid. Wearmouth-Jarrow, too, was enormously wealthy: the *Vita Ceolfridi* and *Historia abbatum* recall its substantial acquisitions of lands and goods.[41] There are also analogies between the purple-leaved gospel book made under Wilfrid for the Ripon church and the Wearmouth-Jarrow Bibles: Amiatinus with its one purple page (fol. 3/IV), and the two volumes placed in the churches of Wearmouth and Jarrow. A possible parallel exists, too, between

Wilfrid's gift to Rome of gold, silver, and jewels and the gifts that the *Vita Ceolfridi* indicates were sent with Amiatinus. It is not stated what these were, but they may have included objects in precious materials.[42]

The only offering to Rome identified in the *Vita Ceolfridi* and *Historia abbatum*, however, is the Bible. Both the specificity of those references and Bede's ideals for the episcopacy deserves thought in view of the emphasis on material finery in the *Vita Wilfridi*. Although Bede refers to the acquisitions for Hexham, Ripon, and especially Wearmouth-Jarrow in positive terms, his writings reveal his conviction that bishops, like monks, should live according to ascetic principles, attending not to luxury but to biblical studies. The Bible, not earthly wealth, should be the main concern of their devotional lives. Bede attributed these virtues to Acca, to whom he dedicated several commentaries besides *On Genesis*,[43] but it is unclear he associated them with Wilfrid. While Acca commissioned the *Vita Wilfridi*, Bede's attitude toward Wilfrid and his cult seems to have been cool; it has been argued that his *Historia abbatum* was informed by a desire to respond to Stephen's work.[44] In this light, it is interesting how the memory of Wilfrid promoted by Stephen appears, in some ways, at odds with Bede's episcopal (and papal) ideology, and accordingly at odds with the conception of the ideal pontiff—and romanness—suggested by the Ezra miniature. One cannot help wondering whether Bede and his fellow monks intended the painting to express to the holy see an understanding of romanizing virtue they saw as different from that of Wilfrid and his allies. Conceivably, Bede felt compelled to clarify his thinking on this issue because of concerns about Wilfrid and his memory. To raise this possibility, though, is again to insist that, although we should not ignore the Ezra portrait's continuities with Mediterranean art, we must be sensitive to its disjunctions. The key to understanding the *romanitas* of this painting lies less in the antique Mediterranean than in early-eighth-century Northumbria.

Early Medieval Romanness

Early medieval artifacts and writings offer irrefutable evidence of the diffusion of cultural traditions from Antiquity and the Mediterranean regions. Despite, though, the influence evident in the literature, art, and architecture, discontinuities with presumed Roman sources are also frequently apparent. By being more sensitive to the ways even the most romanizing characteristics of early medieval sources are sometimes *not* traceable to antique or Mediterranean productions, we can throw a sharper light on their innovativeness and ties to the specific contexts in which they were made and used. Such an approach should facilitate a more nuanced understanding of romanness, in general, in this era—a greater appreciation for the contribution of not only a distant heritage but local circumstances and thought. Amiatinus's Ezra portrait, a classicizing, northern early medieval painting, is obviously informed by antique and Mediterranean sources, including perhaps a picture in the sixth-century Codex Grandior. Yet much as the ancient Jews restored their Temple and Ezra rewrote some of the burned scriptures in a new script, Bede and the Wearmouth-Jarrow artist—who must have recognized the analogy—drew on a range of ancient texts and imagery to create a fundamentally new picture, one they surely believed better for their purposes than any prototype. The forms and style were meant to look Roman, but they were chosen to express romanizing ideals particular to the Wearmouth-Jarrow monks, ideals that seem to have diverged with those of some Northumbrian contemporaries. Attention to the visual evidence of the Ezra miniature, together with its caption and other contemporary texts, offers new insights into the distinctive values of this one center of production.

Early medieval romanness was a mental and spiritual construct as well as the outgrowth of imported antique and Mediterranean conventions. Classical and postclassical writings and objects shaped how different authors and craftsmen thought about Rome, but their individual imaginings were equally if not more important. In the words of Mayke De Jong, what often emerges from our evidence is a "Rome in the mind," despite links to "real" Mediterranean forms, customs, ideas.[45] Throughout the early medieval West, Roman culture was continually invented and reinvented; the copying and imitation of sources, the deliberate, at times radical reworking of that material, and personal reflection on what Rome and its culture *should* be like all played a part. Even the drive for romanness, like so many other facets of the era's cultural history, reveals diversity and disjuncture with the past.

Notes

My thanks to Felice Lifshitz, Mildred Budny, Scott DeGregorio, and Lawrence Nees for helpful comments and criticisms of earlier drafts of this essay.

1. See Eviatar Zerubavel, *Time Maps: Collective Memory and the Social Shape of the Past* (Chicago: University of Chicago Press, 2003), esp. pp. 11–36.
2. The classic study of this "renaissance" paradigm is by Erwin Panofsky, *Renaissance and Renascences in Western Art*, 2 vols., The Gottesman Lectures, Uppsala University 7 (Stockholm: Almqvist & Wiksell, 1960), esp. Text vol., pp. 42–113. Cf. my article, "Amalarius's *Liber Officialis*: Spirit and Vision in Carolingian Liturgical Thought," in *Seeing the Invisible in Late*

Antiquity and the Early Middle Ages, ed. Giselle de Nie, Karl F. Morrison, and Marco Mostert (Turnhout: Brepols, 2005), pp. 327–37 [327–57]. I deal with related issues in my, "Introduction: The End of the 'Dark Ages,'" in *Literacy, Politics, and Artistic Innovation in the Early Medieval West*, ed. Celia M. Chazelle (Lanham, MD: University Press of America Press, 1992), pp. 1–18.

3. Cf. Richard Sullivan, "The Carolingian Age: Reflections on Its Place in the History of the Middle Ages," *Speculum* 64 (1989): esp. 272–78 [267–306].

4. For analysis of these and other problematic tendencies, Geoffrey Koziol, "The Dangers of Polemic: Is Ritual Still an Interesting Topic of Historical Study?" *Early Medieval Europe* 11 (2002): 367–88; Philippe Buc, *The Dangers of Ritual: Between Early Medieval Texts and Social Scientific Theory* (Princeton: Princeton University Press, 2001). Also see Sarah Foot, "Finding the Meaning of Form: Narrative in Annals and Chronicles," in *Writing Medieval History*, ed. Nancy Partner (London: Hodder Arnold, 2005), pp. 88–108; Hayden White, *The Content of the Form: Narrative Discourse and Historical Representation* (Baltimore: John Hopkins University Press, 1987), pp. 1–57.

5. For instance, the discussion of Carolingian culture in the latest edition of H.W. Janson (with Anthony F. Janson), *History of Art: The Western Tradition* (Upper Saddle River, NJ: Pearson/Prentice-Hall, 2004), p. 276: "The fact that these letters [Caroline minuscule] are known today as Roman rather than Carolingian recalls another aspect of the cultural reforms sponsored by Charlemagne: the collecting and copying of ancient Roman literature..." (and so on). My thanks to Lawrence Nees for this reference.

6. This approach seems to me to inform, for example, the discussion of reform under Pippin III and Charlemagne in the otherwise fine book by Yitzhak Hen, *The Royal Patronage of Liturgy in Frankish Gaul: To the Death of Charles the Bald (877),* Henry Bradshaw Society (London: Boydell, 2001), pp. 42–95. In textbooks, a common type of subheading under which such lines of thought are articulated is "The Transmission of Learning": for example, F. Donald Logan, *The History of the Church in the Middle Ages* (London: Routledge, 2002), pp. 59–63.

7. Jennifer O'Reilly, "The Art of Authority," in *After Rome*, ed. Thomas Charles-Edwards (Oxford: Oxford University Press, 2003), pp. 141–89; Mayke de Jong, "Religion," in *The Early Middle Ages: Europe 400–1000*, ed. Rosamond McKitterick (Oxford: Oxford University Press, 2001), pp. 132–42 [131–64].

8. Lawrence Nees, *Early Medieval Art* (Oxford: Oxford University Press, 2002), pp. 9–15.

9. Nees, *Early Medieval Art*, p. 15; Michel Sot, "Le Mythe des origines romaines de Reims au Xème siècle," in *Rome et les églises nationales VIIe-XIIIe siècles*, ed. Claude Carozzi and Philippe George (Aix-en-Provence: Publications de l'Université de Provence, 1991), pp. 55–74.

10. Florence, Biblioteca Medicea Laurenziana, Cod. Amiatino 1, fol. 4/Vr; *La Bibbia Amiatina/The Codex Amiatinus, Complete Reproduction on CD-ROM of the Manuscript Firenze, Biblioteca Medicea Laurenziana, Amiatino 1*, ed. Luigi G.G. Ricci et al. (Florence: SISMEL: Edizioni del Galluzzo, 2000).

11. Bede, *Historia abbatum* (henceforth *HA*) 15, *Vita Ceolfridi* (henceforth *VC*) 20, 37, in *Venerabilis Baedae Historiam Ecclesiasticam Gentis Anglorum, Historiam abbatum, Epistolam ad Ecgberctum, una cum Historia abbatum auctore anonymo*, ed. Charles Plummer, 2 vols. (Oxford: Clarendon, 1896), 1: 379–80, 394–95, 402.

12. Kurt Weitzmann, *Illustrations in Roll and Codex: A Study of the Origin and Method of Text Illustration* (Princeton: Princeton University Press, 1947).

13. Esp. John Lowden, "The Beginnings of Biblical Illustration," in *Imaging the Early Medieval Bible*, ed. John Williams (University Park, PA: Pennsylvania State University Press, 1999), pp. 9–59. Also see John Williams, "Introduction," in Williams, *Imaging*, pp. 1–8; Eva Frojmovic, "Messianic Politics in Re-Christianized Spain: Images of the Sanctuary in Hebrew Bible Manuscripts," in *Imagining the Self, Imagining the Other*, ed. Eva Frojmovic (Leiden: Brill, 2002), pp. 91–128. My thanks to Susan Einbinder for bringing Frojmovic's article to my attention.

14. See John Moreland, *Archaeology and Text* (London, 2001), esp. pp. 94–97.

15. Fol. 4/Vr: "Codicibus sacris hostili clade perustis/ Esdra Deo feruens hoc reparauit opus."

16. Correcting my interpretation in, "Ceolfrid's Gift to St. Peter: The First Quire of the Codex Amiatinus and the Evidence of Its Roman Destination," *Early Medieval Europe* 12 (2003): 155 [129–57]. Compare the high priest (Aaron) in León, Real Colegiata de San Isidoro, Cod. 2, Bible of 960, fol. 50r: Williams, *Imaging*, Color Pl. 15.

17. See, for example, R.L.S. Bruce-Mitford, *The Art of the Codex Amiatinus* (Jarrow: The Rectory, 1966), pp. 13–14; George Henderson, *Vision and Image in Early Christian England* (Cambridge, UK: Cambridge University Press, 1999), pp. 81–87; Mark Vessey, "Introduction," *Cassiodorus: Institutions of Divine and Secular Learning and on the Soul*, trans. James W. Halporn, intro. Mark Vessey, Translated Texts for Historians (Liverpool: Liverpool University Press, 2004), pp. 7–10 [3–101].

18. See Lawrence Nees, "The Originality of Early Medieval Artists," in Chazelle, *Literacy, Politics, and Artistic Innovation*, pp. 77–109.

19. For example, Paul Meyvaert, "The Date of Bede's *In Ezram* and His Image of Ezra in the Codex Amiatinus," *Speculum* 80 (2005): 1107–27 [1087–33]; Jennifer O'Reilly, "The Library of Scripture: Views from Vivarium and Wearmouth Jarrow," in *New Offerings, Ancient Treasures: Studies in Medieval Art for George Henderson*, ed. Paul Binski and William Noel (Stroud: Sutton, 2001), pp. 3–39.

20. Celia Chazelle, "The Three Chapters Controversy and the Biblical Diagrams of Cassiodorus's Codex Grandior and *Institutions*," in *The Crisis*

    of the Oikoumene: The Three Chapters and the Failed Quest for Unity in the Sixth-Century Mediterranean, ed. Celia Chazelle and Catherine Cubitt (Turnhout: Brepols, forthcoming).

21. Cf. Lawrence Nees, "Problems of Form and Function in Early Medieval Illustrated Bibles From Northwest Europe," in Williams, *Imaging*, pp. 151–58 [121–77].

22. Two earlier depictions of Ezra standing are Paris, BnF syr. 341, fol. 212r and a fresco in the Dura-Europos synagogue (photo, Index of Christian Art). My thanks to Dr. Adelaide Bennett for her assistance. No image of a scribe predating the Amiatinus portrait in the Index archive shows him as a Jewish priest or high priest.

23. See I Esdras 7:6, 11, 12, 21; II Esdras 8:1, 4, 9, 13; 12.26, 35. Ezra's high priestly office is mentioned in rabbinic writings and the Old Latin Ezra A' (III Ezra), a book in Grandior but not Amiatinus's Vulgate: III Ezra 9: 39–40, 50, *Biblia sacra iuxta Vulgatam versionem*, ed. Robert Weber, 2 vols. (Stuttgart: Württembergische Bibelanstalt, 1969), 1: 1930; see Cassiodorus, *Institutiones* 1.14.1, ed. R.A.B. Mynors, corrected repr. (Oxford: Clarendon Press, 1961), p. 39. My thanks to Dr. Susan Einbinder concerning the rabbinic texts. IV Esdras 14: 24–48, a text in neither Grandior nor Amiatinus that circulated in early medieval England, records that after the Chaldeans burned the Jerusalem library (IV Kings 25), Ezra miraculously dictated some of the lost scriptures to five scribes who wrote in newly devised letters. Several church fathers mention that Ezra himself rewrote the burned books without attributing to him the high priesthood or a new script. See *The Fourth Book of Ezra*, ed. R.L. Bensly, in *Texts and Studies: Contributions to Biblical and Patristic Literature*, Vol. 3.2, ed. J.A. Robinson (Cambridge, UK: Cambridge University Press, 1895), pp. xxxv–xxxviii, 70–72; Paul Meyvaert, "Bede, Cassiodorus, and the Codex Amiatinus," *Speculum* 71 (1996): 874–76 [827–83].

24. *Bede: A Biblical Miscellany*, trans. W. Trent Foley and Arthur Holder, Translated Texts for Historians (Liverpool: Liverpool University Press, 1999), p. 102 (with my emendations); Bede, *In Regem librum XXX Quaestiones* 7, CCSL 119, ed. David Hurst (Turnhout: Brepols, 1962), pp. 301–02: "Vastata namque a Chaldeis Iudaea et bibliotheca antiquitus congregata inter alias prouinciae opes hostili igne consumpta ex qua pauci qui nunc in sancta scriptura continentur libri postmodum Ezrae pontificis et prophetae sunt industria restaurati. Unde scriptum est de eo, 'Ascendit Ezras de Babilone et ipse scriba uelox in lege Moysi', uelox uidelicet quia promptiores litterarum figuras quam eatenus Hebraei habebant repperit...." On the treatise's date, Paul Meyvaert, "'In the Footsteps of the Fathers': The Date of Bede's *Thirty Questions on the Book of Kings* to Nothelm," in *The Limits of Ancient Christianity: Essays on Late Antique Thought and Culture in Honour of R.A. Markus*, ed. W.E. Klingshirn and Mark Vessey (Ann Arbor: University of Michigan Press, 1997), pp. 267–86.

25. "Ceolfrid's Gift," 152–57 (see above, n16).
26. Scott DeGregorio, "Bede's *In Ezram et Neemiam* and the Reform of the Northumbrian Church," *Speculum* 79 (2004): esp. 18 and n80 [1–25]. Cf. *Epistola ad Ecgbertum*, 3, 7, *Venerabilis Baedae* 1: 406, 411; *Historia ecclesiastica* 2.1 (henceforth *HE*), *Venerabilis Baedae* 1: 74, 77.
27. Meyvaert, "Bede, Cassiodorus," pp. 881–82.
28. See Bede, *De Templo*, CCSL 119A, ed. David Hurst (Turnhout: Brepols, 1969), pp. 143–234; O'Reilly, "Library of Scripture," esp. pp. 22–30; Bianca Kühnel, "Jewish Symbolism of the Tabernacle and Christian Symbolism of the Holy Sepulchre and the Heavenly Tabernacle," *Jewish Art* 12–13 (1986–1987): 147–68.
29. Alan Thacker, "Bede's Ideal of Reform," in *Ideal and Reality in Frankish and Anglo-Saxon Society*, ed. Patrick Wormald et al. (Oxford: Basil Blackwell, 1983), pp. 130–53; see Scott DeGregorio, "'Nostrorum socordiam temporum': The Reforming Impulse of Bede's Later Exegesis," *Early Medieval Europe* 11 (2002): 107–22.
30. *The Earliest Life of Gregory the Great, By an Anonymous Monk of Whitby*, ed. Bertram Colgrave (Lawrence: University of Kansas Press, 1968); *HE* 2.1: 73–81; Alan Thacker, "Memorializing Gregory the Great: The Origin and Transmission of a Papal Cult in the Seventh and Early Eighth Centuries," *Early Medieval Europe* 7 (1998): 59–84.
31. "Nam alii quidam pontifices construendis ornandisque auro uel argento ecclesiis operam dabant, hic autem totus erga animarum lucra uacabat": *HE* 2.1: 77.
32. "Perduxique opus usque dum eiectus Adam de paradiso uoluptatis exilium uitae temporalis intrauit. Aliqua etiam de sequentibus sacrae historiae, si Deus uoluerit auxilio uestrae intercessionis comitante, scripturus, dum primo librum sancti Esrae prophetae ac sacerdotis in quo Christi et ecclesiae sacramenta sub figura, solutae longae captiuitatis, restaurati templi, reaedificatae ciuitatis, reductorum in Hierosolimam uasorum quae abducta, rescriptae legis Dei quae incensa fuerat, castigati ab uxoribus alienigenis populi, et uno corde atque anima in dei seruitium conuersi, ut propheta simul et historicus conscripsit, parum perscrutatus fuero, et aliqua ex his quae commemoraui sacramentis apertiora studiosis, Deo fauente, reddidero": Bede, *In Genesim*, CCSL 118A, ed. C.W. Jones (Turnhout: Brepols, 1967), p. 2. My thanks to Scott DeGregorio for the translation.
33. "Introduction," in *Bede: On Ezra and Nehemiah*, trans. Scott DeGregorio, Translated Texts for Historians (Liverpool: Liverpool University Press, 2006), p. xl.
34. "Sed et vasa templi Dei aurea et argentea, quae Nabuchodonosor tulerat de templo Ierusalem, et attulerat ea in Babylonem, reddantur, et referantur in templum in Ierusalem in locum suum...."
35. "...libere accipe, et sutiose eme de hac pecunia vitulos, arietes, agnos et sacrificia et libamina eorum...."

36. See above, n23.
37. *The Life of Bishop Wilfrid by Eddius Stephanus*, ed. Bertram Colgrave (Cambridge, UK: Cambridge University Press, 1927); henceforth *VW*; *HE* 5.19: 322–30.
38. *VW* 16–17, 22, pp. 32–36, 44–46.
39. *VW* 17, p. 26; see *HE* 5.19: 330.
40. *VW* 63, p. 136.
41. *HE* 5.19, 20: 528, 530; *VC* 7, 9, 20; *HA* 5, 6, 9, 15, pp. 390–91, 394–95, 368–70, 373, 379–80.
42. *VC* 22, p. 395.
43. Plummer, "Introduction," *Venerabilis Baedae* 1: xlix n2.
44. Walter Goffart, *The Narrators of Barbarian History (A.D. 550–800): Jordanes, Gregory of Tours, Bede, and Paul the Deacon* (Princeton: Princeton University Press, 1988), pp. 285–95; Ian Wood, *The Most Holy Abbot Ceolfrid* (Jarrow: The Rectory, 1995), p. 8.
45. De Jong, "Religion," p. 138.

PART II

METHODS: TEXTS AND MANUSCRIPTS
FROM CAROLINGIAN FRANCIA

CHAPTER 6

A CYBORG INITIATION? LITURGY AND GENDER IN CAROLINGIAN EAST FRANCIA

Felice Lifshitz

Examination of eighth- and ninth-century liturgical manuscripts showing locally differentiated baptismal practices informed by gender ideology, which thus undermine notions of the linear evolution of baptismal rites.

Every event and action (including thought) occurs in a particular place.[1] Nevertheless, that fact is not accorded equal weight in all historical explorations. While the preferred method among economic and social historians is immersion in archival sources of indisputable relevance to a given locality, scholars who specialize in other aspects of life have less often considered attention to local variety as a *sine qua non* of their methodology. Whereas certain aspects of religious belief and practice, most notably saints' cults, have been subjected to local or regional analysis,[2] scholarship on another key facet of religious experience, namely the liturgy, has been relatively impervious to the importance of local and regional specificity. Rather than looking for variety, historians of Christian liturgy have generally been primarily interested in the construction of regionally undifferentiated emplotments of change over time. With specific reference to the history of baptism, a common trajectory runs as follows: Augustine of Hippo's doctrine of congenitally transmitted Original Sin soon leads to the universal introduction of infant baptism occurring soon after an individual birth, a practice that strips ethical content from the baptismal rite, rendering it an operation performed on a passive baby, as well as a ceremony primarily concerned with the creation of fictive kinship bonds among the active adults.[3] Even authors who argue that practice diverged from the clerical ideal of immediate infant baptism, nonetheless accept that immediate infant baptism, with its logically concomitant emphasis on god-parentage, did represent a universal clerical ideal.[4]

Yet, synthetic emplotments of liturgical change over time are extremely problematic, for the evidentiary basis on which such syntheses are constructed—editions of liturgical manuscripts—are artificial creations. The production of a critical edition of any text involves, as more and more scholars are realizing, the suppression of evidence attesting to rampant variety.[5] Exclusive reliance upon critical editions of medieval sources (including liturgical ones) yields a misleading picture of a coherent cultural landscape. For instance (according to the editor of "the" Gregorian sacramentary), Cambrai, Bibliothèque Municipale MS 164 is the only accurate copy of a sacramentary sent by Pope Hadrian to Charlemagne.[6] Of the thirty-nine other extant copies of "the" Gregorian sacramentary, eight are labeled by the editor as a "corrected" version, seven as a "reorganized" version, and twelve as a "corrected" version of the "reorganized" version; nine surviving "copies" of "the" Gregorian sacramentary were judged by the editor as too unlike the Cambrai manuscript to be used for the edition at all.[7] Jean Deshusses, the eminent textual scholar responsible for the monumental edition of the sacramentary, certainly understood fully the realities of medieval manuscript evidence. The implications of the evidentiary landscape, however, have not been taken into account in historical scenarios (based on Deshusses's edition) describing the diffusion of "the" *Gregorianum* throughout Francia in the wake of the alliance between Charlemagne and Hadrian.

It is above all in connection with the rite of baptism, the subject of the present essay, that recent scholarship has begun to face squarely the evidence for local and regional liturgical variety. The publication of groundbreaking studies by Glenn Byer and Susan Keefe[8] make it possible for me to explore the liturgy of baptism as a local phenomenon during the Carolingian period east of the middle Rhine, a region about which I am writing a monographic study.[9] To write liturgical history as local history involves, first and foremost, the methodological decision to utilize as sources only specific manuscripts associated with the locality in question. No complete sacramentaries ("Gregorian" or otherwise) survive from the region from the eighth or early ninth centuries, yet we cannot simply cherry-pick evidence from other surviving contemporary sacramentaries in order to supplement the sparse regional evidence. Comparison of an eighth-century sacramentary fragment that does survive from this area, containing the local liturgy for the feast of the Epiphany, with the liturgies for Epiphany in other eighth-century sacramentaries revealed significant variations between the Würzburg-area rite and those in use elsewhere.[10] In the present essay, as in the larger study of which it forms a part, I examine the body of Würzburg-area sources first and foremost from the perspective of gender history. Like the study of liturgy as a localized phenomenon, the examination of liturgy through the lens of gender has not been common. For instance, the liturgy of Visigothic Spain included full-fledged public rites for the partial tonsuring of boys who would not pursue clerical careers, for the full tonsuring of boys who would pursue clerical careers, for the entry into school of all boys destined to receive a formal education, and for the shaving or cutting of an adolescent boy's first beard. Despite the fact that this complex of rites was both exclusive to males and presumably constitutive of Christian masculinity in Visigothic Spain, the only study of these aspects of Visigothic liturgy treats them as relevant to the majority of the faithful in childhood and adolescence, and as manifestations of the need to bless different life stages, while mentioning neither the exclusive maleness of the participants in these rites, nor the very existence of the many females who clearly did not participate in them.[11]

On the specific topic of baptismal liturgy, the paucity of scholarship on the gender aspects of the rite that effectively replaced the Jewish initiation rite of circumcision is almost shocking. Theoretically comprehensive studies of baptismal rites in Late Antiquity and the early Middle Ages are silent on gender issues.[12] Even in a volume of essays dedicated to the exploration of gender and initiation rites, the contribution on Christian baptismal rites virtually ignored gender![13] Sometimes scholars note, but fail to explore the significance of, gendered liturgical practices. Gabriel Ramis, for instance, reports but does not explore the fact that the Antiphonary of León assigned either to fathers or to mothers the task of presenting a child for baptism (albeit preferring that the presentation be made by the father), but assigned exclusively to mothers the role of holding a child during the exorcism portion of the rite.[14] Initiation ceremonies, in conjunction with a long informal process of socialization, are crucial in the creation of identities, including gender identities; with the exception of Christian baptismal rites, such initiation rites have been well studied.[15] Asking questions about gender in connection with Christian baptismal rites would undoubtedly enrich our understanding of European history, but it should be done carefully, avoiding the methodological pitfall of assuming that any surviving liturgical manuscript can provide information valid for all regions.

Particularly worth future exploration is the Sacramentary of Gellone. The manuscript was made in the 790s for the cathedral of Cambrai (the

same see that produced the *Gregorianum*), at the time closely connected
with Charlemagne's court; the manuscript was soon thereafter sent to
Septimania.[16] It happens to include an extremely gendered baptismal rite
that prescribes a system of weekly Lenten-period scrutinies leading up to
baptism on the day before Easter. Each scrutiny consists of many parts,
such as the writing of the names of the catechumens, blessings and sign-
ings of the catechumens, and so forth. At every point, males and females
are treated separately, not only through their physical separation into two
segregated groups but also through the provision of different formulae for
male as opposed to female catechumens. Separate formulae permits the
grammatical underlining of the fact that initiates are in fact both male
and female, since they can be described (for example) as "*hos famulos*"
(these males servants) and then as "*has famulas*" (these female servants).
The substantive differences between the male and female versions of the
rite underline gender difference when, for instance, males are exorcized
(no. 407) in the name of the God who walked on water (a miracle performed for a group of male apostles) and females are exorcized (no. 408)
in the name of the God who raised Lazarus (a miracle performed for some
of Jesus's female disciples, the sisters of Lazarus). Every action is performed
first by, on, or concerning the male catechumens, and then by, on, or
concerning the female catechumens. Thus one acolyte first recites the
creed in Greek over a male initiate, and a second acolyte then recites the
creed in Latin over a female initiate.[17] The baptismal liturgy of the
Sacramentary of Gellone deserves further study along or perhaps in connection with the starkly gendered Visigothic rites described above. It
should not, however, be used as evidence for baptismal practice in all
Latin churches during the eighth and ninth centuries.[18]

To judge by Gisela Muschiol's very recent attempt (the first published
essay on the topic known to me) to begin the examination of "the role of
gender difference in the western liturgy," specialists are far from recognizing local variation as a crucial concern, even if they have embraced
gender as a legitimate category of analysis.[19] In striking contrast to my
modus operandi here, Muschiol utilizes no manuscript evidence whatso-
ever, and eschews all local specificity. She cites, for instance, the ruling of
a (unnamed) sixth-century synod that married women should cover their
hands at communion, and married men wash their hands before communion, as general evidence for a consciousness of gender in the liturgy
of Merovingian Francia.[20] In contrast, I do not feel able to assess the
evidentiary value of this canon without additional information, such as
which synod issued the ruling, which individuals attended that synod,
and in which manuscript(s) the canon is transmitted.

The present essay constitutes an attempt to study Christian liturgy as
both a localized and a gendered practice, on the basis of manuscript

evidence. The relevant manuscripts can now be easily identified, due to recent studies of Carolingian baptismal practice. In 811/812, Charlemagne and his advisors carried out an empire-wide survey concerning the baptismal liturgy. They posed a series of questions such as "for what reason are the nostrils touched?"[21] The inquiry process also stimulated the production of additional discussions of the baptismal rite. The relevant texts, whether directly connected with the inquiry or independent of it, total sixty-one. They have been sorted and associated with authors or institutions by Susan Keefe. Each text, in Keefe's words, "reflect[s] the preferences, concerns, or needs of the specific area in which [it] was copied."[22]

Three of the codices listed by Keefe are relevant to the region east of the middle Rhine: Merseburg, Domstiftsbibliothek MS 136 (Naumburg Domarchiv s.n.), produced at Fulda between 800 and 820; Sélestat, Bibliothèque Humaniste (Bibliothèque Municipale) MS 132, produced in the mid-ninth century at Mainz; and Vatican City, Bibliotheca Apostolica Vaticana, MS Palatinus latinus 485, produced between 860 and 875 at the monastery of Lorsch.[23] The Merseburg and Sélestat manuscripts are examples of what Keefe calls instruction-readers, that is, books produced under episcopal supervision for the instruction of parish clergy.[24] The Vatican manuscript is an example of a schoolbook, used for the instruction of future parish priests; this manuscript was the textbook used at Lorsch.[25] One of the sixty-one baptismal discussions cataloged by Keefe (Text 42) appears both in the Lorsch schoolbook and in the Sélestat instruction-reader (and nowhere else): a discussion of the rite as practiced in the archdiocese of Mainz, either written by archbishop Riculf (787–813) or one of his associates in response to the inquiry of 811/812, or derived very soon thereafter from such a response.[26] The evidentiary value of Keefe's Text 42 for my study is thus quite clear; the Merseburg instruction-reader, however, requires more extensive comment.

Keefe understands all the books in her study as intended for educational purposes, rather than for use in a pastoral context, in part due to the overall rarity of vernacular materials in the compilations. However, two of the four manuscripts in her catalog that do contain vernacular materials (Vatican, Palatinus latinus 485 and Merseburg, Domstiftsbibliothek 136) are relevant to our region. The Merseburg codex is an artificial collection of disparate booklets and leaves. It is the first, originally independent, part of the collection that is of interest here: a *libellus* [little book] spread over twenty-one folios (fols. 3r–23v) in two quires, written at Fulda by a single scribe/author in a short period of time, in a german-insular script typical of the area east of the middle Rhine.[27] This *libellus* contains (among other things) a popular (albeit anonymous) Exposition on the Mass,[28] glosses on the prayers of the baptismal rite,[29] and a baptismal rite.

The rite is complete with red crosses in the margins to remind the celebrant when to make the sign of the cross, and a vernacular baptismal renunciation of Satan and profession of faith (known as the Franconian baptismal vow) for the new initiate.[30] The Franconian dialect of the vow was utilized throughout the area east of the Middle Rhine from Fulda in the north to Lorsch in the south.[31]

The Franconian baptismal vow in the Merseburg manuscript requires the priest to pose a series of questions to the catechumen, each beginning either with "Forsahhistu?" (do you foresake?) or "Gilaubistu?" (do you believe?) (see cover illustration). The interrogation requires, for each question, a statement from the catechumen of either "ih fursahhu" (I forsake) or "ih gilaubu" (I believe). Only after the initiate had many times actively renounced the devil and professed belief, did the priest proclaim: "Exorcizatur malignus spiritus ut exeat et recedat dans locum deo. Exi ab eo spiritus inmunde et redde honorem deo vivo et vero. Accipe signum crucis christi tam in fronte quam in corde. Sume fidem caelestium preceptorum. Talis esto in opibus ut templus dei" (Let the malignant spirit exit and recede, giving its place to God. Go out from him, unclean spirit, and give honor to the living and true God. Receive the sign of the cross of Christ both on your forehead and in your heart. Take up the faith of our heavenly preceptors. Be thus in your works like a temple of God).[32] Philological scholarship on the vernacular portions of the Merseburg manuscript is unanimous in considering the text as intended for use.[33] Furthermore, the vernacular baptismal vow occupies (along with its Latin stage directions) the entire folio in large, clear, and easily readable lettering. There can be little doubt that this rite was meant for practical application.

Another group of manuscripts is also relevant for the understanding of liturgical practice east of the middle Rhine in the Carolingian period. Interest in liturgy during the Carolingian era manifested itself not only in projects such as the baptismal survey of 811/812, but also in engagement with Isidore of Seville's *De ecclesiasticis officiis*, for many centuries the definitive treatise on the Christian liturgy.[34] Twenty-four of the sixty-one early Carolingian discussions of baptism identified by Keefe, including two that appear in both the Sélestat and Vatican manuscripts (Keefe's Texts 42 and 60), made extensive use of Isidore's *De ecclesiasticis officiis*. Two copies of Isidore's treatise survive from the Würzburg area. One, now Würzburg, Universitätsbibliothek M.p.th.q.18, was produced in a lower Main Valley women's scriptorium (one associated with the name of a particular scribe, Abirhilt) in the second half of the eighth century.[35] Another copy of the treatise, now Würzburg, Universitätsbibliothek M.p.th.o.4, was produced at and for the Würzburg cathedral during the second third of the ninth century.[36] This evidence can also help elucidate how local intellectuals perceived gender and liturgy.

Before turning to an analysis of the sources, it is necessary to clarify one point concerning the region under consideration—the area east of the middle Rhine. By the ninth century, the localities in question (along both sides of the Main river valley from Mainz through Würzburg and a bit beyond, including the Odenwald and the Spessart) had long been Christianized and integrated into Francia. The region should not be confused with Saxony to the north or the Slavic territories to the east. Even the area around Fulda, the farthest afield of all the localities relevant to my study, was effectively populated by Christians, although the Fulda monks were active in missions to the Saxons further north. Here I am introducing only the evidence relevant to the long-Christianized Frankish territories. The baptismal rite in the Merseburg manuscript was not intended for use in a missionary effort to adult non-Christians, for the Franconian dialect of the vow was the spoken language of the Rhineland, not of Saxony. A second extant copy of the Franconian vow adapts the language to Bavarian speech patterns, suggesting that the vernacular formula was created at Mainz, a deeply Romanized city, for introduction throughout the already Christianized province, and had no connection with Fulda's missionary duties.[37]

The handful of manuscripts described above represents an extremely fragmentary set of sources. It is clearly impossible to reconstruct fully baptismal experience in ninth-century East Francia. Even studies of late medieval baptism, which benefit from the documentary explosion characteristic of Europe from the thirteenth century onward, must struggle with significant lacunae. One scholar of later medieval baptismal practice, for example, could not determine whether the initiate's biological father participated in the church rite; it is possible his role consisted entirely of entertaining guests at a tavern or inn during and after the ritual![38] Even greater doubts dog the present attempt to understand baptismal practice. Yet, despite the many remaining uncertainties, we must look as closely as possible at baptism, a Christian life event whose significance cannot be overestimated. As Keefe asserted, "the rite of baptism...put its stamp on every individual, not only as part of the Church, but as a member of society...it was the cornerstone of Carolingian society."[39]

Historians have barely addressed, though, the role that gender played in the process of becoming a member of Christian society. Did individuals, at least in the area under consideration during the ninth century, enter Christian society as specifically gendered beings? If so, was the initiation rite itself constitutive of Christian gender identities?

Gender analysis thrives on a consciousness of embodiment and corpo-reality: we must first try to visualize the actual bodies of the individuals in question. The Würzburg area was one of several regions of the Frankish empire to boast a fully functioning catechumenate, a period of instruc-tion culminating in an Eastertide ceremony in which the new initiate is examined concerning her or his apprehension of the basic tenets of the Trinitarian faith.[40] In contrast, church leaders in other areas staged year-round infant baptisms or instituted partial, sometimes dramatically atten-uated catechumenates that did not demand much participation from would-be initiates. The very definition of a catechumen in the archdio-cese of Mainz, to judge by Text 42 in both the Sélestat and Vatican man-uscripts (a text unique to those manuscripts), was a person who had been hearing and learning the truth of the Trinity, but who had not yet been baptized.[41] The existence of a functioning catechumenate is consistent with the need for a vernacular formula for the renunciation of Satan and profession of faith, such as is witnessed in the Merseburg manual. I sug-gest, therefore, that we envision the initiates in question as children of at least three and more likely four or five years of age. Perhaps they were even somewhat older, around six or seven, but they were not adults. In referring to Christian baptismal initiates, the Mainz texts and Merseburg manuscript refer regularly to *pueri* [boys] or *infantes*, words coded to express the relative youth of the initiates.[42]

The biological sex of the initiates is nowhere explicitly mentioned, or even subliminally evoked, in the East Frankish rite, although the rite did include a series of actions performed upon the body of the initiate. Salt and the Eucharist were placed in the initiate's mouth, water on her or his head, and chrism on her or his nostrils and ears. Whereas circumcision targeted precisely a part of the body designed to highlight corporeal dif-ferences between females and males, this baptismal rite targeted body parts that—although certainly potentially gendered—were far less saturated with gendered significance than is a penis. No ritual attention was paid to any parts of the body that could eventually broadcast a per-son's male or female gender identity (breasts, chins and cheeks, throats, waists, shoulders). Furthermore, the Mainz baptismal exposition, found in the Vatican and Sélestat manuscripts, parses the significance of each stage in the baptismal rite without suggestion of gendered distinctions between the natures or capacities of male and female initiates. Every catechumen's ears are touched with chrism in order to permit Jesus and the spirit of wisdom to enter the initiate, which happens through the ears because the ears are the route to every person's intellect.[43] Every catechumen's head is anointed with chrism, to indicate that the new Christian has joined a royal and sacerdotal race.[44] There is certainly no sign of the thoroughgoing gender binary that permeated the Sacramentary of Gellone.

During the ninth century, east of the middle Rhine, all the ritual actions that effected a Christian baptism were performed on the most resolutely non-gendered body parts of the bodies of children, inevitably not yet differentiated along gender lines. Furthermore, all baptisms were performed at once, as part of the Easter ceremonial, rather than strung out throughout the year as a series of lesser events. All the children participated as a single, nonsegregated group in an impressive mass ceremony, whose significance was apparently not understood by priests and liturgical specialists (responsible for interpreting the rite to the congregation) to differ depending upon the biological sex of the new Christian. The initiates, like the audience, could consciously experience and possibly subsequently remember the initiation ceremony.

Baptism provided a stunning sacral moment in which to dramatize gender and have it play a role—or not—in defining the citizens of Christian society. Christians who experienced (from any subject position) the consistently gendered baptismal rite detailed in the Sacramentary of Gellone would, most likely, infer that Christian citizenship was itself a gendered status, one that differed (if only slightly) between males and females. The gendered rite in Gellone lay, effectively, on a continuum with Jewish boys' ritual circumcision, with Jewish boys' torah-study initiation rites, and with the profusion of initiation procedures the world over that have been shown to be central to the creation of the gendered adult personae encountered in every society.[45] When I began this project, I devoted myself to reading the scholarship on gender initiation rites, because—based on my prior knowledge of the Sacramentary of Gellone—I assumed that literature would be both relevant and helpful. It required an epiphany to notice the absence of gendered significance in the East Frankish materials.

Gender analysis thrives on a consciousness not only of embodiment and corporeality, but also of silences, gaps, and absences. Indeed, the absence of any explicit reference to social gender, or to biological sex, in the Würzburg area sources must itself be interrogated. Explicit references to gender are absent, but gender in general is not, for Latin as a language is grammatically gendered. The linguistic evidence of the Fulda *libellus* in the Merseburg manuscript is intriguing. Throughout the booklet, the scribe/author consistently foregrounds the fact that the congregation includes both women and men,[46] yet utilizes exclusively masculine grammatical forms (such as *puer* and *famulus*, along with masculine pronouns and adjectives) in reference to the initiate both during the baptismal rite and in the subsequent discussion of the rite. For instance, the priest is instructed "Quando mittis puerum in fontem, merges eum tribus vicibus" (When you place the boy/child in the font, you submerge him three times; fol. 19r) and "antequam baptizatus ille aliquid gustet, da illi eucharistiam" (Before the one [masculine] who has been baptized tastes anything, give him the Eucharist; fol. 19v). It is one thing for the Würzburg-area materials to treat male and female initiates simultaneously and without distinction of gender; it is, potentially, quite another thing for the author/scribe of the texts to write, grammatically speaking, as if all initiates were best described by masculine gendered words.

The author/scribe considered it neither onerous nor superfluous to utilize both male and female grammatical forms when describing a heterosocial group, for he did so in reference to the congregation, so we must explore the author/scribe's deliberate choice to abandon feminine grammatical forms at this point in the manuscript. The evidentiary base is too sparse to come to any single solid conclusion concerning the significance of this particular silence. However, it may well be that a single solid conclusion would not, in any case, be in order. In other words, it may well be most productive to explore this particular silence with a heightened sensitivity to the fact that the event in question, Christian baptism, is a sacrament and, therefore, on some level a mystery whose significance cannot be fully apprehended through single solid conclusions.

The voluminous cultural anthropological scholarship on gender and "rites of passage" to which I initially turned for help in understanding Christian baptism in ninth-century East Francia was, in this regard, especially unhelpful and misleading. All that scholarship focused on unpacking rituals that created a stark gender binary, such that each individual emerged from the process either fully socially male or fully socially female. I have since found unexpected inspiration in an alternative metaphor for envisioning social identity at the moment of initiation into the Christian community: the hybridity of the boundary-defying cyborg, which merges organism and machine into a single complex being that explodes all binaries, including "men and women." The cyborg, so understood, is primatologist and theorist Donna Haraway's contribution to "the utopian dream of the hope for a monstrous world without gender."[47] Far from being made through the Christian initiation rite of baptism, gender in at least this particular Christian society was effectively unmade. Unlike many other initiation rites constitutive of membership in a given society, rites that create gendered social beings, at least some forms of Christian initiation effectively created non-gendered citizens.

To begin with, the initiates—as small children—were presumably pre-gender already; the masculine forms *puer* and *famulus* may be likened to the German neuter noun *Kind* [child]. The human social status of the child initiate may have been understood by contemporaries to be best expressed through the language used. However, this explanation seems too simplistic and reductive to penetrate to the heart of the significance of a sacramental event, an event that had the power to transform the identities of those who passed through it, at least on a transcendent level. I suggest that the rite itself (not simply the age of the participants in it) required the use of masculine forms to describe the new initiates. All treatments of baptism, including those in the Mainz exposition and in Isidore of Seville's comprehensive treatise (the relevant portion of which is present in the Abirhilt-group manuscript of the text), understand the initiate to be recapitulating and imitating Christ's own journey of death and rebirth. One becomes a Christian by—in this liturgical moment— becoming a Christ, a figure gendered as masculine in mainstream Christian traditions.[48] The social and biological identity of each initiate was, in terms of Christian society, joined to and then overshadowed by that of Christ. Mysteriously the cyborg initiation rendered a female catechumen both male and female (with the masculine grammatical gender predominating), both human and divine. We might even go one step further for, when the female vanishes, so (effectively) does the male. If there is no binary, if there is no dichotomy, there is no distinction of gender. The masculine ceases to be masculine, becoming neuter, and gender is unmade.

The linguistic vanishing of the female and the feminine at the moment of baptism—east of the middle Rhine—reflected a commitment to the full implications of the belief that grace really can erase distinctions of sex. Each Easter season east of the middle Rhine, around 800, clerics taught, and Christians presumably learned, an effectively egalitarian lesson. The lesson did not, of course, purge gender distinctions completely from social life. But the great promise of the sacrament of baptism was fully incorporated into the rite itself, for that one brief shining genderless moment. My suggestion that baptismal practice east of the middle Rhine in the Carolingian period involved a certain willingness to embrace a world without gender, at least on the deepest level of sacramental Christian significance, is based not only on the baptismal materials discussed above, but also on the evidence of the two Würzburg copies of Isidore of Seville's treatise on the liturgy.

The Würzburg Isidore manuscripts diverge in significant ways from the text of the *De ecclesiasticis officiis* as it is believed to have left the hands of Isidore of Seville. For instance, the Abirhilt-group women's manuscript (Würzburg, M.p.th.q.18) omits from its discussion of the baptismal rite Isidore's interpretation of the use of salt in the baptism ceremony, which the Visigothic prelate uses to figure a woman (Lot's wife) as a universal symbol of bad faith.[49] Furthermore, Isidore propounded a starkly hierarchical interpretation of the sacrament of marriage, as a divinely ordained institution intended to assure the subordination of women to men. His discussion contained a string of misogynistic platitudes, all packed into a diatribe against egalitarian gender conceptions and against arrangements in which women dominate men.[50] This section of the treatise does not appear in either of the manuscripts made and utilized east of the middle Rhine. The older manuscript, Würzburg, M.p.th.q. 18, was copied from an exemplar that itself did not contain the chapter on marriage.[51] The younger manuscript, Würzburg, M.p.th.o.4 (made for the cathedral library), is an epitome of the Isidorian treatise, one that reduces the bishop of Seville's discussion of marriage to the single point that Eve was initially created as a comfort to Adam, but that after the two were ejected from paradise, they were commanded to procreate.[52] The cathedral abbreviator was apparently interested in justifying the divine command to engage in sexual activity, but not in expressing a subordinationist ideology of the sacrament of marriage. In such a context, it is possible to imagine that local clerics taught the women and men of the area a nonhierarchical, nonbinary version of gender relations during that most powerful opportunity for Christian pedagogy: the moment of initiation into the community through baptism.[53]

The method employed in the present study could not be more different from that utilized by Gisela Muschiol in her study of gender and the liturgy, which I noted above as the only attempt along these lines known to me. Not only was her method completely dissimilar (for instance, she cites no liturgical texts—properly speaking—at all, whether in manuscript or print form), but the difference in our methods has led or at least contributed to a complete divergence in our conclusions. Muschiol foregrounds, as characteristic of the Carolingian period, a relative decline in the value placed on women's intercessorial prayers as opposed to men's priestly performances of the mass, and Carolingian legislators' attempts to prevent abbesses from performing public, liturgical offices.[54] She asserts that "the Carolingian liturgy became institutionalized in a way which hardly allowed any variability in gender roles."[55] It is not, I think, logically possible to draw that conclusion from the Carolingian-era evidence analyzed in this essay. Whether or not readers find the cyborg metaphor useful for comprehending the complexity of identity at the moment of Christian initiation through baptism, I hope my suggestions will encourage additional attempts to confront overarching emplotments of liturgical history, constructed on the basis of printed editions of texts, with close readings of manuscript evidence.

Notes

1. Josef Bartoš, "Methodologische und methodische Probleme der Regionalgeschichte," *Jahrbuch für Regionalgeschichte* 8 (1981): 11 [7–17]. Versions of this essay were presented at the Universität Bamberg (2000), Florida International University (2000, 2005), and the University of St. Andrews (2002). I am extremely grateful to the cathedral chapter archivist at Naumburg, Frau Nagel, for permitting me to examine, in June of 2000, the manuscript Merseburg Domstiftsbibliothek 136 and to Steffen Hoffman of the Department of Special Collections in the library of the Universität Leipzig, for assistance throughout the summer of 2000. I thank Klaus Van Eickels, Bernd Schneidmüller, Lara Kriegel, Kindon Miek, Judith Stiehm, Julia M.H. Smith, Alan Kahan, Aurora Morcillo, John Coombs, and Kirsten Wood for comments and suggestions, and John Stuart for two years of inspiration. My greatest debt is owed to Celia Chazelle, for her deep understanding of matters liturgical.

2. Thomas F. Head, *Hagiography and the Cult of Saints: The Diocese of Orléans, 800–1200* (Cambridge, UK: Cambridge University Press, 1990); Sharon Farmer, *Communities of Saint Martin: Legend and Ritual in Medieval Tours* (Ithaca: Cornell University Press, 1991); Margaret Cormack, *The Saints in Iceland: Their Veneration from the Conversion to 1400*, Subsidia Hagiographica 78 (Société des Bollandistes: Brussels, 1994).

3. Peter Cramer, *Baptism and Change in the Early Middle Ages, c. 200–c. 1150* (Cambridge, UK: Cambridge University Press, 1993), pp. 113–30 and 138–147; Arnold Angenendt, "Taufe und Politik im frühen Mittelalter," *Frühmittelalterliche Studien* 7 (1973): 143–68; Arnold Angenendt, "Der Taufritus im frühen Mittelalter," in *Segni e Riti nella Chiesa altomedievale Occidentale*, 2 vols., Settimane di Studio del Centro Italiano di Studi sull'alto Medioevo 33 (Spoleto: Centro italiano di studi sull'alto Medioevo, 1987), 1: 296–300 [275–321].

4. Sarah Foot, "'By Water in the Spirit': The Administration of Baptism in Early Anglo-Saxon England," in *Pastoral Care before the Parish*, ed. John Blair and Richard Sharpe (Leicester: Leicester University Press, 1992), pp. 186–89 [171– 92].

5. See the Introduction by Chazelle and Lifshitz, nn21–23.

6. *Le sacramentaire Grégorien. Ses principales formes d'après les plus anciens manuscrits*, ed. Jean Deshusses, 3 vols. (Fribourg-en-Suisse: Academic Press Fribourg, 1971–1982), 1: 80.

7. Deshusses, *Le sacramentaire Grégorien*, 1:35–47.

8. Glenn C.J. Byer, *Charlemagne and Baptism: A Study of Responses to the Circular Letter of 811/812* (San Francisco: International Scholars Press, 1999); Susan A. Keefe, *Water and the Word: Baptism and the Education of the Clergy in the Carolingian Empire*, 2 vols. (Notre Dame, IN: University of Notre Dame Press, 2002).

9. Relevant publications include: Felice Lifshitz, "Gender, Exegesis and Exemplarity East of the Middle Rhine: Jesus, Mary and the Saints in

Manuscript Context," *Early Medieval Europe* 9 (2000): 325–44; Felice Lifshitz, "Demonstrating Gun(t)za: Women, Manuscripts, and the Question of Historical 'Proof,'" in *Vom Nutzen des Schreibens: Soziales Gedächtnis, Herrschaft, und Besitz,* ed. Walter Pohl and Paul Herold (Vienna: Österreichische Akademie der Wissenschaften, 2002), pp. 67–96; Felice Lifshitz, "The Persistence of Late Antiquity: Christ as Man and Woman in an Eighth-Century Miniature," *Medieval Feminist Forum* 38 (2004): 18–27.

10. Now bound as fol. 103 into Würzburg, Universitätsbibliothek M.p.th.f. 42; see Hans Thurn, *Die Handschriften der Universitätsbibliothek Würzburg,* Vol. 3 part 1, *Die Pergamenthandschriften der ehemaligen Dombibliothek Würzburg* (Wiesbaden: Harrasowitz, 1984), pp. 30–31.

11. Jaime Sancho Andreu, "Ritos de la infancia y la adolescencia en el antiguo rito hispánico," *Studia Anselmiana* 105 (1992): 229, 244 [207–45].

12. Victor Saxer, "L'Initiation chrétienne du IIe au VIe siècle: Esquisse historique des rites et de leur signification," *Segni e Riti* 1: 173–96; Angenendt, "Taufritus," in *Segni e Riti,* 1: 275–321.

13. Mark Searle, "The Rites of Christian Initiation," in *Betwixt and Between: Patterns of Masculine and Feminine Initiation,* ed. Louise Carus Mahdi, Steven Foster, and Meredith Little (La Salle: Open Court Publishing Company, 1987), pp. 463, 465 [457–70].

14. Gabriel Ramis, "La iniciación cristiana en la liturgia hispánica," *Studia Anselmiana* 105 (1992): 192 [189–206].

15. Catherine Bell, *Ritual: Perspectives and Dimensions* (New York: Oxford University Press, 1997), p. 37; Thomas O. Beidelman, *The Cool Knife: Imagery of Gender, Sexuality and Moral Education in Kaguru Initiation Ritual* (Washington: Smithsonian Books, 1997); Eugenia W. Herbert, *Iron, Gender and Power: Rituals of Transformation in African Societies* (Bloomington: Indiana University Press, 1993); Bruce Lincoln, *Emerging from the Chrysalis: Studies in Rituals of Women's Initiation* (Cambridge, MA: Harvard University Press, 1981); Richarda Becker, *Die weibliche Initiation im ostslawischen Zaubermärchen: Ein Beitrag zur Funktion und Symbolik des weiblichen Aspektes im Märchen unter besonderer Berücksichtigung der Figur der Baba-Jaga* (Berlin: Otto Harrasowitz, 1990); Ivan G. Marcus, *Rituals of Childhood: Jewish Acculturation in Medieval Europe* (New Haven: Yale University Press, 1996).

16. Paris, BnF lat. 12048. The discussion here is based on *Liber sacramentorum Gellonensis* ed. and int. A. Dumas and Jean Deshusses (CCSL 159–159A; Turnhout; Brepols, 1981) 2 vols; 1: vii, xix–xxi, xxv–xxvi and 2: 48–51, 64–101.

17. *Liber sacramentorum Gellonensis textus,* pp. 68–69.

18. It is in fact so used (albeit without reference to gender) by Angenendt, "Taufritus," in *Segni e Riti* 1: 280–90.

19. Gisela Muschiol, "Men, Women and Liturgical Practice in the Early Medieval West," in *Gender in the Early Medieval World. East and West, 300–900,* ed. Leslie Brubaker and Julia M.H. Smith (Cambridge, UK: Cambridge University Press, 2004), p. 199 [198–216].

20. Muschiol, "Men, Women and Liturgical Practice," p. 205; cf. Julia M.H. Smith, "Religion and Lay Society," in *New Cambridge Medieval History*, ed. Rosamond McKitterick, 7 vols. (Cambridge, UK: Cambridge University Press, 1995–2005), 2: 659 [654–78].

21. Byer, *Charlemagne and Baptism*, pp. 48–49, 51.

22. See Susan Keefe, "Carolingian Baptismal Expositions: A Handlist of Tracts and Manuscripts," in *Carolingian Essays: Andrew W. Mellon Lectures in Early Christian Studies*, ed. Uta-Renate Blumenthal (Washington, DC: Catholic University of America Press, 1983), pp. 169–273 for a list of texts; the quotation is from Keefe, *Water and the Word*, 1: 132.

23. See Keefe, *Water and the Word*, 1: 13–21, 25, 30 and Tables 1; 2: 32, 92–94, 100–03, with the following corrective. Keefe dates the Merseburg manuscript as 820–840, without any rationale for departing from the traditional dating to the very beginning of the ninth century, for which see below n33, as well as Hanns Fischer, *Schrifttafeln zum althochdeutschen Lesebuch* (Tübingen: M. Niemeyer, 1966), p. 11 and pl. 8. Bernhard Bischoff dates the manuscript to the first or second quarter of the ninth century in *Katalog der festländischen Handschriften des neunten Jahrhunderts (mit Ausnahme der wisigotischen)*, ed. Birgit Ebersperger, 2 vols. (Wiesbaden: Harrasowitz, 2004), 2: 183–84.

24. Keefe, *Water and the Word*, 1: 23–26.

25. Keefe, *Water and the Word*, 1: 28-35.

26. "Text 42," ed. Keefe, *Water and the Word*, 2: 546–49. Compare Byer, *Charlemagne and Baptism*, pp. 8, 78; Charles de Clercq, " 'Ordines unctionis infirmi' des IXe et Xe siècles," *Ephemerides Liturgicae* 44 (1930): 101, 120–22 [100–22].

27. The current fol. 1 was added when the codex was bound in its present state. The *libellus* formally begins on what is technically fol. 3, but which is numbered both as fol. 3 (lower right corner) and as fol. 2 (upper right corner, reckoning without the protective sheet).

28. "Expositio in missa," in *Amalarii episcopi opera liturgica omnia*, ed. Jean Michel Hanssens, 3 vols. (Vatican City: Biblioteca Apostolica Vaticana, 1948–1950), 1: 284–338.

29. "Text 43," ed. Keefe, *Water and the Word*, 2: 550–56.

30. Edited by: Adalbert Bezzenberger, "Das Taufritual der Merseburger Hs. No. 58," *Zeitschrift für Deutsche Philologie* 8 (1877): 217–20 [216–26]; Elias von Steinmeyer, *Die kleineren Althochdeutschen Sprachdenkmäler* (Berlin: Weidmann, 1916), no. IV, pp. 23–26; Fischer, *Schrifttafeln*, pl. 8. The "fränkische Taufgelobnis" (Franconian Baptismal Vow) is usually said to be on fol. 16r (according to the numbering in the upper right corners of the pages), but is in fact on fol. 17r (according to the correct numbering in the lower right corners of the pages).

31. Stefan Sonderegger, *Althochdeutsche Sprache und Literatur* (Berlin: De Gruyter, 1987), p. 63.

32. Merseburg, Domstiftbibliothek MS 136, fol. 16r (*recte* 17r).

33. Bezzenberger, "Taufritual," pp. 216–26; Steinmeyer, *Die kleineren Althochdeutschen Sprachdenkmäler*, pp. 23–26; J. Knight Bostock, *A Handbook on Old High German Literature*, 2nd ed., rev. K.C. King and D.R. McLintock (Oxford: Oxford University Press, 1976); Horst Dieter Schlosser, *Die literarischen Anfänge der deutschen Sprache: Ein Arbeitsbuch zur althochdeutschen und altniederdeutschen Literatur* (Berlin: S + W Steuer- und Wirtschaftsverlag, 1977).

34. Isidore of Seville, *De ecclesiasticis officiis*, ed. C.M. Lawson, CCSL 113 (Turnhout: Brepols, 1989); Christopher A. Jones, "The Book of the Liturgy in Anglo-Saxon England," *Speculum* 73 (1998): 659–702. Isidore's dates are ca. 560–636.

35. Bernhard Bischoff and Josef Hofmann, *Libri sancti Kyliani: Die Würzburger Schreibschule und die Dombibliothek im VIII u. IX Jahrhundert* (Würzburg: Kommissionsverlag Ferdinand Schöningh, 1952), pp. 8–9.

36. Bischoff and Hofmann, *Libri sancti Kyliani*, pp. 123–24.

37. Steinmeyer, *Die kleineren Althochdeutschen Sprachdenkmäler*, pp. 23–26.

38. Andrea Reichert, "Wochenbett und Kindertaufe: Die Privatisierung des Alltags in den Satzungen der spätmittelalterlichen Stadt Essen," in *Vergessene Frauen an der Ruhr: Von Herrscherinnen und Hörigen, Hausfrauen und Hexen 800–1800*, ed. Bea Lundt (Cologne: Böhlau, 1992), p. 159 [131–74].

39. Keefe, "Carolingian Baptismal Expositions," p. 171; cf. Byer, *Charlemagne and Baptism*, pp. 1, 37.

40. The procedure to be followed by catechumens in our region is charted (using Keefe's Text 42) in Byer, *Charlemagne and Baptism*, pp. 102–08, 150. For other areas with a functioning catechumenate, see Byer, *Charlemagne and Baptism*, pp. 99, 123–25, 152–57, 163.

41. "Caticuminus dictus est pro eo quod adhuc sanctae trinitatis fidem audit et discit, necdum tamen baptismum recepit": Keefe, *Water and the Word*, 2: 546.

42. The relevant sources also sometimes use the term *famulus* [servant], which is age-neutral.

43. "Text 42," ed. Keefe, *Water and the Word*, 2: 547–48.

44. "Text 42," ed. Keefe, *Water and the Word*, 2: 548.

45. See above, n15.

46. "Memento domine famulorum famularumque tuarum et omnium circumadstantium.... Memento domine famulorum famularumque tuarum et omnium circumadstantium.... deprecat deum patrem ut memorare dignetur omnium ad officium missae sive masculorum sive feminarum advenientium.... Ipsi sunt masculi et femine qui circumstant" (Be mindful lord of your servants male and female and of all those gathered around.... Be mindful of your servants male and female and of all those gathered around...let him [the priest] ask God the Father that he deign to remember all those, whether male or female, who have come to the mass.... They who gather around are male and female): Merseburg, Domstiftbibliothek MS 136, fols. 7v–8r.

47. Donna J. Haraway, "A Cyborg Manifesto: Science, Technology, Socialist-Feminism in the Late Twentieth Century," in idem, *Simians, Cyborgs and Women: The Reinvention of Nature* (New York: Routledge, 1991), p. 181 [149–81].

48. "Text 42," ed. Keefe, *Water and the Word* 2: 548; Isidore, *De ecclesiasticis officiis* II.xxv (xxiiii), ed. Lawson, p. 104; Byer, *Charlemagne and Baptism*, pp. 151, 159–60; Saxer, "L'initiation chrétienne," pp. 190–92; Cramer, *Baptism and Change*, pp. 78–80.

49. See Isidore, *De ecclesiasticis officiis*, ed. Lawson pp. 95–97 for the missing text.

50. Isidore, *De ecclesiasticis officiis* II.xx (xviii), ed. Lawson, pp. 89–95 (especially pp. 94–95).

51. Isidore, *De ecclesiasticis officiis*, ed. Lawson, p. 29.

52. "Deus enim fecit adam et adiutorium aevam cum procreatione sapientiae dicens crescite et multiplicamini et replete terram, sed facta eadem mulier prius pro solatio quam coniugio fuit, donec a paradiso inoboedientia eiceret" (For God made Adam and his helpmate Eve, wisely saying 'grow and multiply and fill the earth' through procreation, but that same woman had earlier been made more for comfort than for marriage, until God threw them out of paradise for disobedience): Würzburg, M.p.th.o.4 fol. 32r.

53. A similar interpretive framework may be relevant to other regions as well, for women in general appear to have been very positively valued by Carolingian authors; see Katrien Heene, *The Legacy of Paradise: Marriage, Motherhood and Woman in Carolingian Edifying Literature* (Frankfurt: Peter Lang, 1997).

54. Muschiol, "Men, Women and Liturgical Practice," pp. 209–11.

55. Muschiol, "Men, Women and Liturgical Practice," p. 216.

CHAPTER 7

ARE THEY NOT LIKE US?
THE CAROLINGIAN FISC IN
MILITARY PERSPECTIVE

Bernard S. Bachrach

Critique of romantic, primitivist concepts of barbarian warrior culture through analysis of contemporary documents revealing Charlemagne's sophisticated bureaucratic machinery and its importance for provisioning the army.

It is now well established that beginning in the eighth century, the economy, that is, the production of goods and services, in Gaul began a process of robust expansion that was accompanied by significant demographic growth.[1] These developments provided immense potential for Charlemagne (d. 814), his father Pippin (d. 768), and his grandfather Charles Martel (d. 741) to sustain a long-term strategy of territorial conquest.[2] A substantial part of the surplus wealth produced by the Carolingian economy was available to the royal government and especially to the army.[3] The vindication of royal rights depended, however, in large part, on the willingness of subjects to obey the law, and the capacity of the government to encourage, if not coerce, obedience.[4]

Charlemagne's personal charisma and that of his family, which developed in the context of a lengthy record of military victories, cannot be ignored when trying to assess the success of the Carolingian government. But emphasis on *fama* and *fortuna*, and on recognition by contemporaries of the role played by God in Carolingian success, explains neither what particular things were done to gain success nor how they were done. Despite his highly romanticized later reputation, Charlemagne was a thorough man, whose personality as a statesman—or better, administrator—was brought out very well over a half-century ago by F.L. Ganshof.[5] By focusing on the prosaic institutions of administration and the "paper trail" created by bureaucrats, some sense of the sound administrative and management structures of Charlemagne's effective government may be gained. Also essential to the enterprise were the functionaries of the royal government, who gained practical literacy in the Carolingian schools. [6]

Royal landed assets were divided into two major groupings. One group of estates was maintained in the possession of the king, and these were administered directly by his government officials located both in the *villae* (estates) in countryside and at court. These directly held and administered estates commonly are considered the royal fisc. A second complex of the king's resources belonged to the fisc, but was held in benefice from Charlemagne by various followers. These men were responsible for the direct administration of these estates, albeit under royal scrutiny. The royal fisc under Charlemagne, excluding both assets taken as a result of the conquest of the Lombard kingdom in Italy in 774 and the *beneficia* (benefices) granted to others, was organized into more than 600 identifiable administrative units.[7]

Some of the units of the royal fisc were single *villae*, each with its own administrative cadre under the direction of a steward.[8] In some cases, though, several fiscal units were joined together into a rather larger grouping with a more complicated administrative structure including an administrative capital, several subordinate *villae*, and/or other smaller administrative structures.[9] The capital *villa* at Annapes, for example, included more than 2,000 hectares, and the entire Annapes-complex amounted to between 2,800 and 2,900 hectares.[10] On the whole, the fiscal *villae* were large and complicated entities with hundreds of free, semi-free, and non-free inhabitants and dependents attached to them in various ways.[11] As a result, the steward in charge of any one of these units was obliged to gather around himself a considerable administrative support staff.

An account of the resources produced on an annual basis by the more than 600 administrative units of the Carolingian royal fisc cannot now be fully recovered, but this information was available in great detail to the Carolingian court. Charlemagne had agents sent from the court to oversee the compiling of inventories of all the *villae* of the royal fisc, and a number of fragments of these severely time-conditioned documents have, fortuitously, survived to serve as one of the sources for the present essay.[12]

Some insight into the wealth and strength of each *villa* can be obtained from the few surviving, fragmented descriptions of the administrative centers where the steward and his staff lived and worked. At Annapes,[13] for example, the administrative center was based within a substantial fortification: a large courtyard enclosed within a very strong wooden wall, entered through a stone gateway and surmounted by a gallery from which the entrance could be defended. Within this larger courtyard there was a smaller courtyard, which was also provided with a wooden wall for its defense. Inside this smaller courtyard was the administrative headquarters, reported to have been a very finely constructed, large stone house with three public rooms, numerous galleries or sleeping quarters, two porticos, a cellar, and eleven small rooms for the unmarried women who worked inside the house and within the confines of the courtyard. Within the inner courtyard there were also seventeen wooden houses, each of which would seem to have had only a single room but were nonetheless provided with what the men who executed the inventory considered to be all required amenities. The entire community was served by a common kitchen, established in its own building. Also within the walls was a separate building for the baking of bread, biscuits, and other such products, plus two storehouses for grain, a stable, and three barns. It must be concluded that both horses and cattle were housed within the confines of the fortification.

Fragmentary descriptions of the administrative centers of other royal *villae* make clear that these too were well fortified. In most cases, there were two concentric walls and stone gate complexes including galleries from which substances such as hot oil could be poured down on attackers.[14] At least one instance, an inventory takes specific note that spikes were affixed atop the walls of the fortification to deter the enemy from scaling the heights.[15] The physical descriptions of Annapes and of several other administrative centers clearly indicate that such installations had the potential to serve as a refuge for the local population of the area in case of enemy attack. It seems likely that each fortified *villa* center played an active role in defense of the realm as a "hard point" to delay hostile operations until a field force could come to the rescue. The requirement that all able-bodied men in the area be prepared to serve as members of the *lantwehr* (local militia) provides additional support for this conclusion.[16] Further support comes from the fact that Charlemagne insisted on the provision of each of these fortified positions with signal fires, guarded and tended around the clock, clearly meant to convey information to some more or less distant headquarters where military units were available.[17] If the fire went out something was amiss, and a relief force could be dispatched.

Charlemagne was well known to have worked diligently throughout his reign to create uniform administrative structures.[18] Thus, he ordered a detailed set of administrative rules and regulations to be issued, which survive in the frequently discussed Capitulary *de Villis*.[19] The breadth of detail exposed by the seventy chapters of this document illustrates the exceptional complexity of the estate-based component of Charlemagne's fiscal administration, every bit as sophisticated as its Roman imperial predecessor in Gaul,[20] and superior to that commanded by the contemporary Byzantine government in those parts of the west that remained under its control.[21]

As noted above, each unit of the royal fisc was administered by a steward; these stewards served at the king's pleasure and were appointed by the central government.[22] They were required to keep in close contact with the royal court on a regular basis, both in person and through a detailed stream of written reports; each steward might well find himself at the royal court at least four or five times each year.[23] Stewards were to be intelligent and careful men, as well as technically competent in a variety of areas, including accounting.[24] They reported directly to a bureaucracy composed of numerous court officials.[25] High levels of control were exercised by the central government with regard to both production at each *villa* and reporting: each steward had to submit a detailed annual report of incomes earned to the royal court at Christmas time, that is, after the year's agricultural cycle had been completed late in the autumn. This took the form of a more or less systematized inventory (but not an exhaustive description) of the *villa*, divided into several score rubrics, which provided Charlemagne and his staff with the information needed to carry on the business of the central government.[26] No inventory formularies or completed inventories are extant, but as already noted, parts of some of the latter type of document do survive. This is especially fortunate, since all such reports were likely of little more than antiquarian value within several years of their drafting. In addition, what appears to be a model of such a formulary survives as a fragment in the Capitulary *de Villis* itself.[27]

The annual Christmas inventory of the income of each *villa* will here be called report Number One. This primary report was supplemented by two other documents, reports Number Two and Number Three, that were intended to be comprehensive. In part A of report Number Two, the steward recorded anything and everything he had appropriated from the resources of the *villa* for the use of the central government.[28] As indicated by a wide variety of other requirements, such a detailed account could, indeed, be quite lengthy.[29] In part B of this same report, the steward was required to register all goods and services he had provided to all persons not connected to the royal court.[30] In part A of report Number Three, the steward was required to record all money payments he made to anyone, and in part B of this same document, he was to provide a list of monies remaining under his direct control in his strongbox.[31] The sources from which all of the money, whether paid out or retained at the *villa*, derived also had to be recorded and reported either in part A or in part B.[32]

In the aggregate, these reports provided the officers of the central government with the total gross income of the royal fisc, the total net income of the royal fisc, and the total expenses of the royal fisc, as well as a register of all individuals with whom the royal government maintained economic relationships through the estates of the fisc, plus a description of all of these relations. Insofar as these documents were retained for a period of two or three years, the court was in a position to track the relative productivity of each of the individual fiscal units, as well as of the fisc as a whole, on a year-to-year basis.[33] Court officials worked with these documents throughout the winter season to establish, for each steward, a set of detailed, written instructions regarding what was to be done at each *villa* during the forthcoming year, based on an estimate of the needs of the royal government.[34] These estimates, in turn, were based on the plans made, also during the winter season, by the king and his advisers for the forthcoming year's activities, for example, the royal itinerary and especially the offensive military operations to be undertaken by one or another royal army.[35] Finally, the court bureaucrats calculated what percentage of the funds in possession of each steward, from the previous year's income, would be needed by the central government, and the stewards were instructed to bring the stipulated amount of cash to court on Palm Sunday, when they also received their instructions for the upcoming year.[36]

Despite the immense administrative detail included in the tripartite set of annual reports, Charlemagne's government recognized that interim reports from the stewards to the central government were also necessary. For example, the quantities of food stuffs (e.g., vegetables, fish, cheese, and butter) sent to the royal court for the Lenten season were to be enumerated, along with an account of what remained at the *villa*.[37] In another bit of detailed micromanagement, each steward was required, by no later than September 1 each year, to send a report to the royal court indicating whether there would be sufficient food on hand to sustain the *villa*'s pigs.[38] Much more information could be adduced regarding the "paper trail" (amounting to thousands of documents) between the stewards of the more than 600 administrative units of the fisc and the royal court. All told, perhaps a dozen written reports, some exceptionally detailed and recording several score items, were required by the central government for delivery to the court from each *villa* each year, in return for which the central government provided the stewards with written instructions.

Finally, each steward was required personally to attend the royal court several times each year or, if this were impossible, to send an acceptable representative.[39]

The *villae* of the royal fisc were organized, first and foremost, to provide logistic support for the army. These *villae* were to prepare special carts that were kept loaded with food for the consumption of the army. At the end of the agricultural year, a set amount of foodstuffs was set aside at each *villa*, the quantities also determined by royal order, for the purpose of supplying the army for the coming year, and a report was submitted indicating the total amount of grain sequestered for military purposes. This same document also reported how much grain was contributed by each homestead and each herder attached to the *villa*.[40] When it came to the matter of supplying the army, the central government clearly wanted to have a detailed record of the working of each *villa* with regard to the personal responsibilities of each dependent.

Each of the *villae* was also assigned to contribute various alcoholic and nonalcoholic beverages to the war effort. The central government even micromanaged the nature of the vessels used for the storage and transport. Beverages were not to be transported in leather bottles, but rather in well-made barrels bound with iron hoops.[41] Not only were the latter more durable than the former; wooden barrels can be constructed to have a far greater capacity than even the largest leather butts. War carts designated to haul food stuffs, officially called *basternae*, were also constructed according to specific orders from Charlemagne.[42] Common carts were not considered suitable for military service. The rough work of a lengthy campaign might, for example, require a supply column to traverse steep mountain roads or cross rapidly running rivers. Charlemagne therefore quite reasonably insisted that each cart be constructed in a superior manner and that it be made waterproof by having a wooden body caulked like a boat and appropriately seamed, probably waxed, animal skins affixed to the open top. Each cart could be expected to negotiate a deep river ford without any water entering the vehicle, especially important when grain or flour was transported. Finally, each cart was to be equipped with a shield (these, in fact, produced at each *villa*), a spear, and a bow with a quiver of arrows for the use of the driver and probably a guard, as well.[43] Thus, a baggage train comprising 300 carts could, for defensive purposes, be arranged in a wagon lager defended by a minimum of some 300 archers, and another 300 lightly armed foot soldiers with shields and spears.

All the *basternae* had to be uniform in terms of their carrying capacity. Each cart was built to hold in weight and/or in volume twelve *modii* (measures) of flour or twelve *modii* of wine, according to the "official measure" determined by the central government and established by legislation.[44] Charlemagne also had mandated that each *villa* have on hand the appropriate devices to calculate this standard set of weights and measures.[45] From this set of regulations, it is plausible to conclude that each of the iron-bound barrels mentioned above was also uniform in size. This uniformity had considerable practical value for military operations. Merely by counting appropriately laden carts, government officials could ascertain the *modii* of grain and/or wine available: the number of carts was multiplied by twelve, a simple task even for those who lacked formal education, based upon the widely used finger calculus.[46]

The standing orders regarding the provision of logistic support for the army were finetuned each year, dependent upon the plans made by Charlemagne's "general staff" during the previous winter.[47] In one of his few surviving military capitularies, Charlemagne reaffirmed the standing order that army carts should provide flour, wine, sides of bacon, and an abundance of other food, plus equipment; and he added that, for the forthcoming campaign, each vehicle was to carry a *mola* (quern) for the grinding of grain. This suggests that the grain for this particular campaign was to be unmilled and would be ground as needed by those charged with providing meals for the soldiers.[48] The equipment carts for this campaign were also to carry, in addition to their normal complement of tools, stone throwing slings (*fundibulae*) and a supply of stones (*petrae*), presumably shaped to a uniform size and weight, for ammunition.[49] Uniform ammunition likely was needed in order to obtain consistent ballistic results. It is noteworthy that the ammunition for the slings was not stored with the slings at the *villae* but was kept in some type of centralized royal arsenal. Twenty loads of *petrae*, each weighing approximately one hundred kilograms, were to be provided for each wagon from already prepared government stocks.[50]

A rare surviving mobilization order issued by Charlemagne casts some light on what constituted the normal complement of tools (*utensilia*) necessary for an army on campaign (*hostem*): among others, the carts (*carris*) are to carry hatchets (*cuniada*), saws for stone cutting (*dolaturia*), augers (*tarratros*), carpenter's axes (*assias*), spades for ditch digging (*fosorios*), and iron shovels (*palas ferreas*).[51] These Carolingian equipment vehicles greatly resemble those of their later Roman predecessors and Byzantine contemporaries. The tools mentioned were just those needed to build fortifications, siege camps, and the normal *castrae* measured out each night for the protection of the column while the army was on the march.[52] Equipment of this kind, for the use of the army, was to be stored in a special building or room at the headquarters of each *villa* belonging to the royal fisc.[53] Apparently, it was not to be employed in the course of the normal exploitation of the lands and other assets of the fisc, but was to be kept solely for military use. The steward was under standing orders to examine the iron tools to ascertain if they were sufficient in number, in good condition, and ready for service on campaign; and he was required to assure that afterward, all this equipment was returned to the above-mentioned storage facility.[54] In light of all the other "paper work" discussed above, it is reasonable to infer that the steward kept written lists of the equipment.

Whereas the preceding paragraphs describe direct support for the army, much produced on the estates of the royal fisc had indirect value for the military. Woollen and linen cloth could be used to make uniforms for soldiers and blankets for both soldiers and horses.[55] During the later Roman Empire, cloth for uniforms and other military uses had been produced in government-run factories, listed in the *Notitia Dignitatum*.[56] Not only did the Carolingian government have access to the *Notitia Dignitatum*, but—like their Roman predecessors—it referred to the installations for weaving cloth with the Greek term *gynaecea* (women's workshops).[57] The Carolingian fiscal *villae* also produced hemp, the basic material for making rope, an essential element of war materiel.[58] Hides of various types were prepared by tanners and had military uses for tents, arrow quivers, and protective shields for war machines such as battering rams and sows.[59] There were also highly specialized leather workers (e.g., saddlers), whose work was needed to produce not only saddles but all types of tack for pack horses, riding horses, draft horses, and war horses. Among the leather workers, there were shoemakers who very likely could prepare the footwear needed for both mounted and foot soldiers.[60] Turners, established at each fiscal *villa*, were of potential value militarily to produce arrow shafts, as well poles or shafts for spears, lances, and pikes.[61] The work of the smiths, who could fabricate all types of arrow and spear points at each *villa*, was also vital to the Carolingians' military efforts.[62] In some areas, the smiths' efforts were enhanced by local surface mining for iron on fiscal resources, and/or the construction of forges capable of maintaining the high temperatures required to produce steel.[63]

Most food stuffs produced at the *villae* were suitable for feeding the troops while on campaign. In addition to various types of grain, however, which, throughout the history of the premodern West, has provided the base of the soldier's diet on campaign, note should be taken of salted meat, smoked meat, and salted fish also prepared by the *villae* of the royal fisc.[64] The various types of wine and beer produced on the estates of Charlemagne's fisc, too, were consumed by the soldiers on campaign,[65] though as Charlemagne was careful to make clear, moderation was required and drunkenness was punished.[66] Food for the beasts of war was also of great importance: the *villae* provided an abundance of hay, as well as various types of grain, including oats for horses.[67]

Although we should not exaggerate the role of mounted troops in Charlemagne's armies, the fiscal *villae* included studs for the breeding of horses.[68] Most of these animals very likely were needed for use as draft horses, pack horses, and riding horses, yet a few were undoubtedly trained for service in war, a highly specialized matter.[69] Detailed instructions were given to the stewards regarding the care of the royal studs; these instructions are very similar to those set out in Vegetius's *Mulomedicina*, a text available to Carolingian society, which epitomized the lengthy traditions of veterinary care as they had developed from ancient times.[70] Close attention was to be paid at each stud farm to the relatively few stallions kept for the servicing of a large number of mares. Their health was of particular concern, especially in the season during which they were to cover the mares.[71] The equestrian staff was also required to pay careful attention to the mares, and special mention is made of the need to separate the new foals from their dams at the proper time.[72] The meadows were to be guarded when the mares were in heat so that the breeding process could be controlled with greater precision.[73] Charlemagne's instructions took into account, as well, the optimum size for a herd of brood mares and mandated that, when this limit was reached, the steward should develop a new stud.[74] All of this work with the king's horses, including taking various animals to the royal palace during the feast of St. Martin, was confided to specialized personnel, some of whom were landless dependents of the royal fisc. Others, both unfree and free, held *mansi* (homesteads) from the fisc as tenements and supported themselves while serving in the stables. Still others were free men who held benefices from the king in the district and served in the stables of the royal fisc.[75]

Although Charlemagne's government was aware of the number of horses of all types on the lands of the royal fisc, including the stud farms, this information has not survived. From the fragments of some surviving inventories, it is possible to grasp the order of magnitude of some of these farms and how the animals were distributed. One steward, for instance, indicates that there were seventy-nine brood mares at the *villa* he administered. Another notes there were fifty-one mares for breeding on his estate, and yet another *villa* is reported to have had forty-four brood mares.[76] Traditionally, mares are put to breeding at three or four years of age and are bred at least until they reach the age of ten, with fourteen being the upper level for the fertility of most mares.[77] If the horse breeding studs at the *villae* of the fisc each serviced an average of fifty brood mares (about eighty-five percent of the average found in the sample above), and about sixty percent of these produced a live and healthy foal each year, the 600 or so units of the royal fisc would have produced some 18,000 horses on an annual basis for direct royal use.[78] The vast numbers of horses mentioned in the narrative sources, especially in connection with the army, and the frequent references to horses in the law codes, makes it very likely that a great many thousands of horses were, in fact, produced each year, not only on the estates of the royal fisc but in studs throughout the realm.[79] All male horses, except for the very few stallions maintained for stud purposes, were, in their third year, either put directly to work or trained for military service as war horses.[80]

In order to explain the effectiveness of early Carolingian armies and their long-term success, it is necessary to temper the romantic-elitist assumptions popularly associated not only with medieval military history in general, but with early medieval military history as well.[81] Primitivist views of the Franks as illiterate and innumerate barbarians living in a "warrior society" are also best jettisoned. Fundamental to romantic and primitivist views is the unproven assumption that "they" are not like "us." From the perspective of medieval military history, the notion of a "warrior society" is a myth, based on the deployment of entertainment literature such as the Beowulf poem as if it were plain text.[82] Finally, it is more misleading than enlightening to compare Charlemagne with Chaka Zulu.[83] Bureaucracy and administration are neither romantic nor elitist, and they go a long way toward countering a primitivist model. Indeed, they tend to narrow the gap considerably between "them" and "us."

By examining here a few aspects of the royal fisc from an administrative perspective, some insight has been gained into the complex bureaucratic structures that undergirded both Charlemagne's government and his army. As everyone should know, an army travels on its stomach. The government that provides adequate supplies on a regular basis and convinces its troops they will be well-treated not only maintains high morale but generally gains success. Like those Roman emperors in the west whom he ultimately succeeded, Charlemagne headed a government that sustained its armies through a highly developed bureaucracy. We can trace its methods and grasp its complexity from the "paper trail" it has left. This brief examination of Charlemagne's fisc in military perspective has revealed but the proverbial tip of an administrative iceberg that supported some two centuries of Carolingian success. Hopefully, it points the way toward a better understanding of the early Middle Ages.

Notes

1. Alfons Dopsch, *Die Wirtschaftsentwicklung der Karolingerzeit vornehmlich in Deutschland*, 2 vols., 2nd ed. (Weimar: H. Böhlaus, 1921–1922); Michael McCormick, *Origins of the European Economy: Communications and Commerce, A.D. 300–900* (Cambridge, UK: Cambridge University Press, 2001), with the proceedings of a colloquium on McCormick's work published as "Origins of the European Economy: A Debate with Michael McCormick," ed. Edward James, *Early Medieval Europe* 12 (2003): 259–323.
2. Bernard S. Bachrach, *Early Carolingian Warfare: Prelude to Empire* (Philadelphia: University of Pennsylvania Press, 2001), pp. 1–50.
3. F.L. Ganshof, "A propos du tonlieu à l'époque carolingienne," in *Settimane di Studio de Centro Italiano di Studi sull'alto medioevo* 6 (1959): 485–508; F.L. Ganshof, "Charlemagne and the Administration of Justice," in F.L. Ganshof, *Frankish Institutions under Charlemagne*, trans. Bryce and Mary Lyon (Providence, RI: Brown University Press, 1968), 71–97; Emile Lesne, *Histoire de la propriété ecclésiastique en France*, 6 vols. (Lille: R. Giard, 1910–1943), 2.2: 411–19, 433–55; Carlrichard Brühl, *Fodrum, Gistum, Servitium Regis: Studien zu den wirtschaftlichen Grundlagen des Königtums im Frankenreich und in den frankischen Nachfolgestaaten Deutschland, Frankreich, Italien vom 6 bis zur Mitte des 14 Jahrhunderts*, 2 vols. (Cologne: Böhlau, 1968), 1: 14–50, 70–74, 97–115; Jean Durliat, "La Polyptyque d'Irminon pour l'armée," *Bibliothèque de l'École des Chartes* 141 (1983): 183–208. Tribute as a part of royal income has been exaggerated due to the work of Timothy Reuter, "Plunder and Tribute in the Carolingian Empire," *Transactions of the Royal Historical Society*, 5th ser., 35 (1985): 75–94.
4. Matthew Innis, *State and Society in the Early Middle Ages: The Middle Rhine Valley, 400–1000* (Cambridge, UK: Cambridge University Press, 2000), supplemented by Bachrach, *Early Carolingian Warfare*, pp. 51–83.
5. F.L. Ganshof, "Charlemagne," *Speculum* 24 (1949): 520–27; repr. in F.L. Ganshof, *The Carolingians and the Frankish Monarchy*, trans. Janet Sondheimer (London: Longman, 1971), 17–27.
6. See the works cited in n3, as well as Karl-Ferdinand Werner, "*Missus-Marchio-Comes*: Entre l'administration centrale et l'administration locale de l'Empire carolingien," in *Histoire comparée de l'administration (IVe–XXVIIe siècles)*, ed. Werner Paravicini and Karl-Ferdinand Werner (Munich: Artemis Verlag, 1980), pp. 191–239; repr. in Karl-Ferdinand Werner, *Vom Frankenreich zur Entfaltung Deutschlands und Frankreichs: Ursprünge, Strukturen, Beziehungen: ausgewählte Beiträge: Festgabe zu seinem sechzigsten Geburtstag* (Sigmaringen: J. Thorbeke, 1984), pp. 108–56; Rosamond McKitterick, *The Carolingians and the Written Word* (Cambridge, UK: Cambridge University Press, 1989); Janet Nelson, "Literacy in Carolingian Government," in *The Uses of Literacy in Early Medieval Europe*, ed. Rosamond McKitterick (Cambridge, UK: Cambridge University Press, 1990), pp. 258–96. Cf. Michael Richter, "... *quisquis scit scribere*,

nullum potat abere labore: Zur Laienschriftlichkeit im 8. Jahrhundert," in *Karl Martel in Seiner Zeit*, ed. Jörg Jarnut, Ulrich Nonn, and Michael Richter (Sigmaringen: J. Thorbeke, 1994), pp. 393–404, who espouses a germanic-primitivist approach, which sees government administration as antithetical to the values and practices of a warrior society.

7. Werner, "*Missus-Marchio-Comes*," pp. 148–49. It is likely, in light of the severely incomplete nature of the surviving sources, that the actual number was much larger than the number identified by Werner.

8. Wolfgang Metz, *Das karolingische Reichsgut: Eine verfassungs- und verwaltungsgeschichtliche Untersuchung* (Berlin: De Gruyter, 1960), pp. 144–54.

9. Metz, *Das karolingische Reichsgut*, pp. 111–12.

10. See F.L. Ganshof, "Charlemagne and the Institutions of the Frankish Monarchy," in Ganshof, *Frankish Institutions*, p. 37 [3–55], with the proviso that the author seriously underestimates the magnitude of the bureaucracy and especially the role played by written documents in government.

11. Metz, *Das karolingische Reichsgut*, pp. 111–19.

12. Ganshof, "Charlemagne and the Institutions," pp. 121 n153, 135 nn261–63 lists more than a dozen orders for inventories. On sources, see Klaus Verhein, "Studien zu den Quellen zum Reichsgut der Karolingerzeit," *Deutsches Archiv fur Geschichte (Erforschung) des Mittelalters* 10 (1954): 313–94 and 11 (1955): 333–92; Metz, *Das karolingische Reichsgut*, pp. 18–72; R.H.C. Davis, "Domesday Book: Continental Parallels," in *Domesday Studies: Papers Read at the Novocentenary Conference of the Royal Historical Society and the Institute of British Geographers: Winchester, 1986*, ed. J.C. Holt (Woodbridge, UK: Boydell Press, 1987), pp. 15–39.

13. For what follows, see *128. Brevium exempla ad describendas res ecclesiasticas et fiscales*, ed. Alfred Boretius, MGH Legum 2.2, *Capitularia regum Francorum* 1 (Hannover: Hahn, 1883), p. 254 cap. 26 [250–56]. Henceforth cited as *Brevium exempla* with chapter numbers. Also see Brühl, *Fodrum, Gistum, Servitium Regis*, pp. 95–97.

14. *Brevium exempla*, cap. 31, 33, 35.

15. *Brevium exempla*, cap. 30.

16. Bachrach, *Early Carolingian Warfare*, pp. 52–54; Bernard S. Bachrach, "Early Medieval Europe," in *War and Society in the Ancient and Medieval Worlds: Asia, the Mediterranean, Europe, and Mesoamerica*, ed. Kurt Raaflaub and Nathan Rosenstein (Cambridge, MA: Center for Hellenic Studies, Trustees for Harvard University, 1999), pp. 290–91 [271–307].

17. *32. Capitulare de villis*, *Capitularia regum Francorum* 1: 85, cap. 27 [82–91]. Henceforth cited as *Capitulare de villis* with chapter numbers.

18. Thomas F.X. Noble, "From Brigandage to Justice: Charlemagne, 785–794," in *Literacy, Politics, and Artistic Innovation in the Early Medieval West*, ed. Celia M. Chazelle (Lanham, MD: University Press of America, 1992), pp. 49–75.

19. The Latin text is most easily available in *Capitularia regum Francorum* 1: 82–91. See, however, *Capitulare de villis*, ed. Carlrichard Brühl, 2 vols. (Stuttgart: Müller and Schindler, 1971), which includes a facsimile of

Wolfenbüttel, Herzog August Bibliothek MS 237 (Helmst. 254) and a German translation.

20. A.H.M. Jones, *The Later Roman Empire, 284–602: A Social Economic and Administrative Survey*, 2 vols. (Norman, OK: University of Oklahoma Press, 1964), 1: 411–27.

21. Thomas S. Brown, *Gentlemen and Officers: Imperial Administration and Aristocratic Power in Byzantine Italy, A.D. 554–800* (London: British School at Rome, 1984), pp. 109–25.

22. *Capitulare de villis*, cap. 60.

23. *Capitulare de villis*, cap. 20, 35.

24. 77. *Capitulare Aquisgranense, Capitularia regum Francorum* 1:172, cap. 19 [170–72]. Henceforth cited as *Capitulare Aquisgranense* with chapter numbers.

25. *Capitulare de villis*, cap. 27, 45.

26. *Capitulare de villis*, cap. 62; Ganshof, "Charlemagne and the Institutions," p. 36.

27. *Capitulare de villis*, cap. 62.

28. *Capitulare de villis*, cap. 55.

29. For example, *Capitulare de villis*, cap. 8, 15, 17, 20, 23.

30. *Capitulare de villis*, cap. 55, 62.

31. *Capitulare de villis*, cap. 55, 62.

32. *Capitulare de villis*, cap. 55, 62.

33. *Capitulare de villis*, cap. 4, 7, 37.

34. *Capitulare de villis*, cap. 7, 62.

35. Bernard S. Bachrach, "Charlemagne and the Carolingian General Staff," *The Journal of Military History* 66 (2002): 313–57; Bernard S. Bachrach, "Adalhard's *De ordine palatii*: Some Methodological Observations Regarding Chapters 29–36," *Cithara* 39 (2001): 3–36.

36. *Capitulare de villis*, cap. 28.

37. *Capitulare de villis*, cap. 44.

38. *Capitulare de villis*, cap. 25.

39. *Capitulare de villis*, cap. 15, 20, 28.

40. *Capitulare de villis*, cap. 30; for discussion of a useful analogue, see Durliat, "La Polyptyque d'Irminon pour l'Armée," 183–208.

41. *Capitulare de villis*, cap. 68.

42. *Capitulare de villis*, cap. 64.

43. *Capitulare de villis*, cap. 45, 62, 64.

44. Jean-Pierre Devroey, "Units of Measurement in the Early Medieval Economy: The Example of Carolingian Food Rations," *French History* 1 (1987): 68–92.

45. *Capitulare de villis*, cap. 9.

46. E. Alföldi-Rosenbaum, "The Finger Calculus in Antiquity and in the Middle Ages: Studies on Roman Game Counters I," *Frühmittelalterliche Studien* 5 (1971): 1–9; Bachrach, *Early Carolingian Warfare*, p. 206.

47. *Capitulare de villis*, cap. 64; *Capitulare Aquisgranense*, cap. 10; Bachrach, "Charlemagne and the Carolingian General Staff," 313–57.

48. *Capitulare Aquisgranense*, cap. 10.

49. *Capitulare Aquisgranense*, cap. 10; Bachrach, *Early Carolingian Warfare*, pp. 109–10.

50. *Capitulare Aquisgranense*, cap. 10. The carrying of artillery seems to have required a special order; see, for example, *75. Karoli ad Fulradum Abbatem Epistola, Capitularia regum Francorum* 1: 168.

51. *Karoli ad Fulradum*, p. 168.

52. Vegetius, *De re militari* 1.24 and 3.8, ed. and trans. Leo F. Stelten (New York: Lang, 1990).

53. These tools are mentioned in the formularies completed as part of the inventory process; see *Capitulare de villis*, cap. 42.

54. *Capitulare de villis*, cap. 42.

55. *Capitulare de villis*, cap. 62; Bachrach, *Early Carolingian Warfare*, pp. 166–69.

56. S.T. James, "The *fabricae*: State Arms Factories of the Later Roman Empire," in *Military Equipment and the Identity of Roman Soldiers: Proceedings of the Fourth Roman Military Equipment Conference, 1986*, ed. J.C. Coulston (Oxford: Oxford University Press, 1988), pp. 257–331; John Haldon, *Warfare, State and Society in the Byzantine World, 565–1204* (London: UCL Press, 1999), pp. 140–41.

57. M.D. Reeve, "*Notitia Dignitatum*," in *Texts and Transmission: A Survey of the Latin Classics*, ed. L.D. Reynolds and P.K. Marshall (Oxford: Oxford University Press, 1983), pp. 253–57; *Capitulare de villis*, cap. 43.

58. *Capitulare de villis*, cap. 62.

59. *Capitulare de villis*, cap. 62; Bachrach, *Early Carolingian Warfare,* pp. 108–15.

60. *Capitulare de villis*, cap. 45, 62.

61. *Capitulare de villis*, cap. 45, 62.

62. *Capitulare de villis*, cap. 45, 62.

63. *Capitulare de villis*, cap. 45, 62.

64. *Capitulare de villis*, cap. 34, 62, 66.

65. *Capitulare de villis*, cap. 45, 62.

66. *Capitulare de villis*, cap. 62; Bachrach, *Early Carolingian Warfare*, pp. 135–36.

67. *Capitulare de villis*, cap. 62.

68. Bernard S. Bachrach, "Charlemagne's Cavalry: Myth and Reality," *Military Affairs* 47 (1983): 181–87, repr. in Bernard S. Bachrach, *Armies and Politics in the Early Medieval West* (Aldershot: Variorum, 1993), pp. 1–20; Bernard S. Bachrach and Charles R. Bowlus, "Heerwesen," in *Reallexikon der Germanischen Altertumskunde*, ed. Heinrich Beck et al., 28 vols. (Berlin: Walter De Gruyter, 2001), 14: 122–36; R.H.C. Davis, *The Medieval Warhorse: Origin, Development and Redevelopment* (New York: Thames and Hudson, 1989), pp. 51–53.

69. Carroll Gillmore, "Practical Chivalry: The Training of Horses for Tournaments and Warfare," *Studies in Medieval and Renaissance History* n.s. 13 (1992): 7–29.

70. Ann Hyland, *Equus: The Horse in the Roman World* (New Haven: Yale University Press, 1990), pp. 30–60; J.K. Anderson, *Ancient Greek Horsemanship* (Berkeley: University of California Press, 1961).

71. *Capitulare de villis*, cap. 13.

72. *Capitulare de villis*, cap. 14.

73. *Capitulare de villis*, cap. 14; Davis, *The Medieval War Horse*, pp. 52–53.

74. *Capitulare de villis*, cap. 14.

75. *Capitulare de villis*, cap. 15, 50.

76. *Brevium Exempla*, cap. 25, 31, 33.

77. Hyland, *Equus*, p. 33.

78. Hyland, *Equus*, p. 31, suggests that about 60% of mares foaled each year under natural circumstances.

79. Ann Hyland, *The Medieval Warhorse from Byzantium to the Crusades* (Conshohocken, PA: Combined Books, 1994), pp. 64–65.

80. Ann Hyland, *Training the Roman Cavalry: from Arrian's 'Ars Tactica'* (Dover, NH: Alan Sutton, 1993), p. 24.

81. For the traditional romantic-elitist treatment of warfare that still survives to mislead non-specialists, especially those wedded to a "Germanist" view of the Middle Ages, see Reuter, "Plunder and Tribute," pp. 75–94. A useful antidote is provided by Bachrach, "Charlemagne's Cavalry: Myth and Reality," pp. 1–20; and Bachrach and Bowlus, "Heerwesen," pp. 122–36.

82. Steven C. Fanning, "Tacitus, Beowulf and the *Comitatus*," *The Haskins Society Journal* 9 (2001): 36–38 [17–38]; Roberta Frank, "Scaldic Verse and the Date of Beowulf," in *The Dating of Beowulf*, ed. Colin Chase (Toronto: University of Toronto Press, 1981), pp. 123–39. See the continued dedication to these myths by Guy Halsall, *Warfare and Society in the Barbarian West* (London: Routledge, 2003) pp. 34, 144, where drinking bouts and feuds are emphasized.

83. Karl J. Leyser, *Rule and Conflict in an Early Medieval Society: Ottonian Saxony* (Bloomington, IN: Indiana University Press, 1978), observes regarding Zulus, "Yet, one or two lessons about the place of sacral kingship...in early medieval kingdoms...can perhaps be learned from these models" (p. 102). For a more detailed discussion and critique of the use by medievalists of sub-Saharan models constructed by modern anthropologists, see Bernard S. Bachrach, "Anthropology and Early Medieval History: Some Problems," *Cithara* 34 (1994): 3–10; also see Philippe Buc, *The Dangers of Ritual: Between Early Medieval Texts and Social Scientific Theory* (Princeton: Princeton University Press, 2001).

CHAPTER 8

THE CAROLINGIAN CREATION OF A MODEL OF PATRILINEAGE

Constance Brittain Bouchard

Reevaluation of Carolingian historical writings, and the role of women in their genealogies, challenging assumptions that the patrilineal family model was invented in the twelfth century.

Medieval noble families are often conceptualized using a paradigm derived from twelfth-century France: straight-line lineages organized around male inheritance.[1] In this essay I argue that this vision of family structure, although never a straightforward description of reality, was first created ca. 800 CE by publicists at the Carolingian court. It proved so compelling that all who wished subsequently to assert their right to rule had to present a similar model of their families, and so convincing that modern scholars have allowed this model to shape their own understanding of Charlemagne's family tree. My discussion of how this family tree may be read and understood by modern historians is intended as a reminder that one cannot easily apply methodologies originally developed for the High Middle Ages to earlier periods. It is also a warning against treating medieval people's descriptions of their past as a transparent window into what had happened, rather than into what they thought—or wished—had happened.

Those in the twelfth century who wrote the histories of their ancestors tended to pare away collateral branches and put the emphasis on the line of inheritance, which normally meant the male line. Although modern historians of the High Middle Ages used to accept this patrilineal model as normative, it has recently been questioned. In particular, a number have pointed out that women as well as men played a significant role in both their natal and marital families. Widows could and did act as lords in their own right, sometimes even after their sons were grown. Noblemen might identify more with their mother's than father's relatives if the former group was more powerful.[2] Even when power and property went preferentially to men rather than women, younger sons were not necessarily marginalized. And inheritance never functioned in reality as a simple succession of fathers and sons, both because of serious disagreements between potential heirs and because of premature deaths of sons, or a failure to have sons at all. Most notably, the succession of kings in England from the late eleventh century to the end of the twelfth involved inheritance by a son, a brother, a nephew, a cousin, a son, and a brother. In two-thirds of the cases, the new king was not the product of the sort of father–son succession modern scholars have thought was normal.[3]

Here I challenge the paradigm of a standard medieval patrilineal family structure from another direction: such a mode of family organization was not as prevalent among the nobles of the early Middle Ages as either their twelfth-century descendants or modern scholars have assumed. The replacement for this paradigm, however, is emphatically not a treatment of early medieval families as amorphous with ill-defined boundaries,[4] because nobles themselves appear to have had an excellent idea of who were and were not their relatives. Instead, it is necessary to look at how and when early medieval noble families sought to create a model—accurate or not—of straight-line male descent.

I argue that a "model" of patrilineage with an emphasis on a single, straight line of men (without detours, for instance, off to cousins) was the conscious creation of the Carolingian court, promulgated in part to justify Pippin the Short's removal of the Merovingian dynasty in the mid-eighth century. Neither a self-evident description of how all early medieval noble families thought of themselves, nor something that emerged for the first time in the twelfth century, during Georges Duby's "male Middle Ages,"[5] this paradigm of patrilineal descent was developed as part of Carolingian efforts to justify why they and they alone should be kings of the Franks.

Specifically, publicists for the Carolingian dynasty attempted, at the end of the eighth century and beginning of the ninth, to create an image of unproblematic descent from Bishop Arnulf of Metz and Pippin I to Charlemagne. But if one examines the *genealogiae* thus produced, the accounts are far from uniform, are in fact oddly contradictory. Further, the sources that these publicists themselves used, many still available, indicate that the rise of the family of the mayors of the palace and their ascension to the throne were much more dynastically complex than the *genealogiae* suggest. The family tree contains more twists and turns than acknowledged; indeed, a whole group of relatives in Italy, never considered before in a Carolingian context, seems to have as much right to be attached to the Pippinids as does the lineage's supposed founder, Arnulf of Metz.

Scholars now take for granted that France was ruled by three discrete, successive dynasties that succeeded each other in the turning-point years of 751 and 987, but this characterization is a product only of the eleventh century, when it was first proposed by a chronicler at Sens. Although the modern term "the Carolingians" was in use in the High Middle Ages, it postdates the death of the last Carolingian king by a good century. As late as 1200, a scribe compiling the cartulary of Echternach, who could accurately reconstruct a *genealogia* leading from Pippin of Herstal to Charles the Fat, had no collective noun to give this group, calling them "our Pippins and Charleses" (Pippinos et Carlos nostros).[6] His lack of a handy patrilineal name for this *gens* should serve as a warning against too ready an assumption that the men of the eighth and ninth centuries so categorized their relatives.

In this context it is striking to note that the great lords found in the records of Merovingian Gaul seem devoid of the patrilineal consciousness indicated by the twelfth-century *genealogiae*. They may appear abruptly in the records as well-established men of enormous wealth, often making gifts of vast holdings by testament to the Church,[7] and then disappear again, with no mention of their ancestors. An example is Wideradus, who died ca. 720 and is best known as the founder of Flavigny. He distributed a large amount of property in central Burgundy, located within a giant square some 120 kilometers on a side, to four basilicas: St.-Andoche of Saulieu, Ste.-Reine of Alise, St.-Férreol of Grigny/Vienne,[8] and especially to St.-Prix (Praeiectus) of Flavigny.[9] Wideradus mentioned that his late father Corbo had been a *vir illuster* and that he himself had "heirs," to whom he left some property according to the Roman law of *falcidia*, but he was otherwise unspecific about his family, either ancestors or younger relatives.[10] Abbo, a younger contemporary of Wideradus, gave even more property in 739 to the monastery of Novalesa, which he had founded, property in most of the dioceses between Mâcon and the Mediterranean. But despite the high status this gift implies—and the likelihood that he was the final *patricius* of Provence—little is known about his family connections. He names several aunts, uncles, and cousins, his late parents Felix and Rustica, his paternal grandfather Marro and maternal grandparents Maurinus and Dodina from whom he inherited and was descended; but they are given no more attention than the names of the people from whom he acquired property through purchase. Likewise, he did not look toward the future of his family unit, for he mentioned no relatives of a generation younger than his.[11]

One could argue that donors like Wideradus or Abbo had few secular heirs, or they would not have been giving their property to the church. But the evidence does not suggest that generous donors were typically the last in their families. Rather, it generally indicates they had plenty of relatives, even if they did not use donation charters as excuses to recite the list. Twelfth-century donation charters normally mention numerous relatives: not necessarily everyone to whom the donor was related, but usually patrilineal ancestors and living relatives who would share in the spiritual benefit of the gift.[12] Testaments from the first half of the eighth century, though, are not nearly as concerned with enumerating family members.

These testaments, of powerful landowners who seem (by later standards) curiously uninterested in their paternal ancestry or the continuity of the family unit, reflect a long-standing pattern. Bishop Bertram of Le Mans, who died in the first decades of the seventh century, was certainly not the last living person in his family, but he showed little concern for previous generations. His unusually long testament names not only two late brothers but also three living nephews, four grand-nephews, and four cousins ("parentes," three men and a woman), one with two sons of his own. Bertram had inherited or otherwise acquired property spread over much of western Francia, from the mouth of the Seine south nearly to the Pyrenees.[13] Yet his testament fails to identify the ancestors from whom he received it. When Adalgisel-Grimo, a deacon from a powerful noble family, drew up his testament in 634, he noted that he had *parentes* and *propinqui*, but he named none of them other than his nephew Bobo, a "duke" (*dux*).[14]

Although given the scantiness of Merovingian-era documents one must beware arguing from silence, the existing evidence suggests that patrilineal ancestry was not a major concern for the great lords.[15] The only group of relatives in which one can perceive dynastic consciousness is the Merovingian royal family. Only those descended in the male line from the sea-serpent of legend could sit on the Frankish throne—and they could do so even if underage, even if illegitimate.[16] It did not matter if they had to be recalled from the monastery to fill a royal vacancy, as long as their fathers were of the royal lineage. In contrast, royally born women of the sixth and seventh centuries are almost invisible in the records; we know, for example, of one daughter but five sons of Clovis, and one daughter but seven sons of Clovis's son Clothar. This emphasis on a continuing line of legitimate male descendants makes the Merovingian dynasty distinct from any contemporary group of relatives.

When the Carolingians deposed the last Merovingian king, however, they felt compelled to duplicate the sense of a long male lineage. It was only at this point, I argue, that any powerful kin group other than the Merovingian rulers sought to conceptualize itself as derived from a long line of men. Once Charlemagne's family had done so, anyone trying to challenge them needed a similar reconceptualization.

The Carolingians

Later Carolingian publicists, especially Einhard, tried to suggest that the deposition of Childeric III, whom Pippin had tonsured and put into a monastery, was an almost inevitable result of Merovingian ineptitude, but it was certainly more than a reaction to a newly emergent weakness in the ruling line. The mayors of the palace had been choosing the kings, rather than vice versa, for over a generation before 751. Pippin's father, Charles Martel, had deliberately sought out two Merovingians to make kings when his royal lords died: Clothar IV was so obscure that modern scholars cannot agree on who his father was; Theoderic IV had to be brought out of the cloister. For the final years of his life, even after the death of Theoderic IV, Charles continued to rule as mayor of the palace rather than having himself crowned.[17] Similarly, Pippin initially chose a Merovingian king to serve, one who (unlike Charles's kings) may have had a son and was thus in a position to continue the royal line.[18] During the decade between the death of Charles Martel and his own coronation, though, Pippin seems to have changed his mind.

The novel and complex acts and rituals that accompanied the last Merovingian's deposition and the coronation of Pippin the Short, according to the written records, suggest the difficulty of the decision.[19] Besides the usual election, placing someone on the throne not of the Merovingian line took consecration with a chrism, reflecting both Old Testament models and, probably, the baptism of Clovis with holy oil,[20] and it took, especially, the concurrence of the pope. The question was not simply the replacement of one king by another, but the establishment of the Carolingian lineage as a valid alternative to the Merovingian. Such an establishment was shaky enough that it also required, three years after Pippin's initial coronation in 751, the personal appearance of the pope in Francia to preside over more rites.

As detailed in a contemporary text known as the *Clausula de Pippino*,[21] Pope Stephen II anointed and blessed Pippin in 754 along with his wife and sons, Charles (Charlemagne) and Carloman, at a ceremony that included the consecration of the church dedicated to the first apostle to Gaul, Saint Denis. The pope also issued a highly unusual proclamation: from then on, no one "from any other loins" should become king of the Franks. Everything that ritual could do was done to equate the fruit of Pippin's seed with the leadership and continued well-being of the Franks. That such added ritual was thought necessary indicates how fragile the equation was.

The participation of Pippin's family in the papal blessing was repeated three years later in a 757 letter from Stephen II to Pippin preserved in the *Codex Carolinus*: "May you be blessed, my esteemed son…and may the Lord guard and in all things protect your beloved offspring, my spiritual sons, Lord Charles and Carloman, established by God as kings of the Franks and patricians of the Romans, with their most Christian mother, the most excellent queen, your dearest wife…May God expand your seed and bless it."[22] The biblical parallels with the seed of Abraham were unmistakable. For the popes as for the Carolingians themselves, Pippin's sons had been established as kings along with their father; the mother who bore them took part in the divine blessing; and the benediction was to be extended to the next generation.

As a family affair, kingship demanded a glorious ancestry for Pippin and Charlemagne as well as a glorious future for Pippin's seed. The Merovingian dynasty, after all, had traced a clear line of descent from the first Frankish kings four centuries earlier, a descent spelled out by Gregory of Tours and the chronicler Fredegar. They had a collective name, the *gens Meroingorum*, used by Einhard,[23] although there would be no such name for the group modern scholars call the Carolingians for two more centuries. Specifically, the Carolingians had to be reconceptualized as a male-line dynasty, one in which power had *always* passed smoothly from father to son, without long detours or dead-ends. Toward the end of the eighth century, Paul the Deacon said that a new "lineage" (*prosapia*) had taken up Frankish rule; by making this comment in the context of the deeds of Charlemagne's great-grandfather, he implied this had happened a century and a half earlier.[24] In equating family and royal rule for Pippin and his son Charlemagne, though, Paul was doing something markedly different than had chroniclers of the Merovingians. With the Merovingian kings, male kinship gave one a right to rule, but there is nothing in contemporary accounts, or for that matter in modern reconstructions of their family tree, that can be construed as straight-line inheritance (exclusively father to son) in the male line. Yet this is what Carolingian publicists sought to create.

The first effort to construct such a male-line dynasty for the family was that of Paul the Deacon writing in the 780s, about a generation after Pope Stephen had blessed Pippin's seed. Paul embedded his *genealogia* of Charlemagne within an account of the bishops of Metz, based, he said, on what the king had told him of his family's history.[25] Charlemagne, according to Paul, had stated that he was the great-great-great-grandson (*trinepos*) of the blessed Arnulf of Metz, whom Paul said was of the "race" (*stemma*) of the Franks. Arnulf, he continued, was father of Anschisus, father of Pippin of Herstal. He did not name the wives of Arnulf or Anschisus or, indeed, any wives or brothers as he carried the line of descent onward from Pippin of Herstal to Charles Martel to Pippin the Short to Charlemagne. Charlemagne is the first person in this family tree whose wife is named, indicating how thoroughly the account is one of a male lineage. Charlemagne's son Pippin, Paul explains, was named for his grandfather, and his son Charles for his father and great-grandfather, reinforcing the image of a male-line dynasty.

Paul the Deacon was certainly correct that Anschisus—or a man with a name only slightly different from that—was father of Pippin of Herstal; Pippin named his father Ansegesil (*Ansgisilius*) in his own charters.[26] Yet Paul's father–son connection between Arnulf of Metz and Anschisus/Ansegisel is not attested by any contemporary source; in fact, he was the first to put it forward. Paul had probably read Fredegar's chronicle, which shows Bishop Arnulf and Pippin I acting together in the first decades of the seventh century, without, however, suggesting there was any tie of blood or marriage between them. The "continuations" of Fredegar's account call Ansegisel a noble Frank, but again do not suggest a family connection with Arnulf.[27] There is no way to disprove definitively what could be the lineage's oral memory, but there is enough evidence suggesting otherwise to justify the doubt recently cast on accepting Arnulf as Charlemagne's first male-line ancestor.[28]

Curiously, Paul gave no explanation here of how the transition from Merovingian to Carolingian kings took place.[29] He had spoken in his *Historia Langobardorum* of the previous kings of the Franks as having "degenerated from their accustomed strength and skill" in the early seventh century, precisely the time of Bishop Arnulf—far earlier than any other source would put Merovingian decadence. Then, he said, the mayors of the palace took over "whatever the kings used to do," and due to "heavenly disposition...the Frankish realm was translated to this lineage."[30] But the *Historia* is reticent about exactly what this transfer involved or when it occurred; the implication appears to be that it was in the seventh century, though Paul must have known that Charlemagne's father Pippin, the first king of the dynasty, was not crowned for another century.

The *Gesta* of the bishops of Metz are even vaguer on the transition. The topic of Merovingian decline never arises, and there is no mention that Pippin the Short deposed the last king of that dynasty. This very silence is telling. Paul seems to want to suggest that the Carolingians had already enjoyed over a century and a half of rule by the time he wrote. The absence of reference to the deposition of the last Merovingian, in both the *Historia* and the *Gesta*, may well indicate that the transfer of the crown in 751 from one lineage to another was still a highly sensitive issue in the late eighth century, one Paul did not care to touch.

Paul's version of a Carolingian dynasty, though, as found in a male-line descent from Arnulf of Metz, was not the only one proposed at Charlemagne's court. A quite different version is found in the so-called Annals of Metz, composed twenty years or so after the *Gesta*, possibly by Charlemagne's sister.[31] Although Arnulf of Metz appears in this account, he is not Ansegesil's father, only a "paternal relative" of Pippin of Herstal.[32] That Arnulf is mentioned but not placed in the family tree must indicate a deliberate rejection of Paul the Deacon's version of Carolingian ancestry.

It was more challenging for the annalist of Metz to create a plausible male-line dynasty reaching from Charlemagne back to the early seventh century; the Annals covered the maternal, rather than paternal, ancestry of Pippin of Herstal (Charlemagne's great-grandfather), yet an agnatic family tree was still the goal. The appearance of women in the *genealogia* composed by the annalist, the chief basis for the modern argument that the author was female, should not obscure the effort to build a family tree in which male descent took precedence. It is especially striking that this annalist should have sought to reconceptualize Pippin of Herstal's maternal relatives as an agnatic group because Pippin seems to have acquired most of his wealth and influence through women. It has recently even been argued that the real seventh-century Pippin was the product of a matrilineage,[33] a sharp contrast with how he and his family were remembered at the beginning of the ninth century.

The Annals open with the succession of Pippin of Herstal to the "principality" (*principatus*; the office of mayor of the palace) of his father, Ansegesil. But then almost immediately the annalist turns to Begga, Ansegesil's wife, a "glorious mother" (gloriosa genitrix) for Pippin and "worthy of all praise" (cunctis laudibus digna). Begga, the annalist tells us, was daughter of Pippin I, and although this account (like Paul the Deacon's) was written 150 years after the fact, it is essentially confirmed by sources much closer to the events (unlike Paul's). While the annalist had no choice but to discuss Begga, who was the link between Pippin of Herstal and Pippin I, the Annals also include Saint Gertrude, Begga's sister, and Pippin I's wife, Itta, known from seventh-century sources.[34]

Despite the inclusion of these women, the overall purpose was to create an image of male-line descent, as shown most clearly by the efforts to turn Pippin of Herstal's maternal grandfather into the moral equivalent of a paternal grandfather. Pippin I, we are told, had "no offspring of the masculine sex, and thus left both his name and his principality to his grandson Pippin" (of Herstal).[35] But Pippin I *did* have a son, Grimoald I, mayor of the palace in the 650s.[36] This Grimoald, though, was not of the line that led to Charlemagne, doubtless why he was quietly left out of the story. Grimoald had been mayor, but the eventual accession of his sister's son to that office had nothing to do with his ultimately failed efforts to rule through an infant Merovingian.[37] Pippin of Herstal commemorated this maternal uncle through the name of his second son, Grimoald II, but he himself became mayor of the palace only a generation after the first Grimoald's death.

Again in contrast to Paul the Deacon, the annalist of Metz made the Merovingian kings part of the story. Although no more impressed by them than Einhard would be when writing some two decades later, the annalist's Merovingian rulers are active figures, cruel and untrustworthy perhaps, but never figures of fun. When they stopped being active and cruel, they stopped being mentioned. The last Merovingians simply do not appear, and the account of the consecration and coronation of Pippin the Short does not note that a final Merovingian king first had to be removed. This version of Carolingian family history avoids the problem of justifying the transfer of the crown from one lineage to another by not referring to it.

Two major versions of Charlemagne's ancestry were thus already in existence when Einhard wrote not long after Charlemagne's death: one emphasizing Pippin of Herstal's paternal ancestry, one his maternal ancestry, but with the clear intention of making Pippin I into a virtual paternal relative. Although modern scholars typically conflate these two accounts, when written they were meant to be different. Perhaps wanting to avoid choosing between them, Einhard discussed none of Charlemagne's ancestors before his father, Pippin the Short, though he mentioned that Pippin's father and grandfather had also been mayors of the palace. In spite of their divergences, Paul the Deacon, the annalist of Metz, and Einhard clearly all tried to create a version of Carolingian ancestry that emphasized the men. All versions also radically pruned the family tree of brothers and cousins,[38] simplifying it into a straight-line story of fathers and sons: the kind of story typically told in twelfth-century *genealogiae*.

The efforts around the year 800 to create a coherent dynasty for Charlemagne, in which his great-grandfather was the grandson of one of two seventh-century figures, Pippin I or Arnulf of Metz, ignored some other seventh-century figures whom modern scholars might treat as part of the extended Arnulfing/Pippinid group, if they followed the same methods they usually use to construct family trees. Exactly the same sort of evidence exists to infer that these figures were part of the familial group as used by historians to create genealogies of other "clans," especially name similarities,[39] but they do not appear in modern treatments of the Carolingians. The pruned and simplified version of Charlemagne's ancestry established in the early ninth century has undergone very few more recent modifications.

The overlooked family group, traceable back to the late sixth century, is described by Fredegar (see figure 8.1) and marked by the name Grimoald, also a Pippinid name. Two brothers, Grimoald and Gundoald, had a sister, Theudelinda, who married King Agilolf of the Lombards and was the mother of the succeeding Lombard king; her daughter married the next two kings after Agilolf, who assumed office in part through marrying this daughter. Theudelinda's brother Gundoald also went to Italy and married a noble Lombard wife, having sons by her.[40] A brief seventh-century history of the Lombards, one of Paul the Deacon's sources for his Lombard history, suggests this family group was Bavarian. Garipald and Waldrada of Bavaria are identified as the parents of Queen Theudelinda of Lombardy and Gundoald (and presumably their brother

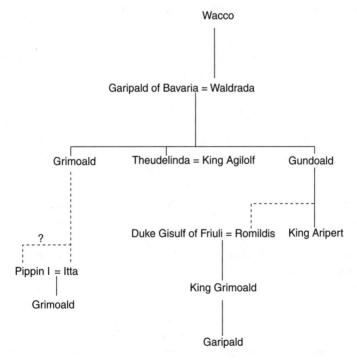

Figure 8.1 Possible Lombard relatives of the Pippinids.

Grimoald), and it is noted that Waldrada was the daughter of King Wacco of the Lombards.[41] Although Fredegar calls Theudelinda's family Frankish, not Bavarian or Lombard, she was likely the daughter of the duke of Bavaria and his wife.

Paul the Deacon also describes another Lombard group that must have been related to this family: the family of Duke Gisulf of Friuli, whose son Grimoald was adopted by the duke of Benevento and became king of Lombardy in the second half of the seventh century, having a son named Garipald. For Paul, the wife of Duke Gisulf, Romildis, became the focus of a wildly misogynist story. She conceived a lust for the manly form of the chieftain of the Avars and opened the gates of Friuli to his hordes; but he, more honorable than she even though a barbarian, gave her to a dozen of his Avar henchmen to enjoy and then had her killed, a suitable punishment for having betrayed her people.[42] The question here, though, is the family origins of Romildis.

Name similarities suggest she was the daughter of Theudelinda's brother Gundoald. Gundoald is known to have had multiple sons, one of whom, Aripert, was briefly king of the Lombards. Given the propensity in seventh-century Lombardy for men to acquire authority through their wives, a daughter of Gundoald would have been a valuable prize. Having tarred her so thoroughly for excess libido, Paul is perhaps understandably uninterested in talking about her family. But if Romildis was Gundoald's daughter, this would explain why one of her sons was named Grimoald, the name of her paternal uncle, and why King Grimoald named his own son Garipald, the name of her grandfather.[43]

Although Fredegar does not say what became of Theudelinda's second brother, Grimoald, he lived at the right time to be the father of Pippin I—or perhaps of Pippin's wife Itta. His name of course appears among Pippin's and Itta's children, and Fredegar stressed that this Grimoald was a noble Frank, whose sister came close to marrying a Merovingian king before marrying the Lombard king instead. If this Grimoald was related to the Pippinids, it would add another whole collection of relatives to the Carolingian family tree, and also give a precedent for the Carolingian–Lombard marriage alliances of the eighth century. Paul the Deacon does not draw any connection between the Frankish-Bavarian-Lombard Grimoald group (largely known through his own account) and the Carolingians, but then he had nothing to say about any of the maternal ancestors of Pippin of Herstal. I would not try to argue definitively that Grimoald (brother of Theudelinda) was Pippin I's father or father-in-law, given the sparse evidence, though he certainly could have been. That the ninth-century authors did not do so either suggests they mined Fredegar's account with a clear idea of what they intended to find.

The point of this genealogical exercise, trying to work out the connections between a group of (probable) Franks in Lombardy who seem potentially connected with Charlemagne's Pippinid ancestors, is not mere antiquarianism, adding extra names to the Carolingian family tree. Rather, it is to demonstrate that by and large, modern scholars have looked only for Carolingian relatives attached to his ancestry by narrative sources written specifically for Charlemagne's court. Thus although Charles Martel had a number of sons and brothers who do not appear in these texts yet are well attested in contemporary documents, even working out his family connections has been a relatively recent event. That I can propose ancestors of Charlemagne in Lombardy, using evidence widely available to scholars for a century, and have my suggestions be novel, indicates the enormous influence the family trees created at the Carolingian court still exercise. It also indicates that the kind of patrilineal family consciousness later centuries took for granted was not the norm in the seventh century; the contemporary sources that discuss Pippin I say nothing of his ancestry. Paul the Deacon, the annalist of Metz, and Einhard all tried to create pictures of male-line descent for Charlemagne, but they were hampered by using sources that did not define earlier people, even the powerful, by their male forebears.

Defining families by a clearly marked line of males was a new development around the year 800, in part an attempt to create a genealogy for the Carolingians parallel to that of the Merovingians, but in part much more restrictive. The deliberate paring away of branches of the family tree meant that male cousins were excluded if they were not the fruit of Pippin's loins, even if by the Merovingian definition of who was and who was not family they would have been included. This new kind of definition was not immediately accepted, as can be demonstrated by Charlemagne's cousin Wala, son of a half-brother of Pippin the Short. When the so-called Astronomer was writing a biography of Louis the Pious, he suggested that Wala was considered a potential rival to Louis upon Charlemagne's death in 814.[44] The fear that he might plot against Louis was immediately assuaged, the biographer continued, when Wala hurried to submit himself to Louis, but the incident raises an interesting issue. Despite probable concubines in Wala's immediate ancestry, the Astronomer expected his readers to recognize him as a plausible source of a sinister plot. In the mid-ninth century, there was at least some sense that any male connected through male relatives to Pippin the Short and Charlemagne might potentially be king, even though Wala's father Bernard, as Pippin's half-brother, had never taken part in any of the papal blessings and was in no way a product of Pippin's loins. The deliberate effort to create a Carolingian male-line *gens* comparable to the

Merovingian was beginning to be accepted by the time of Charlemagne's grandsons, yet not necessarily as narrowly as those creating the *gens* would have preferred. Once the Carolingians had defined themselves patrilineally, their potential rivals had to do so, as well. The Merovingians had been unique as a male-defined kindred, but when one family set out to challenge that uniqueness, all possible royal lines had to follow suit. The Carolingians were more willing than their royal predecessors to mention women in constructions of their families, but those who sought to replace them needed a patrilineage of their own to which they could point. What has obscured this development is the lack of success of Boso, the first non-Carolingian for over a century crowned in Charlemagne's old *regnum*. Boso built up enough power and authority through service to Charles the Bald to challenge Charles's successors; Boso's coronation in 879 and rebellion against those successors indicate an intention to create a kingdom he could pass to his son and grandson, his own royal dynasty. He and his relatives never succeeded, but it was certainly not for lack of trying.[45]

More indicative than Boso's failed efforts is the Council of Quierzy (877), with its suggestion that counties held *in beneficium* from Charles the Bald could be passed on by heredity to the counts' sons. The one-time scholarly assumption that Quierzy marked the "birth of feudalism" or "the end of centralized government," along with the more recent arguments pointing out, quite rightly, that at the time it was not considered to mark any significant change in royal administration,[46] have masked what may be its most important feature. Land had always been viewed as hereditary, even if there were major discussions over who had the right to inherit from whom and in what circumstances. Now ruling office, in this case a count's authority but in the broader sense kingship, was assumed to be unproblematically hereditary. Quierzy did not create this assumption, but its canons show how thoroughly the idea had become accepted. By the time of Charlemagne's grandsons, multiple noble families, not only the Carolingians, defined themselves by the male line of descent.

Once the publicists of the Carolingian court had made the case that these kings, and they alone, were chosen to rule the Franks, and that this right of rulership passed by blood to the males of the next generation, then those who would challenge them, or even rule under them, were obliged to accept a similar sort of family consciousness. Agnatic descent as the idealized model shaping noble families, whether or not realized, was an invention not of the eleventh century as scholars once claimed,[47] but, it seems, of the eighth and ninth centuries.

Notes

1. Georges Duby, *The Chivalrous Society*, trans. Cynthia Postan (Berkeley: University of California Press, 1977), pp. 101–03.
2. *Aristocratic Women in Medieval France*, ed. Theodore Evergates (Philadelphia: University of Pennsylvania Press, 1999). See also Constance Brittain Bouchard, *"Those of My Blood": Constructing Noble Families in Medieval Francia* (Philadelphia: University of Pennsylvania Press, 2001), esp. pp. 175–80. For a particularly influential lady-lord, see Fredric L. Cheyette, *Ermengard of Narbonne and the World of the Troubadours* (Ithaca: Cornell University Press, 2001).
3. Marjorie Chibnall, "'Clio's Legal Cosmetics': Law and Custom in the Work of Medieval Historians," *Anglo Norman Studies* 20 (1998): 31–43.
4. An idea first put forward by Karl Schmid fifty years ago and rarely challenged using French sources: "Zur Problematik von Familie, Sippe und Geschlecht, Haus und Dynastie beim mittelalterlichen Adel," *Zeitschrift für die Geschichte des Oberrheins* 105 (1957): 1–62.
5. Georges Duby's *Mâle Moyen Age* was published in English as *Love and Marriage in the Middle Ages*, trans. Jane Dunnett (Chicago: University of Chicago Press, 1994).
6. *Historia Francorum Senonensis*, 750, 987, ed. Georg Heinrich Pertz, MGH SS 9 (Hannover: Hahn, 1851), pp. 364, 368; *Geschichte der Grundherrschaft Echternach im Frühmittelalter*, ed. Camillus Wampach, 2 vols. (Luxembourg: Luxemburger Kunstdruckerei AG, 1929–1930), 2 (1930): 4–8.
7. Ulrich Nonn, "Merowingische Testamente: Studien zum Fortleben einer römischen Urkundenform im Frankenreich," *Archiv für Diplomatik* 18 (1972): 1–129.
8. I identified St.-Férreol as in Besançon in, *The Cartulary of Flavigny, 717–1113*, ed. Constance Brittain Bouchard, Medieval Academy Books 99 (Cambridge, MA: Medieval Academy of America, 1991), p. 2. However, it seems more likely that it was the heart of the monastic complex at Grigny, on the west bank of the Rhône, across from Vienne. See Ian Wood, "A Prelude to Columbanus: The Monastic Achievement in the Burgundian Territories," in *Columbanus and Merovingian Monasticism*, ed. H.B. Clarke and Mary Brown, British Archaeological Reports, International Series 113 (Oxford: BAR, 1981), pp. 6–7 [3–32].
9. On St. Praeiectus: Paul Fouracre and Richard A. Gerberding, *Late Merovingian France: History and Hagiography, 640–720* (Manchester: Manchester University Press, 1996), pp. 254–70; on his relics at Flavigny: Hugh of Flavigny, *Chronicon*, ed. Georg Heinrich Pertz, MGH SS 8 (Hannover: Hahn, 1848), pp. 351–52.
10. *Cartulary of Flavigny*, pp. 19–28, no. 1.
11. Patrick J. Geary, *Aristocracy in Provence: The Rhône Basin at the Dawn of the Carolingian Age* (Philadelphia: University of Pennsylvania Press, 1985), pp. 41, 65, 71, 115.

12. Stephen D. White, *Custom, Kinship, and Gifts to Saints: The "Laudatio Parentum" in Western France, 1050–1150* (Chapel Hill: University of North Carolina Press, 1988).

13. Margarete Weidemann, *Das Testament des Bischofs Bertramn von Le Mans vom 27. März 616: Untersuchungen zu Besitz und Geschichte einer frankishen Familie im 6. und 7. Jahrhundert* (Mainz: Römisch-Germanischen Zentralmuseum, 1986), pp. 7–49, especially pp. 16, 24, 34, 36, 42; for the extent of his property, see map p. 84.

14. Wilhelm Levison, "Das Testament des Diakons Adalgisel-Grimo vom Jahr 634," *Trierer Zeitschrift* 7 (1932): 73–84 [69–85].

15. Alexander Callander Murray, *Germanic Kinship Structure: Studies in Law and Society in Antiquity and the Early Middle Ages* (Toronto: University of Toronto Press, 1983), pp. 39–77, 109, 137, 218; Bouchard, "*Those of My Blood*," p. 68.

16. John Michael Wallace-Hadrill, *The Long-Haired Kings, and Other Studies in Frankish History* (London: Methuen and Co., 1962), pp. 155–231.

17. Martin Hartmann, "*Pater incertus*? Zu den Vätern des Gegenkönigs Chlothar IV. (717–718) und des letzten Merowingerkönigs Childerich III. (743–751)," *Deutsches Archiv für Erforschung des Mittelalters* 58 (2002): 1–15.

18. Childeric, whom Pippin deposed in 751, was the last known Merovingian king. He may have had a son named Theoderic, mentioned only in the *Chronique des abbés de Fontenelle* 10.4, ed. Pascal Pradié (Paris: Les Belles Lettres, 1999), p. 124. This source says that Theoderic, like his father, entered St.-Bertin, where he disappears from history.

19. More broadly, on Carolingian efforts to conceptualize their history and accession to power, see Rosamond McKitterick, *History and Memory in the Carolingian World* (Cambridge, UK: Cambridge University Press, 2004).

20. For Pippin's anointing, see also Janet L. Nelson, *Politics and Ritual in Early Medieval Europe* (London: Hambledon Press, 1986), pp. 289–91. She downplays its novelty, pointing out that since bishops had taken part in the elections of Merovingian kings, Pippin's enthronement cannot be called the first to have touched on the sacred. But the anointing was treated at the time as novel: not as some switch from profane to sacred, but as a legitimation of transfer from one lineage to another.

21. Ed. Bruno Krusch, MGH SSrM 1.2, new ed. (Hannover: Hahn, 1969), pp. 15–16. For the text's authenticity, see Robert-Henri Bautier, "Sacres et coronnements sous les Carolingiens et les premiers Capétiens: Recherches sur la genèse du sacre royal français," *Annuaire-Bulletin de la Société de l'histoire de France* (1989), repr. in idem., *Recherches sur l'histoire de la France médiévale: Des Mérovingiens aux premiers Capétiens* (Hampshire: Variorum, 1991), II, p. 12 n13 [7–56]. McKitterick points out that "contemporary" is not strictly accurate; the Clausula, by its own evidence, was written some fifteen years after Pippin's coronation, and the text may have been reworked later: *History and Memory*, pp. 140–41.

22. "Benedictus es, eximie fili...et tuos amantissimos natos meosque spiritales filios, domnum Carolum et Carolomannum, a Deo institutos reges Francorum et patritios Romanorum, cum christianissima eorum matre, excellentissima regina dulcissimaque coniuge....Dilatet Deus semen vestrum et benedicat....": *Codex Carolinus* 11, ed. Wilhelm Gundlach, MGH Epp 3, Epp Merovingici et Karolini aevi 1 (Berlin: Weidmann, 1892), p. 505. Alain J. Stoclet, about the last scholar to argue against the authenticity of the "Clausula," makes an unconvincing effort to explain away this blessing of Pippin's wife and children: "La 'Clausula de unctione Pippini regis': Mises au point et nouvelles hypothèses, *Francia* 8 (1980): 34–35[1–42].

23. Einhard, *Vie de Charlemagne* 1, ed. Louis Halphen (Paris: Les Belles Lettres, 1938), p. 8.

24. Paul the Deacon, *Gesta episcoporum Mettensium*, ed. Georg Heinrich Pertz, MGH SS 2 (Hannover: Hahn, 1829), pp. 264–65.

25. Paul the Deacon, *Gesta*, pp. 264–65. See also McKitterick, *History and Memory*, pp. 60–83; Walter Goffart, "Paul the Deacon's *Gesta episcoporum Mettensium* and the Early Design of Charlemagne's Succession," *Traditio* 42 (1986): 59–93.

26. *Diplomata maiorum domus regiae* 4–6, ed. Georg Heinrich Pertz, MGH DD imperii 1 (Hannover: Hahn, 1872), pp. 93–95.

27. Fredegar, *The Fourth Book of the Chronicle with Its Continuations*, ed. John Michael Wallace-Hadrill (London: Nelson, 1960), cont.3: 83.

28. For example, Fouracre and Gerberding, *Late Merovingian France*, pp. 311, 339; and Roger Collins, *Charlemagne* (Toronto: University of Toronto Press, 1998), pp. 24–25.

29. See also McKitterick, *History and Memory*, p. 124.

30. "Hoc tempore aput Gallias Francorum regibus a soli[ta] fortitudine et scientia degenerantibus, hi qui maiores domui regalis esse videbantur administrare regi potentiam et quicquid regibus agere mos est coeperunt; quippe cum caelitus esse[t] dispositum, ad horum progeniem Francorum transvehi regnum.": Paul the Deacon, *Historia Langobardorum* 6.16, ed. L. Bethmann and G. Waitz, MGH SSRL (Hannover: Hahn, 1878), p. 170.

31. *Annales Mettenses priores*, ed. B. de Simson, MGH SSRG 10 (Hannover: Hahn, 1905). See Yitzhak Hen, "The *Annales* of Metz and the Merovingian Past," in *The Uses of the Past in the Early Middle Ages*, ed. Yitzhak Hen and Matthew Innes (Cambridge, UK: Cambridge University Press, 2000), pp. 175–90; McKitterick, *History and Memory*, p. 125.

32. "agnatione propinquus": *Annales Mettenses priores* 688, p. 3.

33. Ian Wood, "Genealogy Defined by Women: The Case of the Pippinids," in *Gender in the Early Medieval World: East and West, 300–900*, ed. Leslie Brubaker and Julia M.H. Smith (Cambridge, UK: Cambridge, University Press, 2004), pp. 234–56.

34. *Annales Mettenses priores* 688, pp. 1–2. For the couple Pippin I and Itta, see the seventh-century *Vita S. Geretrudis* 1, ed. W. Wattenbach, MGH SSRM 2 (Hannover: Hahn, 1888), p. 454. The *vita* states that Saint Gertrude was one of their daughters; Begga was another, according to *De*

virtutibus S. Geretrudis 10, MGH SSRM 2: 469. The only detail not given in the Gertrude-material is that Begga married Ansegesil. See also Fouracre and Gerberding, *Late Merovingian France*, pp. 309–11.

35. "Sane quia huic masculini sexus proles defuerat, nepoti suo Pippino superstiti nomen cum principatu dereliquit": *Annales Mettenses priores* 688, pp. 2–3.

36. Fredegar, *Fourth Book* 85–86, pp. 71–72. See also Richard A. Gerberding, *The Rise of the Carolingians and the "Liber historiae Francorum"* (Oxford: Oxford University Press, 1987), p. 65.

37. For Grimoald's "coup," see Matthias Becher, "Der sogenannte Staatsstreich Grimoalds," in *Karl Martell in seiner Zeit*, ed. Jörg Jarnut, Ulrich Nonn, and Michael Richter, Beihefte der Francia 37 (Sigmaringen: Jan Thorbecke, 1994), pp. 119–47.

38. For the complicated history of Charlemagne's ancestral family, see Eduard Hlawitschka, "Die Vorfahren Karls des Grossen," in *Karl der Grosse: Lebenswerk und Nachleben*, ed. Wolfgang Braunfels, 5 vols. (Düsseldorf: L. Schwann, 1965–1968), 1 (1965): 51–82.

39. Karl-Ferdinand Werner, "Untersuchungen zur Frühzeit des französischen Fürstentums (9–10. Jahrhundert)," *Die Welt als Geschichte* 18 (1958): 256–89; 19 (1959), 146–93; 20 (1960), 87–119.

40. Fredegar, *Fourth Book* 34, p. 22.

41. *Origo gentis Longobardorum* 4, 6, MGH SSRL, pp. 4–5. The couple Duke Garipald of Bavaria and his wife Waldrada also appear in Gregory of Tours, *Libri historiarum* 4.9, ed. Bruno Krusch and Wilhelm Levison, MGH SSRM 1.1 (Hannover: Hahn, 1951), pp. 140–41.

42. Paul the Deacon, *Historia Langobardorum* 4.37, MGH SSRL, pp. 129–30. See also Walter Goffart, *The Narrators of Barbarian History (A.D. 550–800): Jordanes, Gregory of Tours, Bede, and Paul the Deacon* (Princeton: Princeton University Press, 1988), pp. 404–05.

43. According to Paul the Deacon, the two sons of King Aripert fell out after his death. One called on Grimoald to help him against his brother, promising his sister as a reward: *Historia Langobardorum* 4.51, MGH SSRL, p. 138. If Grimoald's mother was, like Aripert, the offspring of Gundoald, he would have been first cousin of the quarreling sons of Aripert, and it might have made sense to ask for his assistance. It is not clear whether Grimoald ever married the promised sister. (She would of course also have been his first cousin, but prohibitions on consanguinity were not nearly as clear in the seventh century as they would be in the ninth, and, of course, someone plotting fratricide would have considered consanguinity a trivial concern.)

44. *Vita Hludowici imperatoris* 21, MGH SS 2: 618.

45. Bouchard, *"Those of My Blood,"* pp. 74–97.

46. See especially the arguments of Janet L. Nelson, *Charles the Bald* (London: Longman, 1992), pp. 248–51.

47. Bouchard, *"Those of My Blood,"* pp. 175–80.

CHAPTER 9

POLITICAL HISTORY

Jason Glenn

A case study in the evolution of the use of medieval narratives for the study of political culture in the early Middle Ages.

While on a research trip in the summer of 1833, Georg Heinrich Pertz visited the Bamberg Staatsbibliothek.[1] There, he consulted a manuscript whose title page indicated it contained a history written by the thirteenth-century author, Richer of Senones.[2] It did not take long for the editor of the *Monumenta Germaniae Historica* to realize the text was mislabeled. "Having perceived the age of the work from the first," he said in the introduction to the edition he published shortly thereafter,

> in the first lines, hardly without the utmost joy, I soon recognized the tenth-century author, to this point unpublished, whose name had been cited by [Johannes] Trithemius [in the fifteenth century]. So that I might transcribe it, I easily obtained it from the illustrious man Jaeck, who learnedly presided over the library and favorably supported our studies in things German. And thus the book, coming out of the shadows in which it was concealed for more than eight hundred years, now bursts forth, and its author will take his place among the eminent historians of the Middle Ages.[3]

Pertz had before him a history of conflicts among west Frankish magnates in the tenth century, an autograph manuscript composed in the 990s by another Richer, a monk of Saint Remigius, just outside the walls of Reims. As his words suggest, Pertz seemed to sense that the history of the tenth century would never be the same. He was right. From the appearance of Pertz's edition in 1839 to the present, scholars of this period and region have had to grapple with the prospects and problems that Richer's narrative presents.

The story of the scholarly reception and use of Richer's text across nearly two centuries, the main focus of this essay, is instructive for illustrating the evolution of the modern study of medieval historiography and political history. In a concluding section, we also consider briefly how analysis of Richer's work and, implicitly, early medieval narrative histories in general offers fruitful points of entry into the political culture of the early Middle Ages and has significant implications for the ways we write its political history.

Pertz's edition of Richer's work attracted much attention from scholars throughout Europe and received a particularly warm welcome in France.[4] Within months of its publication, Benjamin Guérard of the Institut de France reviewed it enthusiastically in the *Journal des savants*.[5] As Guérard summarized Richer's work, he skimmed briskly over the first half, which, he explained, was largely based on the annals kept from 919 to 966 by the canon Flodoard at the cathedral of Reims.[6] The annals had long been published and had been recently translated into French, so they and the early history of the century were accessible to readers of the *Journal*.[7] Guérard went into greater detail as he summarized the second half of Richer's work, on the last third of the century; in these "new and original parts," according to the reviewer, Richer shed new light on an otherwise little known period of the French past.[8]

Like Guérard and other members of the Institut, members of the Société de l'Histoire de France recognized the importance of Richer's work for their national history. They commissioned from Joseph Guadet a French translation that appeared with a reedition of the Latin text in 1845.[9] Guadet shared Guérard's enthusiasm for Richer's work and concluded his introduction with a quotation from Flodoard's French translator, François Guizot, who had lamented the state of historical writing in the dark age of the tenth century, when contemporary historians were unable to pull together disparate events into a well-ordered narrative. Gaudet explained that Guizot's words were written before the discovery of Richer's manuscript and thus asked rhetorically whether the translator would write such words now that Richer's work had been discovered. He claimed Guizot would have made "an honorable exception" in the case of the monk.[10]

Richer had burst forth from the shadows of obscurity and was poised to fulfill Pertz's prophesy.[11] By the 1870s, his place among the great historians of the Middle Ages may have appeared secure, at least in France. Toward the end of the decade, Ernest Babelon sought "to popularize"

Richer's work in his own history of the west Frankish kingdom from the late ninth century to the end of the tenth, *Les derniers Carolingiens d'après Richer et d'autres sources originales*.[12] As the title suggests, Babelon's work is based in large part on Richer's text; indeed, at times it seems almost a paraphrase. Richer's history had become for this student at the École des Chartes, if not the authoritative text, at least the principal one for this obscure period in France's past. But such perceptions soon changed.

During the academic year 1887–1888, Arthur Giry, maître de conférences at the École Pratique des Hautes Études in Paris, gave a lecture on the reign of Charles the Bald (840–877).[13] His study of the sources and his critique of previous scholarship, he asserted, had led to new, exciting results, particularly for the chronology of Charles's reign. The findings, he suggested, also shed light on the subsequent period recounted by Richer. From the reign of Charles the Bald to the reign of Hugh Capet (987–996), according to Giry, "France was made" and became conscious of its "national existence." French scholars had not yet adequately studied this period of French history, he noted, and he expressed regret that the French did not have anything comparable to the German *Jahrbücher*.[14] Fearing that France's early history, too, would be written by the Germans, he suggested a collaborative project to research, inventory, classify, and critique the available historical sources for the era.

Giry's appeal did not fall on deaf ears. At the end of the year, a group of students approached him with a plan to put together a "Régeste carolingien" under his direction. When they gathered the following fall, Giry and his students set a two-fold agenda: they would compile critical editions of the royal acts from the period and compose a series of monographs similar to the *Jahrbücher*, which would establish a narrative history of the Carolingian royal dynasty from Charles the Bald to its demise at the end of the tenth century. The editors of the acts would follow a uniform format, and the authors of the monographs agreed to uniform principles: to present a critical summary of their sources with an extensive bibliography; to follow the most precise chronology possible; to include even seemingly insignificant facts; to document all statements with references to their sources in footnotes; to acknowledge all *lacunae* in the history and the poverty of sources where appropriate; to place any discussions that strayed from the narrative in appendices; and to end each volume with an alphabetical index of names and subject matter. Whereas most of these features may now be common practice in academic writing of history, they represent a stark contrast to much previous French scholarship on the period; Babelon's book, for instance, did not aspire to such standards. Thanks to the rigor of the editors and authors, the collected royal acts and monographs—like the work of those German scholars from whom they hoped to reclaim their national history—remain to this day essential to the study of late-ninth- and tenth-century west Francia and beyond.

The first monograph appeared in 1891. Perhaps its author, Ferdinand Lot, used Babelon's title as an attempt to right what he deemed an historiographical wrong. Like Babelon, Lot employed Richer's text extensively in his own *Les derniers Carolingiens*, but it was not his most central or important source.[15] In fact, he was decidedly ambivalent about its value. Like some contemporaries of Pertz and Guérard, Lot recognized that portions of Richer's work, particularly the material not found in Flodoard's annals, were historically unreliable; Richer's account only became "more sure" beginning with the 970s, when he was a contemporary or witness to events.[16] In contrast to his French predecessors, however, Lot was unwilling to look past these supposed shortcomings with unabashed excitement. In a dispassionate, analytical tone, he suggested that even for the period in which Richer's work became more reliable, there were "improbabilities," and overall, the style had an "unbearable archaism."[17] Lot's ambivalence was perhaps best expressed in his concluding remark that, "In spite of all of its deficiencies, [Richer's] chronicle is a precious source. Let us not accept blindly all its contents, but let us also refrain from systematically rejecting, as do certain historians, all the information it furnishes."[18]

Lot neither named these historians nor cited their work, but he did identify them. "Richer," he explained, "has a very poor reputation among German historians who accuse him of partiality, of chauvinism, and of French flightiness and vanity."[19] Lot was not exaggerating. With the possible exception of Pertz, nineteenth-century German scholars were generally far less forgiving of Richer's apparent inaccuracies than were their French counterparts. They questioned the reliability of his work, and their questions often betrayed a deeper hostility toward the French. Even Pertz, who praised Richer as a historian, was frustrated at times by the "errors" he found in the text.[20] He noted, for instance, that Richer sometimes credited the Franks with victory when they had been vanquished, and he suggested that Richer sought to make the German kingdom appear under the dominion of the French king, Charles the Straightforward (893–929).[21] These misrepresentations Pertz attributed to French patriotism: "We have learned from such things that Richer is zealous for his fatherland (*patriae*) beyond what is to be endured, and [he is] given to a vainglory which, found still in the emissaries of Napoleon, arouses popular indignation."[22] The bite of this comparison to the Bonapartists, who whipped up French national sentiment after Napoleon's death, would have been clear to both French and German scholars of Pertz's day. This was at a time of intense nationalist fervor in both countries, only decades removed from Napoleon's military expansion through Europe and his restructuring of the German states.

Throughout the century, German scholars generally accepted and even elaborated Pertz's explanation for Richer's supposed errors and, like Pertz, viewed him as a French nationalist.[23] In 1863, Karl Wittich contended that the later Carolingians could not get over their loss of Lotharingia to their German rivals, the Ottonians, to the east—kings from each dynasty had laid claim to it throughout the tenth century.[24] From Wittich's perspective, writing less than a decade before Lotharingia came under German control (after the Franco-Prussian War), that territory had belonged to the Ottonians; the Carolingians, he maintained, continually sought to take it back, and Richer more than others had championed their cause. Not only did Richer grant Charles the Straightforward dominion over Lotharingia, as Pertz suggested; according to Wittich he invested Charles's grandchildren with authority over the region. Richer shared the Carolingians' arrogance and expressed "a decided nationalism." "Like other French clerics of his day," Wittich stated, "he was through and through French.... Each folio shows his carelessness, his vanity, as well as a strange addiction...to decorating in his own way the content of his dry, often fragmentary or dark sources." Wittich concluded by suggesting that Richer takes an "absurd pleasure in the external form" often imitated from the ancients. In short, Richer's work was little more than an historical novel (Geschichtsroman).[25]

The characterization of Richer's text by Wittich, Pertz, and other nineteenth-century German scholars did not go over well in France. In the early 1840s, one of Guérard's colleagues at the Institut de France explained away Richer's supposed errors as a result of his poor sources.[26] To the later and more hostile German attacks on Richer's work, Gabriel Monod, one of Lot's masters at the École Pratique des Hautes Études, presented an impassioned, colorful defense. Rather than try to refute German allegations, Monod accepted, even revelled, in the nationalistic terms of the debate, proudly noting in 1885 that Richer's exaggeration of Carolingian power and disdain for the Germans led him to commit errors and falsehoods. "This disdain, which makes us smile," Monod elaborated is the first expression of an incipient national sentiment. Although Richer, faithful to the memory of Caesar, speaks only of the Gauls, he is the first French historian [Monod's emphasis]. So he is by the vivacity of his national sentiment, as also by his concern for literary form, style, and composition."[27] Here and elsewhere in his article, Monod relished in Richer's "hostility towards Germany"[28] and saw in Richer's supposed national sentiment an expression of his enmity toward the German kings who had appropriated the legacy of the Carolingian empire for themselves. In Monod's view, Richer's work and hostility represented an attempt to claim back some of that legacy, if not territory, for France. Monod thus appears to project his own nationalist sentiments onto Richer, and he interpreted them as we might interpret his own.

By the last decade of the nineteenth century, Monod, Wittich, Pertz, and their colleagues in France and Germany had placed Richer in the crossfire of a debate fuelled by their sense of nation and their views of their own national histories. Ferdinand Lot attempted, to a certain extent, to pull him out. We saw above that Lot, like Monod, reacted against the German historians who rejected "all of the information [Richer's work] furnishes." Rather than defend Richer on the nationalistic terms established by the Germans and accepted by his own master, however, Lot proposed an explanation for the text's supposed errors that depoliticized it: Richer's bias for the Carolingians with respect to the Ottonians had been overstated, and in any case he did not express particularly strong Carolingian sentiments. Commenting on the unreliability of even the more reliable portion of Richer's history—an assessment he would have likely applied to the work as a whole—Lot said the inaccuracies were due less to political bias than a desire to imitate the great Roman historians and use their discourses.[29]

The suggestion that it was the monk's shortcomings as a literary stylist, not his political inclinations or national sentiment, that colored the passages in which previous scholars had seen evidence of French nationalism had a profound impact on the work's subsequent use inside and outside France; but much of that influence was indirect. Authors of the subsequent monographs produced at the École Pratique des Hautes Études generally accepted Lot's assessment.[30] In the 1930s, Robert Latouche, who published a new French translation and revised edition of the text that remained standard throughout the twentieth century,[31] took Lot's analysis to the extreme. In an article written as he prepared his edition and translation, he labeled Richer an "imitator of Sallust." "We must renounce the position which represents Richer as blinded by political passion," he elaborated, "to do so renders, at once, too much insult and too much honor to a monk who appears to have submitted only to influences of a literary nature."[32] In the introduction to his edition, Latouche remarked that "events only interest him [Richer] in so far as they furnish him with the material for a narrative, dissertation, or speech."[33] Latouche thus wound up, ironically, with more or less the same conclusion as had Wittich, that is, that Richer's text is, in essence, a work of historical fiction.

Richer's work had not changed in the century between the editions of Pertz and Latouche, but its perceived utility had. The optimism that

welcomed its discovery as a sort of missing link for the transition from
Carolingian to Capetian rule had given way to a resignation that, with
the possible exception of certain passages in which Richer describes
events from his own lifetime, it was unreliable for the reconstruction of a
political narrative. With good reason. Richer did not aspire to the scientific standards of his nineteenth-century audience. Indeed, comments he
wrote into the lower margin of the first page of his manuscript—a short
qualification of comments made in his prologue, perhaps in response to a
critique leveled by contemporary readers—suggest he did not conceive of
his work as a transparent report of the information that he found in
Flodoard's annals, witnessed, or heard reported:[34]

> If I am charged with ignorance of the unknown past, I do not deny that I
> have taken some things from a certain *libellum* of Flodoard, a priest of
> Reims; but this history demonstrates most clearly that I have not set down
> those same words, indeed, but used some in place of others in a style
> (*schema orationis*) quite distinct. I think that I have done well enough by the
> reader if I have arranged all things credibly, clearly, and briefly.[35]

These comments speak to a self-consciousness that permeates Richer's
history about his role as author. He was aware that his words and *schema
orationis* shaped the content of his narrative. For him, the annals were the
raw material from which he forged it, and he seems to have recognized
and expected his audience to accept that the narrative would be, at some
level, his own.

While Richer may have been more self-aware in this regard than were
his nineteenth- and early-twentieth-century counterparts, as in their case
his assumptions, agendas, and biases perhaps led him to read sources in
particular ways as he tried to make sense of the events they described.
This is not to suggest that Richer—or the modern scholars who have
struggled with his text—necessarily sought to subjugate any historical
reality to particular ideological agenda; rather, his present and historical
concerns informed his relationship to his own sources as both present and
historical concerns have done and continue to do for his modern counterparts.

Beginning in the second half of the twentieth century, scholars more
interested in political ideology than chronology *per se* began to find a use
for the work of Richer. Some acknowledged an apparent contradiction in
his attitudes toward the two west Frankish royal dynasties of the tenth
century, Carolingian and Capetian (a.k.a. Robertian). Indeed, scholars
from the nineteenth through the mid-twentieth century had frequently
asserted that Richer favored the Carolingians,[36] a view based in large part

on the convergence of two historiographical traditions. On the one hand, the supposition that Richer was a French nationalist who favored Carolingian over Ottonian claims to Lotharingia, as we saw with Wittich and Monod, led to interpretations of his favor as an expression of pro-Carolingian sympathies. On the other hand, beginning with Pertz, scholars have observed that Richer's father served loyally two Carolingian kings; they are therefore inclined to see similar loyalties in Richer.[37] There are also instances in which Richer seems to sympathize with the Carolingians in conflicts between members of the two dynasties.[38] Taken together, these observations have led many scholars to see Richer as a Carolingian supporter. Dissenters, most clearly Lot, observed that Richer was generally receptive to the accession of King Hugh Capet in 987 and that he was a disciple of Archbishops Adalbero (969–989) and Gerbert (991–998) who, respectively, orchestrated Hugh's accession and sided with him in the subsequent civil war against a Carolingian claimant. In this view, Richer is supposed to have been sympathetic to the Capetians and therefore to have shared the views not of his father, but of his masters.[39]

Rather than take sides in such a historiographical debate, a number of scholars working on kingship and national consciousness during the past five decades have tried to make sense of the apparent conflict in Richer's sympathies. In the 1950s, for instance, Gian Andri Bezzola sought to explain why a supposed devotee of the Carolingians would appear receptive to the accession of a man who effectively ended their rule. Richer, he noted, portrayed some members of each dynasty in a favorable light and represented others in less sympathetic terms. He concluded that Richer supported neither the Carolingians nor the Capetians *per se*, but that the depiction of individual kings varied according to their personalities and, above all, the context for their actions. His apparently contradictory partisanship, Bezzola suggested, derived from his notion of legitimate rulership, based principally but not exclusively on dynastic tradition, a notion that led him to favorable depictions of the kings—Capetian or Carolingian—who had legitimacy on their side.[40] Two decades later, Joachim Ehlers suggested that during the tenth century a national consciousness began to grow within the west Frankish kingdom. He saw the first signs of this consciousness in the declining importance of the Carolingian tradition as it related to kingship and argued that the monarchy shed its affiliation with the Carolingian or any other dynasty and came to be identified instead, with the realm itself. The first parts of Richer's history, Ehlers argued, displayed a Carolingian tradition still in place, but in the last third of the century, particularly in his unfavorable depiction of the last Carolingian king, Louis V (d. 987) and apparent support of Hugh Capet, Richer dissociated the monarchy from the dynasty.[41]

Although perhaps unintended, Ehler's analysis implicitly presented an alternative explanation for the coexistence of Richer's supposedly conflicting sympathies: Richer merely told it like it was. The changes in kingship catalyzed by the incipient national consciousness manifested themselves, in Richer's work, as apparent support for one or the other dynasty.

Whereas Bezzola sought to link the difficulty to Richer's internal struggle with the elements of legitimate rulership, Ehlers's analysis linked it to a cultural transformation documented somewhat transparently by Richer. Both scholars acknowledged the previous concerns about the verisimilitude of Richer's work, but they sought to move beyond them. They are not alone. Over the past fifty years Richer's work has increasingly been viewed as a testament to the ideals, values, and mentalité of his day. In the past few decades, a number of historiographical monographs have treated his work as a text whose author's influences, intentions, and agendas are not obstacles but worthy objects for study in their own right and for insight into the political and intellectual culture of the west Frankish lands in the tenth century.[42]

Such a shift in the ways Richer's work has been viewed and used—a shift from source to text[43]—reflects a broader development within historical studies, as the field of medieval historiography has grown from its roots in the *Quellenkritik* of the nineteenth and early twentieth centuries and in the *Ideengeschichte* of the mid-twentieth century.[44] Today, scholars inspired by the so-called linguistic turn seek to understand the contexts in which, and audiences for which, medieval authors wrote, as well as the personal, pragmatic, and literary concerns they brought to their work. In innovative and creative studies focused on single authors, œuvres, and groups of authors or writings, historians now consider what can be learned about not merely the events described but aspects of the worlds in which the texts were produced. The study of the manuscripts in which the texts were written, copied, and transmitted; of the ways writers used their sources; and of the circumstances in which the texts were created and read (or heard) have deepened our understanding of what it meant to write history in the early Middle Ages. It has also sensitized us to the meanings and uses of the past for those who lived in that era.

This recent work has significant implications for, among other things, our conception of early medieval politics and the workings of power, as it offers opportunities to confront an epistemological conundrum fundamental to historical inquiry in general, one that underlies recent debates concerning our approaches to the study of early medieval political culture:[45] can our source material give us access to the world it appears to describe, or is it merely textual representation or even mediation without clear resonance in a historical reality of that world? There have been serious theoretical explorations of this problem.[46] Much recent work is based on the premise, often implicit, that whatever the precise relationship of texts to the realities they may appear to present, the texts' creation, like the linguistic and intellectual conventions they betray, are themselves a reality; their production tells us something about the world in and for which they were written.[47] In particular, whether we treat our narrative sources as windows onto social or political realities or as constructs divorced from the realities they profess—or find some reasoned position between these two extremes—we can often use their narrative constructions to glimpse what it meant to experience and engage in contemporary political culture. The acknowledgment of authorial subjectivity in our sources may render them problematic for use in the ways that our nineteenth-century predecessors and even some recent historians might like. But it frees us to see in texts what mattered to their authors and how it mattered. We have therefore the opportunity to imagine a world in which they and their concerns could exist and thus to develop a more textured understanding of that world.

Richer's work provides opportunities for such an exploration. The above-quoted comments etched into the lower margin of his prologue remind us that Richer was self-conscious about the ways he worked with his sources. Since we have access to his principal source, the annals of Flodoard, we can reflect on how he used this material, that is, what aspects he chose to ignore, what he decided to include, and how he shaped it into a narrative of his own "in a style quite distinct." Examination of their works suggests, for example, that what distinguished Richer's text from his source was not merely the *schema orationis*; he consciously sought, with that *schema*, to transform the memory of events Flodoard had first recorded. In particular, it seems, he wanted to mute the political sympathies Flodoard had expressed for Robertian kings and their supporters in their conflicts with the Carolingian ruler Charles the Straightforward. Both Charles and his Robertian opponents competed for the throne from the late ninth century into the 920s when Flodoard began to keep the annals—the conflict may have led Flodoard to write in the first place. In his account of the conflict between Charles and Robert I for the throne in 922/923, Flodoard chose to identify Robert as "king" and stopped using the title for Charles from the point of Robert's coronation in opposition to him. Seven decades later, Richer was more sympathetic to the Carolingian's plight and, at least in the revisions he made to his autograph manuscript, presents Charles's greatest Robertian adversary as a "tyrant" who coveted the throne.[48]

Such a contrast in sympathies might seem insignificant were it not for the circumstances surrounding the composition of Richer's manuscript and his dedication of it to Archbishop Gerbert. Richer wrote and rewrote his history during the 990s, in the wake of the election of another Robertian, Hugh Capet, and his son Robert. Their elevation to the throne, which in retrospect marked the end of Carolingian rule, sparked a serious challenge from a Carolingian claimant, Charles of Lotharingia. Leaving aside the details of the conflict that ensued, it should be noted that Reims stood at the center of power plays by the leading secular and ecclesiastical figures in the kingdom for much of the tenth century, most intensely from the mid-980s through the 990s. King Hugh elevated Gerbert to the archiepiscopal see after he captured the previous archbishop, Arnulf (989–991, 999–1022), a Carolingian bastard who had betrayed the king and led the resistance to the Capetian. Because Richer dedicated his history to Gerbert, praised his intellectual ability and accomplishments, and does not present Arnulf or Charles in the most favorable light, it has often been supposed that Richer shared Gerbert's political orientation. And why not? To support the Capetians during the conflict, all the more so once Hugh and his son Robert had seemingly secured their hold on the throne in the early 990s, would appear, at least in hindsight, the path of least resistance. But this supposition perhaps assumes too much homogeneity within the community of Reims, that people necessarily shared the allegiances of the community leaders, and that the Capetians had secured their position and support in Reims. [49]

The very existence of Richer's work asks us to be cautious about these assumptions. Although, as Bezzola and Ehlers noted, he does not withhold critique of individual Carolingians or praise of Robertians/ Capetians, Richer's use of sources, his literary allusions, and the evolution of his manuscript as the political winds shifted around him reveal a man with an enduring commitment to the Carolingian dynasty past and present, an affinity or allegiance expressed carefully—even veiled, at times—and yet consistently in his narrative. Moreover, his work and other texts provide evidence of the shifting alliances and allegiances among the elite and permit us to see, albeit less clearly, how less prominent members of the religious and intellectual community had a stake in the power plays of the magnates. They, too, took and switched sides and had opportunities to reap benefits and suffer consequences for their choices.

Richer wrote within and for such a community. He was no mere observer of the world around him. And it is too simplistic to suppose that he served as mouthpiece for the man to whom he dedicated his work, expressed some shared set of family or factional ideals, or represented the views of other people within his community or of a larger Frankish nation. He was an individual within a dynamic community. Although his text is not overtly polemical or of unqualified advocacy—he expresses his affinities subtly—we can imagine that his version of the "unknown past" perhaps rubbed some members of the community the wrong way, perhaps those who had internalized Flodoard's presentation of the earlier conflicts between Carolingian and Robertian claimants or those who supported the elevation of Hugh Capet and Robert in Richer's day. His marginal addendum to the prologue suggests as much, that is, that his work elicited some critique, to which he responded with a defense of his knowledge of the past, a citation of his main source, and an explanation that he chose to write in his own words and *schema orationis*. But this passage tells us more. Richer wrote with the assumption that his history would be read and/or heard by other members of his community, people with a stake in the events he described. To write in this fashion was to enter the political arena.

However inaccurate the information Richer presents, students of medieval political culture are fortunate to have his work. But to use it requires us to adapt some what our approach to the study of political history and the ways we use our narrative sources. Richer's world consisted not merely of secular and ecclesiastical magnates or their henchmen, but also of the people who experienced and witnessed their power at all levels of the society. It is often difficult to know how the leading figures within this world thought or even what they did and why, to say nothing of the problems we confront if we wish to know how nonelites experienced and understood the power dynamics in which they participated, if only passively at times. Yet we can get closer to those who wrote the narratives that described and, in some ways, shaped those dynamics. In other words, if we understand the political community to include the authors of our narrative sources as active participants, their work may permit us to glimpse at least some dynamics within that community, dynamics difficult to detect when we imagine our texts either as literary creations or treat them principally as sources for information about events and key figures. Just as the nineteenth-century scholars who struggled to make sense of—and expressed disappointment at—the "errors" they saw in Richer's work participated, through their own work, in the larger politics of Franco-German relations of their day, Richer, as an author, engaged and thereby participated in the local and larger politics of tenth-century Francia. The very act of writing as he did and when he did, represents a political act in and for a world of political actors. To understand the political meaning and implications of the Capetian accession; the century of competition among Robertians, Carolingians, and other magnates that led to it; or the civil war it ignited—to write the political history of early medieval France or the early Middle Ages—we must broaden our enquiry. We must let our focus wander, at least periodically, from those who have traditionally held our attention to those who made history political.

Notes

In addition to the editors of this volume, I wish to thank Courtney Booker, Scott Bruce, Andrew Fogleman, Sharon Marcus, Rosamond McKitterick, William North, Ramzi Rouighi, and Jay Rubenstein for comments on earlier drafts of this essay.

1. Georg Heinrich Pertz, "Reise nach Franken und Baiern vom 24. Juli bis 29. August 1833," *Archiv* 7 (1839): 105–08.

2. MS Bamberg, Hist. 5.

3. "Primo intuitu vetustate operis perspecta, mox primis etiam lineis haud sine maximo gaudio scriptorem saeculi decimi hucusque ineditum, et cuius tantum nomen a Trithemio proditum fuisset, agnovi, quem ut describerem a V. Cl. Iaeck, qui magno litterarum commodo bibliothecae ditissimae praeest et summo in rem Germanicam favore studiis nostris suffragatur, facillime impetravi. Prodit igitur iam liber, tenebris quibus per octingentos amplius annos tegebatur evolutus, atque inter historicorum medii aevi praecipuos locum suum ipse sibi vindicaturus": *Richeri historiarum libri IIII*, MGH SS 3, ed. Georg Heinrich Pertz (Hannover: Hahn, 1839), p. 566 [561–657].

4. By the middle of the 1850s, two French translations, including re-editions of Pertz's edition, a German translation, and a doctoral dissertation from Oslo had appeared: Richer, *Histoire de son Temps*, trans. Joseph Guadet, 2 vols. (Paris: J. Renouard, 1845–1846); *Richeri historiarum quatuor libri*, ed. and trans. Auguste Maurice Poinsignon (Reims: Académie impériale, 1855); *Richers vier Bücher Geschichte*, trans. Karl von der Osten-Sacken, intro. Wilhelm Wattenbach, Die Geschichtschreiber der deutschen Vorzeit 37 (Berlin: Besser, 1854); Eduard Reimann, "De Richeri vita et scriptis," unpublished dissertation (Oslo, 1845).

5. Benjamin Guérard, review of *Richeri historiarum*, ed. Pertz, *Journal des savants* (1840): 470–89, 535–56.

6. Guérard, review, 482–89.

7. "La Chronique de Flodoard," trans. François Guizot, in idem., *Collection des mémoires relatifs à l'histoire de France depuis la fondation de la monarchie française jusqu'au 13e siècle*, 31 vols. in 17 (Paris: J.L. Brière, 1823–1835), 6 (1824): 67–162. The Latin *Annales* of Flodoard was edited by D. Bouquet in *Recueil des historiens des Gaules et de la France* 8 (Paris: Palmé, 1752) pp. 176–215. Also see *Les Annales de Flodoard*, ed. P. Lauer, Collection de textes pour servir à l'enseignement de l'histoire 39 (Paris: Picard, 1906), pp. xxix–xxxii, with earlier editions; and *Flodoardi annales*, MGH SS 3: 363.

8. Guérard, review, 553.

9. For the development of the project, see *Histoire de son Temps*, 1: xvii–xviii. As Guadet acknowledges (1: ix–x), the edition is, except for a few minor changes, that of Pertz.

10. Guadet claims to quote from Guizot, "Notice sur Flodoard": *Histoire de son Temps*, 1: cx–cxi. He gives no complete bibliographic reference. The statement is not found in Guizot, "Chronique."

11. *Richeri historiarum*, ed. Pertz, p. 566, quoted above at n3.

12. Paris: La Société Bibliographique, 1878.

13. See Giry's preface to Ferdinand Lot, *Les derniers Carolingiens: Lothaire, Louis V, Charles de Lorraine, 954–991* (Paris: Honoré Champion, 1891), pp. ix–xii.

14. *Jahrbücher der Deutschen Geschichte*, 36 vols. (Leipzig: Dunker and Humblot, 1863–1909).

15. Lot, *Derniers*, pp. xvi, xviii, calls Flodoard's *Annales* the most important source for the early years of Lothar's reign, and the letters of Gerbert the most important overall.

16. Lot, *Derniers*, pp. xvii–xviii. As for the verisimilitude of Richer's work, I note only the early scholarly analysis here; subsequent scholars have generally acknowledged the unreliability of at least the early portions and cited these studies: *Richeri historiarum*, ed. Pertz, pp. 563–65; Guérard, review, 483; Roger Wilmans, *Jahrbücher des Deutschen Reichs unter der Herrschaft König und Kaiser Otto's III, 983–1002* (Berlin: Dunker and Humbot, 1840), pp. 39–63, 175–86; *Histoire de son Temps*, 1: cii–cx; Wattenbach, *Richers vier Bücher*, pp. xiii–xiv.

17. Compare Lot, *Derniers*, pp. xvii–xviii to: Guérard, review, 470–89, 535–56 ; *Histoire de son Temps* 1: v–cxi; Babelon, *Derniers*, pp. v–xi; Gabriel Monod, "Études sur Hugues Capet," *Revue historique* 28 (1885): 347–54.

18. Lot, *Derniers*, p. xviii.

19. Lot, *Derniers*, p. xvii. Lot here echoes Monod, who singles out Roger Wilmans as particularly accusatory: "Études sur Hugues Capet," 348.

20. *Richeri historiarum*, ed. Pertz, pp. 563–65.

21. *Richeri historiarum*, ed. Pertz, pp. 563–64. See Richer, *Historiae*, MGH SS 38, ed. Hartmut Hoffmann (Hannover: Hahn, 2000), fol. pp. 83–85, 58–63. Pertz discusses a passage to which Richer made changes in his manuscript. For analysis of these changes and further references, see Jason Glenn, *Politics and History in the Tenth Century: The Work and World of Richer of Reims* (Cambridge, UK: Cambridge University Press, 2004), pp. 183–89.

22. *Richeri historiarum*, ed. Pertz, p. 564.

23. Gian Andri Bezzola, *Das ottonische Kaisertum in der französischen Geschichtsschreibung des 10. und beginnenden 11. Jahrhunderts* (Graz: H. Böhlaus, 1956), p. 109.

24. Wittich, "Richer über die Herzoge Gislebert von Lothringen und Heinrich von Sachsen," *Forschung zur Deutschen Geschichte* 3 (1863):

107–08 [107–41]; cf. Hartmut Hoffmann, "Die Historien Richers von Saint–Remi," *Deutsches Archiv* 54 (1998): 470–74 [445–532].

25. Wittich, "Richer über die Herzoge," 107–08.

26. *Histoire de son Temps*, 1: ciii–cvii, registers and critiques this defense.

27. Monod, "Études sur Hugues Capet," 253–54.

28. Monod, "Études sur Hugues Capet," 248.

29. Lot, *Derniers*, pp. xvii–xviii. Lot was not the first scholar to note Richer's stylistic reliance on antique authors; cf. *Richeri historiarum*, ed. Pertz, p. 565. The use of this idea as an explanation for Richer's seeming inaccuracies represents a change of emphasis.

30. For example, Auguste Eckel, *Charles le Simple* (Paris: Honoré Champion, 1891), p. ix.

31. *Histoire de France*, ed. and trans. Robert Latouche, 2 vols, Classiques de l'histoire de France au Moyen Age 12, 17 (Paris: Belles Lettres, 1930, 1937). The next and most recent edition of Hoffmann (see above, n21) appeared in 2000.

32. Robert Latouche, "Un imitateur de Salluste au Xe siècle: l'historien Richer," *Annales de l'Université de Grenoble, section lettres droit*, n.s. 6 (1929): 300 [289–306]. For further discussion of and references regarding Richer's use of Sallust, see Glenn, *Politics and History*, pp. 118–25.

33. "Richer a été beaucoup moins mêlé qu'on ne l'a cru à la vie politique de son temps: très livresque, les événements ne l'intéressent que dans la mesure où ils lui fournissent la matière d'une narration, d'une dissertation, d'un discours": *Histoire*, ed. and trans. Latouche, 1xi.

34. For Richer's sense of the genre of his work, see Hoffmann, "Die Historien Richers," 456–65; for further discussion of the prologue, see Glenn, *Politics and History*, pp. 176–79, 212–14.

35. "Sed si ignotæ antiquitatis ignorantiæ arguar, ex quodam Flodoardi presbyteri Remensis libello, me aliqua quidem sumpsisse non abnuo, at non verba quidem eadem, sed alia pro aliis longe diversissimo orationis scemate disposuisse res ipsa evidentissime demonstrat. Satisque lectori fieri arbitror, si probabiliter atque dilucide breviterque omnia digesserim": Richer, *Historiae*, ed. Hoffmann, pp. 35–36. This text incorporates revisions Richer made to the marginal note; see the critical apparatus and fol. 1r at the end of this facsimile edition.

36. Bezzola, *Ottonische Kaisertum*, p. 114 n32.

37. On Richers father, Richer, *Historiae*, ed. Hoffmann, pp. 162–64 and 174–75. For Pertz's comments, *Richeri historiarum*, ed. Pertz, pp. 561–62.

38. In *Histoire de son Temps*, 1: cv–cvi, Guadet reluctantly acknowledges one such case and expresses his disappointment in Richer for it.

39. See, for example, Lot, *Derniers*, p. xvii, Monod, "Études sur Hugues Capet," 253; Bezzola, *Ottonische Kaisertum*, p. 114.

40. Bezzola, *Ottonische Kaisertum*, pp. 114–23.

41. Joachim Ehlers, "Karolingische Tradition und frühes Nationalbewußtsein in Frankreich," *Francia* 4 (1976): 218–23 [213–35].

42. In addition to Glenn, *Politics and History*, and Hoffmann, "Die Historien Richers," see B. Schneidmüller, "Widukind von Corvey, Richer von Reims und der Wandel politischen Bewußteins im 10. Jahrhundert," in *Beiträge zur mittelalterlichen Reichs- und Nationsbildung in Deutschland und Frankreich*, ed. Carlrichard Brühl and Bernd Schneidmüller (Munich: Oldenbourg, 1997), pp. 83–102; Michel Sot, "Richer de Reims a-t-il écrit une *Histoire de France?*" in *Histoires de France, historiens de la France : Actes du colloque international, Reims, 14 et 15 mai 1993*, ed. Yves-Marie Bercé and Philippe Contamine (Paris: Honoré Champion, 1994), pp. 47–58; Hans-Henning Kortüm, *Richer von Saint-Remi: Studien zu einem Geschichtsschreiber des 10. Jahrhunderts* (Stuttgart: Steiner Verlag Wiesbaden, 1985); Wolfgang Giese, *"Genus" und "Virtus": Studien zu den Geschichtswerk des Richer von Saint-Remi* (Augsburg: W. Blasaditsch, 1969).

43. On this shift, Robert Stein, "Literary Criticism and the Evidence for History," in *Writing Medieval History*, ed. Nancy Partner (London: Hodder Arnold, 2005), pp. 67–87.

44. Glenn, *Politics and History*, pp. 9–16.

45. Two debates, in particular, seem to hinge on this problem: (1) about the existence or degree of a "feudal revolution" ca. 1000; (2) about the utility of the study of ritual for understanding early medieval political culture. See Glenn, *Politics and History*, pp. 10–12.

46. Gabrielle Spiegel, "Towards a Theory of the Middle Ground: Historical Writing in the Age of Postmodernism," in *Historia a Debate: actas del Congreso Internacional "A Historia a Debate" celebrado el 7–11 de Julio de 1993 en Santiago de Compostela*, ed. Carlos Barros, 3 vols. (Santiago de Compostela: Historia a Debate, 1995), 1: 169–76, repr. in idem., *The Past as Text: The Theory and Practice of Medieval Historiography* (Baltimore: Johns Hopkins Press, 1997), pp. 44–56; Gabriel Piterberg, *An Ottoman Tragedy: History and Historiography at Play* (Berkeley: University of California Press, 2003), pp. 50–68; Stein, "Literary Criticism."

47. David Warner, "Ritual and Memory in the Ottonian *Reich*: The Ceremony of *Adventus*," *Speculum* 76 (2001): 256–57 [255–83]. Mary Rouse and Richard Rouse, *Authentic Witnesses: Approaches to Medieval Texts and Manuscripts* (Indiana: Notre Dame University Press, 1991), pp. 1–4; Philippe Buc, *Dangers of Ritual: Between Early Medieval Texts and Social Scientific Theory* (Princeton: Princeton University Press, 2001), pp. 259–60; and recent work cited in Glenn, *Politics and History*, pp. 11 n44, 13 n50, 14 n51.

48. See Glenn, *Politics and History*, pp. 176–214.

49. See Glenn, *Politics and History*, pp. 89–167.

PART III

PERIODIZATION: FROM THE
"FALL OF ROME" AND PIRENNE
TO KABBALAH

CHAPTER 10

DRAWING A LINE UNDER ANTIQUITY: ARCHAEOLOGICAL AND HISTORICAL CATEGORIES OF EVIDENCE IN THE TRANSITION FROM THE ANCIENT WORLD TO THE MIDDLE AGES

Michael Kulikowski

Examination of conflicting textual and archaeological paradigms for the transition from antique to medieval in Spain, arguing that historians should respect the independent validity of both types of evidence.

All periodization is a matter of drawing lines in the past; artificial but necessary if we are to parcel out history into manageable objects of study. Even though we know that our periodizations are artificial heuristic devices rather than substantive barriers between sections of past time, it is easy for them to become normative, whether in the courses we teach, the conferences we go to, or the books we read. Given this tendency, it is worth making the most of our periodizations and giving them some logical substance. The attempt to draw a line between Antiquity and the Middle Ages is ultimately a legacy of Renaissance humanists who believed themselves to be reviving the one while rejecting the other. Why should we perpetuate their distinction when we no longer accept the value judgment behind it? One answer might be that the categories ancient and medieval articulate a meaningful difference. After all, that the second and eighth centuries bore little resemblance to one another is not open to serious dispute. What is debatable, by contrast, is the way in which the divergences between those centuries arose. That problem is immeasurably complicated by the fact of the Roman Empire and the disappearance of its western portions. Try as we might, it has proved difficult to avoid eliding what is essentially a political problem—why the western empire ceased to function and then disappeared during the 400s—with the more encompassing problem of how, why, and when the deep structures of Antiquity, however we define them, became something new.

In practice, most attempts to deal with one of these problems become tangled up with trying to answer the other. One need not reach back to Gibbon, Lot, or Rostovtzeff to see this.[1] The editors of the European Science Foundation's Transformation of the Roman World series assume that the disappearance of imperial government, or its replacement by something else, is the same question as why ancient society came to an end.[2] Indeed, if we pick up Alexander Demandt's exhaustive catalog of explanations for the "Fall of Rome," we find that most of them are not really about Rome's fall at all, but about all sorts of political, social, economic, or institutional changes that historians have linked to the political fact of the western Roman empire's disappearance.[3] This sort of conceptual slippage is still everywhere in evidence: Bryan Ward-Perkins's recent Fall of Rome maintains that the political disappearance of the empire in the West corresponds to a collapse of civilization itself, and J.H.W.G. Liebeschuetz's Decline and Fall of the Roman City consistently equates the transformation of classical civic norms with political collapse.[4]

Now, it is worth stressing that there is nothing intrinsically wrong with using a political event like the disappearance of the western empire as a tool of periodization. The tendency to subdivide the human past according to political events is deeply rooted in Indo-European culture, traceable at least as far back as the Hittite king-lists that mark the passage of time by the passing of royalty. Many alternative chronologies and tools of periodization have been proposed over the past century, but most are at heart reactions against our long tradition of histoire événementielle, and thus deeply informed by it.[5] Moreover, periodizing the past by reference to political events can work quite well. It has a real advantage over changes to social habits or to institutions, which can rarely be dated with even rough precision: was the Ostrogothic praetorian prefecture still Roman? And if so, does that mean that the Ostrogothic kingdom was still Roman, that Rome had not fallen? Drawing lines in the past by reference to big political events is artificial, but it avoids just such imponderable questions and can therefore function as a useful symbolic shorthand.

This sort of periodization, though, becomes deeply unhelpful when used as a normative framework to which other sorts of historical change are pegged, for obvious reasons: change in social and institutional life is almost always slower—and less precisely dateable—than is the course of political events, so linking the one too rigidly to the other will inevitably distort some part of the evidence. That problem may be obvious, but it can be compounded by a rather less obvious corollary: the subordination of evidence from other disciplines to a periodization drawn from political history. This is all too frequently the fate of archaeological evidence—as it is of epigraphy, paleography, diplomatic, and the many other disciplines traditionally regarded as auxiliary sciences. Late ancient and early medieval historians regularly turn to the archaeological record for the simple reason that there is not enough textual evidence to answer even basic historical questions. But unless done with requisite care, the appeal to the other disciplines can distort more than it clarifies. In particular, historians have to recognize the autonomy of other disciplines on which they draw, so that they neither expect nor demand answers those disciplines are incapable of answering.

Archaeology and the Historian

However much historians use archaeological evidence and however much archaeologists use historical sources to make sense of their finds, history and archaeology are autonomous disciplines. This is largely a function of the methodologies required by literary and material sources respectively. In simple terms, the historian is concerned with the succession of moments in time, the archaeologist with residual patterns of material change, almost always observable only over long periods.[6] The historian, whether interested in the course of events, the gradual evolution of one person's thoughts, or the development of institutions, typically deals in evidence that is the product of one moment in time and can be studied as such. This means that he or she—regardless of research interests and at whatever distance from a purely narrative approach—is inseparably wedded to the precise chronology of the past. The historian asks questions in terms of events, moments in time. The archaeologist, by contrast, cannot do this, and thus the discipline must frame its questions in a different way. The material evidence of the past does not generally permit us to see moments, and this is true even of evidence that is the product of a precise, discernible point in time. Even where we can date the creation of a piece of material evidence—say, a coin-type minted in only one place for a few days—we cannot necessarily date its deposition. Even where we can date the moment of deposition, we can rarely describe the circumstances in which it took place. Archaeological facts can almost never have a place in the sequence of precise chronological moments with which the historian deals as a matter of course. Instead, what archaeology can document is material change over time. Archaeological evidence allows us to infer that, over time, the condition of a site, or human behavior at that site, changed from one thing to another. But despite that documentation of change, our understanding of it is static. We know that something happened, leaving us its residual traces, but not how it happened moment by moment, proximate cause by proximate cause. The dynamism, the forward momentum, at the core of the historical approach is necessarily absent from the archaeological approach. A static picture of change may seem a paradox, but that is precisely what archaeology reveals to us.

It is, furthermore, a static picture of change that we can almost never correlate to the sequence of events—the moments of change in time— indicated in our narrative and documentary evidence. Consider, for instance, destruction layers. Most archaeological sites display evidence of destruction at some point in their development. There is always a temptation to link such signs to one or another cataclysmic event recorded in our historical evidence. Yet to put the material evidence of destruction in realistic perspective, one need only imagine any modern city. Several buildings burn down each week, many others have bits and pieces torn up in the course of remodeling. The same thing was true in Antiquity and the Middle Ages. Historically significant events, let alone historically knowable events, do not determine the fate of such buildings. A given burnt foundation is just a burnt foundation, not necessarily an index of anything else. That same burnt foundation *might* be a result of some important historical event. But we cannot assume that it or any other piece of material evidence corresponds to the historical record except where we have an ironclad stratigraphic reason for doing so. Most of the time we do not.

Let us take as an example the southwestern Spanish city of Mérida, the Roman Emerita Augusta founded in 25 BC, the capital of the Roman province of Lusitania, and a city of great importance until the destruction of its walls by the Córdoban emir Muhammad I in 868.[7] Partly because it is now a sleepy provincial town, Mérida's ancient and medieval remains are well preserved and have been excavated with exemplary care since the late 1980s; two extensively excavated and published neighborhoods are the zone of the Morería and the area around and beneath the church of Saint Eulalia.[8] The Morería excavations preserve several blocks of the Roman city, two in their entirety. The church of Saint Eulalia preserves a suburban villa property, over which there later developed a large necropolis, including several mausolea and numerous burials that pre-dated the erection of the earliest basilica. Both sites display evidence of a substantial destruction phase in the fifth century. At the church of Santa Eulalia, mausolea were razed to ground level, simpler grave markers were systematically demolished, and the entire zone was leveled. In the

Morería, many *domus* were badly damaged. Two bodies lay crushed beneath the roof tiles of one; in another, a body had been buried according to normal rites that, given the universal Roman horror of intramural burial, suggests a period of siege in which it was impossible for people inside the walls to reach the age-old cemeteries outside them. At both the Morería and Santa Eulalia, all the attested destruction took place at the same time, though it is impossible to state that the destruction layers at the Morería and Santa Eulalia are contemporary with one another. The excavator of Santa Eulalia, however, has repeatedly asserted that the destruction at both Santa Eulalia and the Morería can be correlated to a known, well-dated historical event: the attack on the city of Mérida by the Suevic king Hermigarius in 429, attested by the chronicler Hydatius.[9]

Though possible, this connection is unlikely. In the Morería, close dating of the destruction phase is impossible, because trenches with good stratigraphy contain no diagnostic artifacts—the type of ceramic wares that changed shape rapidly enough to allow for very close dating. At Santa Eulalia, the stratigraphy is less good, but dateable material exists in greater quantity. This consists of various ceramics, some possibly dating as early as the 420s, but the preponderance of which date from later in the century. The 429 date drawn from the literary source is not really in keeping with what the archaeological evidence taken on its own terms would suggest. What is more, even if the material evidence did show an earlier date than it does, there would still be no good reason to suppose that it documented the attested Suevic siege. For most of the fifth century, Mérida stood at the center of Spain's most disputed region. It was the diocesan capital—the chief Roman administrative site in the whole peninsula—and hence a grand prize. Our record of narrative events consists of a single chronicle, which demonstrably leaves out information its author might have been expected to know.[10] Why should the destruction attested in the archaeological record bear any necessary connection to the handful of historical episodes preserved in Hydatius, rather than to some other episode of violence of which we lack all mention? In fact, nothing in the evidence compels us to make such a connection, or even suggests that we should. Although the material destruction at Mérida illustrates how, in the unstable conditions of the fifth century, even a great Spanish city might experience moments of appalling violence, it tells us nothing one way or another about the specifics of the city's narrative history.

The thoroughness of the main site report on Santa Eulalia makes it possible to check the excavator's conclusions against the record of his evidence, and to reach a conclusion that differs from his. But that is only true of the full site report: the many excellent overviews of late antique

Mérida published in the last few years all baldly state that the material evidence confirms Hydatius's report of a Suevic sack.[11] That is a perfect illustration of a problem of which historians must be constantly aware. At the vast majority of late Roman and early medieval sites, particularly in the Mediterranean, site reports on the scale of the Santa Eulalia excavation do not exist. Thus the conclusions and assumptions of excavators remain impervious to examination; we are compelled either to accept or reject their conclusions on faith, without access to the evidence that would allow us to make an informed choice.[12] From the historian's point of view, this causes the greatest difficulties in matters that concern the chronology of an archaeological site's development. The importation of fixed chronological markers from textual sources into the archaeological chronology of a site is very common, as it is in many early medieval artifact typologies: the sequence, that is, of attested forms of particular varieties of artifact, for instance brooches, belt buckles, or knives. It is certainly true of the highly refined typology of Spanish late antique personal ornament informing many studies of the Visigoths.[13] Unfortunately, introducing historical data into the archaeological evidence in this way will often lend a fatal circularity to any argument dependent on it. We have already looked at destruction strata as an example of the interpretative limits of archaeological evidence, but let us now see what happens when those limits are not respected: if an archaeologist dates a stratum of ash at a particular site to a particular year because a literary source reports a rebellion in that year, and if a historian then uses that site report as corroborative evidence for the scale of damage done by the rebellion, they have between them created a perfect evidentiary circle. If the site report gives only a bare date for that stratum of ash, without explaining how the date was arrived at, the circularity is invisible. What is worse, networks of evidence and interpretation created in this way are self-authenticating, because archaeological results framed on a certain historical premise cannot help but corroborate that same historical premise.

This scenario is anything but hypothetical, as we can illustrate by reference to another Spanish example, the Frankish invasion of the third century. Three literary sources—Jerome, Aurelius Victor, and Eutropius, all derived from the same lost original—state that at an imprecise moment during the reign of Emperor Gallienus (r. 253–268), Franks from Germany invaded Gaul, penetrated beyond the Pyrenees, and sacked Tarragona.[14] This is one of only three historical events recorded during the Spanish third century, and in the 1950s it came to be regarded as the key event in Spain's "third-century crisis."[15] Very soon, the invasion became an anchor to which masses of archaeological evidence could be attached, evidence used both to confirm and to exaggerate the effects of the invasion.[16]

A second barbarian invasion was imagined, dated to 273 or 276, and attributed to the Alamanni.[17] This invasion was supposedly attested by the various signs of destruction in the archaeological record that could not plausibly be attributed to Franks in the year 260. For a very long time, it was the universal practice at Spanish sites to date all evidence of destruction to the third century and link it to these invasions, either the first, attested one or the later, invented one. The third century therefore became a sort of dead zone for excavators, who attributed to it all demolished buildings, traces of fire, or leveled foundations. For this reason, masses of material evidence seemed to confirm historians' assumptions for the very good reason that the material evidence was excavated, recorded, and published within the framework of those assumptions. As a result, most work on third-century Spain has been rendered useless by a circularity of argument from which it is impossible to escape.

This sort of contamination of archaeological evidence and its chronology, whether at the time of excavation or publication, is precisely the sort of error that historians are most likely to be blind to. Despite the flowering of alternative methodologies within the historical profession over the past thirty years, most historians are still, in the first instance, reared on literary and documentary evidence. Consequently, they tend to be unconsciously prone to accept as natural the primacy of literary and documentary over material evidence. How does one guard against this trap? One extreme approach would be to discard archaeological evidence altogether, and many historians will perhaps feel most comfortable doing so. But there is another way forward, and that is for the historian to know the evidentiary basis on which the arguments and conclusions of a given archaeological report rest. In particular, we need to understand where dates in site reports come from. When confronted with a site report in which it is impossible to check the basis of an excavator's conclusions, the historian must proceed with extreme caution. If a report asks us to accept as an archaeological date a year already familiar to us from our literary evidence, and fails to explain the archaeological basis for that date, we should presume we are looking at a fossil of the literary evidence that has entered the archaeologist's findings in the process of either excavation or interpretation. In such cases, though the date might indeed be more or less correct, it is methodologically compromised and we must discard it. If, on the other hand, a site report has presented the basis for its conclusions, the historian is put in a position to evaluate those conclusions and make up his or her own mind.

This is not to say that the historian needs to, or can, do the work of an archaeologist. Historians are not trained to deal with the technicalities of dating material evidence, whether typologically or by the available scientific methods, most typically carbon-14 dating. For such purposes we are chiefly, and rightly, in the hands of specialists. Yet the historian can and should strive to understand the characteristics of those kinds of artifact that dominate the region he or she studies, particularly those regarded as chronologically diagnostic. The historian must also read full excavation reports, rather than summaries, abstracts, or popularizations, which will, by their very nature, omit the documentation essential for testing their conclusions. Once these precautions are observed, it becomes possible to use archaeology as a separate, autonomous category of evidence. Rather than a supplement to traditional textual sources, it can offer an independent alternative to them, one that can be studied on its own terms before being brought into dialogue with other sources.

An Alternative Approach

To see what this can mean, think about the disappearance of the Roman city. Just when the ancient city ceases to be recognizable as such, and instead becomes something else, is a problem that has inspired several colloquia and one large work of synthesis in recent years.[18] Ancient culture—the high culture of our written sources and the political and religious culture of the elites who shaped events—was a definitively urban culture. Change in the ancient city, therefore, is basic to understanding differences between the ancient and medieval worlds, even if we reject the axiom, embraced quite candidly in Liebeschuetz's recent synthesis, that any change from a normative classical cityscape must represent decline. The Spanish evidence is now sufficiently reliable to provide illustration. Whether superimposed on preexisting townscapes or created *ex nihilo* in a new location chosen by Roman government, Spanish cities had become remarkably homogeneous by the mid-second century CE, each equipped with the basic furnishings of a Roman city: an orthogonal street grid with a forum or fora at its center, public baths, theatre, amphitheatre, and, if the city was large enough, circus.[19] After the second century, very little new monumental construction is attested, with the exception of the imperial palace of Cercadilla at Córdoba and urban wall-circuits, some twenty of which can be dated with certainty to the period 280–320.[20]

The general absence of new monumental construction need reflect nothing more than satiety, and it by no means constitutes decline in and of itself. The real question is the balance between maintenance, disuse, and alteration in the second-century cityscape. Most older archaeological reports peg changes in the cityscape to a chronology drawn from the ancient literary sources. Thus, the cessation of public building is linked to the one major narrative event known from the late second century, the invasion of southern Spain by Moors during the reign of Marcus Aurelius; city walls are reflexively dated to 260, the year of the Frankish invasion discussed above; the evidence collectively tends to be read in a Rostovtzeffian model of third-century crisis, in which the glorious urban culture of the empire was barbarized and ruralized by the rise of the peasantry and the army, until barbarian invasions in the third and fifth centuries destroyed the peninsula's cities once and for all Archaeological evidence dug and dated on the basis of such chronological and interpretative suppositions can hardly avoid confirming them, and duly does so. For many historians and archaeologists, the fourth-century Spanish city is a place of ruins, abandoned by all but imperial administrators and bishops.

This interpretative model remains substantially intact in Spanish historical literature and has informed recent works of synthesis in English and German. But the past two decades' archaeological work in Spain has revolutionized our understanding of these questions. With sites now dug on their own terms, and published so that their evidence is open to examination, a whole new set of data has turned old interpretations and chronologies on their heads.[21] It has become clear that the first major change to the second-century cityscape involved the occupation of certain types of public space by private construction, chiefly the extension of residences into the porticoes of public streets or the remodeling of larger townhouses to take over the surface area of minor cross-streets. Although such changes altered early street plans, they frequently correspond to signs of general growth in most large Spanish cities, including the upgrading of townhouses on new, richer plans, and the remodeling of temples. Chronologies vary, but this sort of change is visible across the entire third century and well into the fourth. In the same period, amphitheatres and circuses everywhere were maintained and in use, public baths and theatres widely but not universally so. The early fourth century brought massive construction at a few key cities, mostly imperial administrative capitals such as Mérida and Tarragona, but also trading centers such as Barcelona or Gijón and other cities such as Complutum (Alcalá de Henares), the importance of which is hard to gauge. In the same period, many cities of much lesser importance were walled for the first time or had their early imperial walls substantially rebuilt.

After the start of the fourth century, however, there seems to be a gradual divergence between cities with imperial administrative patronage and the many others without it. The basic shape of the second-century city remained intact everywhere in Spain until the fifth century. But in cities with no permanent imperial establishment, the physical infrastructure underlying the plan of the city deteriorated. This is true even of grand cities like Zaragoza, where by the 370s all the secondary sewers had silted

up; even in the main forum, the drainage conduits no longer carried
wastewater into the sewers and thence to the Ebro River. Parallel processes are visible throughout Spain's cities, and the chronology everywhere seems to be very late fourth century. There are no functional
changes to urban space, no reimagining of city plans, merely the physical
decay of what existed. Similar changes take place in the most important
and well-connected cities, but they do so later, and more suddenly. In
Tarragona, the great imperial forum had lost its grandiose rectangular
articulation by the 440s when, in at least one substantial section, its paving stones were torn up and carted off, replaced by a domestic rubbish pit.
In contrast, another corner of the same forum was still used for imperial
honorific inscriptions down to 472, the year of our last imperial dedication in all of Spain.[22]

This covering over of the large public spaces—spaces with social and
symbolic as well as functional purpose—implies the disintegration of the
social function that once made them necessary. Across Spain, though, no
new model of urbanism replaced the old one until the end of the fifth, or
more frequently, middle of the sixth century. Only then do the intramural
zones of Spanish cities come to be occupied with a new form of monumental building: Christian churches. This is a point of some significance.
Despite the fact that Spain was thoroughly Christianized by the end of the
fourth century, Christian cult and episcopal power remained suburban
and extramural. The first Spanish churches are assumed to have been mar-
tyrial, as they are located in the suburban cemeteries where martyrs were
interred and where martyr cults are attested by the fourth century.[23] But
it is very striking that long after Christianity had come to occupy a central
role in the lives of Hispano-Romans, its physical locus remained outside
the old intramural centers of urban life. Only when the old public spaces—the temples and fora—had lost all their social content did the physical
manifestations of Christian authority come to occupy central intramural
spaces. Thus at Tarragona, an episcopal church and palace were built at the
apex of the hill on which the city stood, once the site of a large imperial
cult precinct, the walls of which were knocked down to put up the *episco-
pium*.[24] But this construction took place around the year 500, half a century after there had ceased to be imperial government in Spain.

Which of these stages of change one decides to take as the dividing
line between Hispano-Roman Antiquity and the Spanish Middle Ages is
in some ways irrelevant, particularly if one must choose between the
years in which the old public shape of the city disappeared and those in
which a new urban order replaced it. Even if one develops a rationale for
choosing one date rather than the other, there is still the problem of the
fuzziness of archaeological dates, the fact that these general trends have

different chronologies in different parts of the peninsula. Regardless, the important thing to notice is how very little the rhythms of change to Spanish urbanism have to do with the narrative of Spanish history. Modern archaeological techniques have redated the period of major physical deterioration in most Spanish cities to the late fourth, rather than the third century. Neither the exaggerated barbarian invasions of the third century, nor Diocletian's administrative reform of the 290s can be placed in an immediate causal connection with the decay of the urban infrastructure observable in the material record. When that decay becomes visible, it corresponds to no known event in the historical record, nor to any attested institutional or administrative change. In the same way, the disuse of the imperial fora at Tarragona and elsewhere in the 440s takes place a good twenty years before the last signs of imperial administration disappear from Spain. The fourth-century decay of the Spanish cityscape similarly fails to correspond to the archaeological evidence for the monetary history of the peninsula, which received its last significant shipments of coined money in the late 390s, or the system of military supply, the *annona militaris*, which almost certainly disappeared in the 410s.[25] Trade to and from the peninsula likewise obeys a very different chronology, whether in the interior, which begins to show a certain dislocation from Mediterranean and Atlantic networks by the 420s, or on the coasts, where old contacts with North Africa and Asia Minor only disappear in the mid-sixth century.[26]

All of this demonstrates something we know but sometimes ignore for the sake of simplicity: different approaches to the past give different answers and different chronologies to questions of periodization. When different perspectives and categories of evidence are interrogated on their own terms, it becomes possible to read them against each other without introducing circularity to the argument. Taken on its own, the archaeological record confirms what perhaps we all suspect, that the end of the western Roman empire is just an epiphenomenon of a much larger process of change.[27] But where it stands in relation to that process, as cause or as consequence or as something in-between, is a question best approached with full consciousness of what certain types of evidence can and cannot do.

Notes

1. Gibbon's *Decline and Fall of the Roman Empire*, the first volume of which appeared in 1776, laid out the problem in the terms it retains to this day, although the basic question of the fall of Rome was of much longer standing. The influence of Michael Rostovtzeff, *A Social and Economic*

History of the Roman World (Oxford: Clarendon Press, 1926), was enormous. The influence of Ferdinand Lot, *The End of the Ancient World and the Beginnings of the Middle Ages* (New York: A.A. Knopf, 1931) was disproportionately large in America because of its reprinting as a widely circulated Harper Torchbook (New York) in 1961.

2. Transformation of the Roman World, 14 vols. (Leiden: Brill, 1998–2005).

3. Alexander Demandt, *Der Fall Roms: Die Auflösung des römischen Reiches im Urteil der Nachwelt* (Munich: Beck, 1984).

4. Bryan Ward-Perkins, *The Fall of Rome and the End of Civilization* (Oxford: Oxford University Press, 2005); J.H.W.G. Liebeschuetz, *The Decline and Fall of the Roman City* (Oxford: Oxford University Press, 2001).

5. Into this category we may place sociological approaches derived from Max Weber, the groundbreaking works of the *annalistes*, the anthropology of Clifford Geertz, and virtually every historical fad of the past thirty years, from cliometrics to Pierre Bourdieu.

6. Books on archaeological theory and practice are too numerous to list here, but all historians should read Bruce G. Trigger, *A History of Archaeological Thought* (Cambridge: Cambridge University Press, 1990).

7. For an excellent introduction to the city's Roman history, see now *Mérida: Colonia Augusta Emerita*, ed. Xavier Dupré Raventos, Las capitales provinciales de Hispania 2 (Rome: L'Erma di Bretschneider, 2004).

8. The Morería has been published piecemeal; we still await a promised monographic treatment. The most important treatments are in the six volumes so far of *Mérida: Excavaciones Arqueológicas* (Mérida: Consorcio Ciudad Monumental Histórico-Artística y Arqueológica de Mérida, 1996–). On Santa Eulalia, see Pedro Mateos Cruz, *La basílica de Santa Eulalia de Mérida. Arqueología y urbanismo*, Anejos de Archivo Español de Arqueología 19 (Madrid: Consejo Superior de Investigaciones Científicas, 1999). A fuller synthesis, with earlier literature, appears in Michael Kulikowski, *Late Roman Spain and Its Cities* (Baltimore: The Johns Hopkins University Press, 2004), pp. 209–14.

9. Hydatius, *Chronicle 80, The Chronicle of Hydatius and the Consularia Constantinopolitana*, ed. and trans. R.W. Burgess (Oxford: Clarendon Press, 1993).

10. Kulikowski, *Late Roman Spain*, pp. 153–56; Javier Arce, "El catastrofismo de Hydacio y los camellos de la Gallaecia," in *Los últimos romanos en Lusitania*, ed. Agustín Velázquez, Enrique Cerrillo Martín de Cáceres, and Pedro Mateos Cruz, Cuadernos Emeritenses 10 (Mérida: Museo Nacional de Arte Romano, 1995), pp. 219–29.

11. For example, Pedro Mateos Cruz, "*Augusta Emerita*, de capital de la *Diocesis Hispaniarum* a sede temporal visigoda," in *Sedes regiae (ann. 400–800)*, ed. Gisela Ripoll and Josep M. Gurt (Barcelona: Reial Acadèmia de Bones Lletres, 2000), pp. 491–520; Pedro Mateos Cruz and Miguel Alba Calzado, "De *Emerita Augusta* a Marida," in *Visigodos y Omeyas: Un debate*

entre la Antigüedad Tardía y la alta Edad Media, ed. Luís Caballero Zoreda and Pedro Mateos Cruz, Anejos de Archivo Español de Arqueología 23 (Madrid: Consejo Superior de Investigaciones Científicas, 2000), pp. 143–68.

12. Certain traditions of excavation are less problematical than others in this respect: partly on theoretical grounds and partly because of the local economics of publishing, British, Dutch, and German archaeologists have an older tradition of comprehensive documentation and publication than do French, Italian, or Iberian counterparts.

13. In a series of works since the mid-1980s, most recently *Toréutica de la Bética (siglos VI y VII d.C.)* (Barcelona: Reial Acadèmia de Bones Lletres, 1998), Gisela Ripoll López has developed and refined a typology rigidly periodized by reference to dates drawn from the literary evidence of Hydatius, the *Consularia Caesaraugustana*, and III Toledo.

14. Aurelius Victor, *Liber de caesaribus* 33.3, ed. F. Pichlmayer (Leipzig: Teubner, 1911); Eutropius, *Breviarium ab urbe condita* 9.8, ed. C. Santini, 2nd ed. (Stuttgart: Teubner, 1992), p. 58; Jerome, *Chronicle*, s.a. 264, ed. R. Helm (Berlin: Akademie-Verlag, 1956), p. 221. The source is the lost fourth-century *Kaisergeschichte* posited by Enmann. Orosius, *Historiae* 7.41.2, ed. C. Zangemeister (Vienna: Gerold, 1882) derives from a different ultimate source.

15. For example, Blas Taracena, "Las invasiones germánicas en España durante la segunda mitad del siglo III de J.C.," *Congreso Internacional del Instituto de Estudios Pirenaicos* 1 (Zaragoza: Consejo Superior de Investigaciones Científicas, 1952), pp. 4–13; Miguel Tarradell, "Sobre las invasiones germánicas del siglo III de J.C. en la península ibérica," *Estudios Clásicos* 3 (1955): 95–110; Alberto Balil, "Las invasiones germánicas en Hispania," *Cuadernos de trabajos de la Escuela Española de Historia y Arqueología en Roma* 9 (1957): 97–143; José Sánchez Real, "Las invasiones germánicas," *Boletín Arqueológico* 57 (1957): 6–12.

16. See for instance the many widely read works of J.M. Blázquez, for example, "Der Limes im Spanien des vierten Jahrhunderts," *Actes du IXème congrès international d'études sur les frontières romaines, Mamaïa, 6–13 septembre 1972* (Bucharest: Editura Academiei Republicii Socialiste Romînia, 1976), pp. 485–502; idem., *Economía de la Hispania romana* (Bilbao: Ediciones Najera, 1978). Also many overviews of Hispano-Roman history, for example, Alberto Balil, "Aspectos sociales del Bajo Imperio," *Latomus* 24 (1965): 886–904; idem., "De Marco Aurelio a Constantino: una introducción a la España del Bajo Imperio," *Hispania* 27 (1967): 245–341.

17. Taracena, "Invasiones germánicas."

18. *Towns in Transition: Urban Evolution in Late Antiquity and the Early Middle Ages*, ed. Neil Christie and S.T. Loseby (Aldershot: Ashgate, 1996); *La fin de la cité antique et le début de la cité médiévale de la fin du IIIe siècle à l'avènement de Charlemagne*, ed. Claude Lepelley (Bari: Edipuglia,1996); *Recent Research in Late-Antique Urbanism*, ed. Luke Lavan, Journal of Roman

Archaeology Supplement 42 (Portsmouth, RI: Journal of Roman Archaeology, 2001); Liebeschuetz, *Roman City*.

19. This evidence is treated at greater length in Kulikowski, *Late Roman Spain*, chaps. 2, 3. Juan Manuel Abascal Palazón and Urbano Espinosa, *La ciudad hispano-romana: privilegio y poder* (Logroño: Ibercasca, 1989) remains the most effective short introduction.

20. The main publication of Cercadilla is Rafael Hidalgo Prieto, *Espacio publico y espacio privado en el conjunto palatino de Cercadilla (Córdoba): el aula central y las termas* (Córdoba: Junta de Andalucía, 1996). For town wall circuits, see Carmen Fernández-Ochoa and Ángel Morillo Cerdán, "Walls in the Urban Landscape of Late Roman Spain," in *Hispania in Late Antiquity: Current Approaches*, ed. Kim Bowes and Michael Kulikowski (Leiden: Brill, 2005), pp. 299–340, with earlier literature.

21. For what follows, see Kulikowski, *Late Roman Spain*, chap. 5; and idem., "Cities and Government in Late Antique Hispania: Recent Advances and Future Research," in *Hispania in Late Antiquity*, pp. 31–70.

22. TED'A (Taller Escola d'Arqueologia), *Un abocador del segle V d.c. en el fòrum provincial de Tàrraco*, Memòries d'Excavació 2 (Tarragona: Ajuntament de Tarragona, 1989) is the basic study.

23. See Pedro Castillo Maldonado, "*Angelorum participes*: The Cult of the Saints in Late Antique Spain," in *Hispania in Late Antiquity*, pp. 151–88, which summarizes and revises the author's *Los mártires hispanorromanos y su culto en la Hispania de la Antigüedad Tardía* (Granada: Universidad de Granada, 1999).

24. Javier Aquilué Abadías, *La sede del Collegi d'Arquitectes: una intervencion arqueológica en el centro histórico de Tarragona* (Tarragona: Collegi d'Arquitectes de Catalunya, 1993).

25. For the coinage see especially Fernando López Sánchez, "Coinage, Iconography and the Changing Political Geography of Fifth-Century Hispania," in *Hispania in Late Antiquity*, pp. 487–518; for the *annona*, Fernández-Ochoa and Morillo, "Walls in the Urban Landscape."

26. Paul Reynolds, *Settlement and Pottery in the Vinalopó Valley (Alicante, Spain) A.D. 400–700*, British Archaeological Reports, International Series 588 (Oxford: Tempus Reparatum, 1993); idem., *Trade in the Western Mediterranean, AD 400–700: The Ceramic Evidence*, British Archaeological Reports, International Series 604 (Oxford: Tempus Reparatum, 1995). Both brought up to date in idem., "Hispania in the Late Roman Mediterranean: Ceramics and Trade," in *Hispania in Late Antiquity*, pp. 369–486.

27. A point comprehensively missed in the reductive arguments of Peter Heather, *The Fall of the Roman Empire* (London: Macmillan, 2005), which appears to regard barbarian invasion as the single necessary cause of Roman collapse.

CHAPTER 11

MITTELEUROPA: THE MAKING
OF EUROPE BETWEEN BYZANTIUM
AND THE LATIN WEST, CA. 800–1025

Charles R. Bowlus

*Critique of the periodization schemes of Henri Pirenne and Francis Dvornik,
arguing that the transition from antique to medieval resulted from Carolingian
expansion and Byzantine responses in central Europe.*

Shortly before his death in 1935 Henri Pirenne wrote, "It is therefore
strictly correct to say that without Mohammed Charlemagne would
have been inconceivable."[1] According to him, an expanding Islamic
empire cut the symbiotic between the Greek East and the Latin West,
bringing what had been a slow death of classical civilization to an abrupt
end, and ushered in the Middle Ages. Almost thirty years later Francis
Dvornik agreed both that outside forces had separated the Latin West
from the Greek East, and that this separation was decisive in extinguishing
classical civilization. Calling attention to *Mitteleuropa* (central Europe: the
Carpathian Basin and the Balkans), he insisted that the migration of Avars
and Slavs into the Roman province of Illyricum (ca. 550–600) had
divided the eastern and western parts of the Roman Empire well before
the rise and expansion of Islam. "Illyricum," he asserted, "instead of
being a bridge between West and East, became the battle field on which
the two forces of Christendom waged the first great struggles which led
to that complete separation so fateful for the whole of Christendom and
all of mankind."[2]

In the last half-century both paradigms have gone out of fashion, giving way to scenarios positing that the main currents of medieval civilization first became evident at the turn of the first millennium.[3] Some Carolingianists are now seeking a place for themselves in the club of Late Antiquity,[4] although a recent guide to the postclassical world seems to exclude them, defining Late Antiquity as 250–800 CE, "a distinctive and quite decisive period of history that stands on its own."[5] Thus, late Carolingian rulers, nobles, churchmen, their followers, and dependents are now consigned to a limbo between Late Antiquity and the Middle Ages.

A subspecies of this currently dominant paradigm holds that a hallmark of western civilization is its propensity to use military force to replicate its way of life across the face of the planet. For some scholars, the expansion of medieval Europe has become a synonym for "the making of Europe," the title of a seminal book by Robert Bartlett.[6] Although there is no unanimity concerning when this process began, most date its origins ca. 950–1100.[7] If, on the other hand, one defines western civilization (as Bartlett does) in terms of military expansion followed by the transplantation of western institutions into conquered regions, a strong case can be made that the Carolingian era did indeed witness the origins of the expansion/making of Europe and, hence, the beginnings of the Middle Ages. Bernard S. Bachrach has shown that the early Carolingians created a well-oiled military machine that enabled them to piece back together the Frankish kingdom.[8] Then, building on the work of his ancestors, Charlemagne extended his power beyond the Frankish realm and established his direct rule over Saxony and Lombard Italy.[9] Finally, in the decade prior to his imperial coronation in 800, he destroyed the khaganate of the Avars who had ruled the Carpathian Basin for more than two centuries, establishing his rule in *Mitteleuropa*, Dvornik's Illyricum.[10]

This essay holds that the Carolingian conquest of *Mitteleuropa* was more important in the transition from Antiquity to the Middle Ages than has been recognized. It was not the settlement of Slavs and Avars in Illyricum that drove a wedge between "East" and "West," but rather Charlemagne's intrusion into *Mitteleuropa*, which was an ambitious undertaking to reshape the region politically and ecclesiastically on a Latin western model. Carolingian expansion into the Carpathian Basin and the Balkans gave rise to apprehensions in Constantinople and compelled the Byzantines to turn their attention, albeit reluctantly, to their northern neighbors, whom they had treated with benign neglect for two centuries.

In the first half of the seventh century, strategic considerations required that Emperor Heraclius (610–641) and his successors leave the diverse peoples of *Mitteleuropa* to their own devices.[11] The empire relied on a strategic doctrine of defense-in-depth, which was effective in protecting urban assets but inadequate for offensive operations aimed at conquests.[12] The loss of territory in the seventh century forced the state to become totally focused on defending its capital.[13] Despite an ideological claim that the Danube was still the frontier, the empire maintained a defensive posture vis-à-vis the peoples settled north of the Haemus Mountains. The principal threats to imperial survival were in the east, first from the Persian Empire and then the Umayyad Caliphate. In contrast, west of the Bosporus no major power threatened Byzantium after the failure of the Avars (as allies of the Persians) to take Constantinople in 626.[14] The Bulgars, who established their rule along the lower Danube ca. 680, represented a nuisance that could be contained by diplomacy, patronage, and the judicious use of limited military force. In the Balkans there existed a hodgepodge of barbarian ethnicities designated by the Byzantines as Slavs and/or Antes.[15] They occasionally pillaged imperial territory, but they did not menace Constantinople. On the Black Sea, Aegean, and Adriatic, the empire used its navy to convey diplomats to fortified coastal enclaves, whence they established communications with barbarian leaders whom they persuaded with "gifts" to attack the enemies of Byzantium whenever the need arose.[16] But emperors did not use their armies to impose the trappings of Byzantine civilization upon the barbarians of *Mitteleuropa*.

Analogously, Byzantine clergy did little to extend the state religion beyond the environs of the capital. There is no evidence of a concerted Byzantine effort to Christianize *Mitteleuropa* in the seventh and eighth centuries.[17] Residual Christian populations may have tried to win over their pagan neighbors and conquerors, and there must have been some activity on the part of freelance missionaries who ventured on their own into pagan lands; the Byzantine state, however, made no attempt to establish episcopal organizations there. Although Emperor Leo III (717–743) declared ca. 730 that all of Illyricum came under the ecclesiastical jurisdiction of Constantinople, he and his successors took no steps to establish a hierarchical church in *Mitteleuropa*.[18] Numerous artifacts unearthed by archaeologists do offer testimony that the peoples of the region were influenced by interactions with their Byzantine, Lombard, and Frankish neighbors.[19] Nevertheless, these outsiders did not impose the symbols of their civilizations on the barbarians.

Defensive military strategies also predominated in the Frankish kingdom throughout the seventh century. Although Merovingian kings had attempted to extend their rule across the Alps into Italy prior to 600, their subsequent wars north of the Alpine barrier were waged to establish and maintain tributary relationships, not to conquer, convert, or govern. What is more, this realm fragmented in the mid-seventh century, leaving the task of reconstituting the Frankish kingdom to the early Carolingians. These rulers, though, showed little interest in pushing their conquest beyond the *regnum Francorum* (kingdom of the Franks: Gaul and western and southern Germany) until Charlemagne occupied Italy, Saxony, and, in 791, unleashed his juggernaut against the Avar realm, destroying it in little more than a decade.[20]

The significance of this conquest was obvious to contemporaries. Einhard wrote that, with the exception of the victory over the Saxons, Charlemagne's Avar war was his greatest triumph, which "he waged with more vigor and greater preparation than all of the others."[21] Despite this testimony, Rudolf Schieffer sums up recent scholarship on the subject, asserting that the wars against the Avars were simply "a rush for booty (*Beutezug*) with only a half-hearted intention to conquer."[22] Dieter Hägermann, who also uses the word *Beutezug* to describe these expeditions, thinks that the conquest was primarily undertaken for the prestige to be gained from a quick and easy victory over a pagan people, and had no strategic motives.[23] The Avar treasure certainly did represent a splendid haul of booty, but we must not be blinded by it so as to overlook other factors. Einhard himself emphasized that Charlemagne was determined to conquer all the land of the Avars, including "both Pannonian provinces, the part of Dacia east of the Danube, as well as Istria, Liburnia, and Dalmatia with the exception of cities which Charles gave to the emperor of Constantinople for reasons of friendship and because of a treaty that he had made with him."[24]

An important piece of literary evidence revealing the geographic extent of Charlemagne's ambitious plans for the Carpathian Basin comes from a long panegyric written by Patriarch Paulinus II of Aquileia, on the occasion of the death in 799 of Erich, margrave of Friuli, who led many of the Avar expeditions.[25] The poem begins with the rivers of the region mourning Erich's demise. They include the Danube, Sava, Tisza, and a river named *Marua*, a reference to the Maros/Mures, a tributary of the Tisza near Szeged.[26] According to Paulinus, Erich's realm stretched from Sirmium in the east to Pula (Istria), Aquileia, and Cividale in the west, and from the Drava in the north to the interior of Dalmatia in the south. The poem also contains a reference to Scythia, that is, the great plain between the Danube and the Tisza that Paulinus saw with his own eyes when he participated in the 796 expedition to destroy the Avar Ring.[27] Following this campaign, the patriarch presided over a synod on the banks of the Danube, where plans were laid for an ecclesiastical organization in *Mitteleuropa*.[28]

The conquest of *Mitteleuropa* became a strategic necessity when Charlemagne committed himself to an imperial revival.[29] His Byzantine rivals could use the cities of Dalmatia as diplomatic bases, from which (for instance) to entice Avars and Slavs to disrupt communications between the Frankish kingdom and Italy. Charles was forced to abandon any attempts to conquer outright Byzantine enclaves along the Dalmatian coast, not (as Einhard asserted) because of his "friendship with the emperor," but rather because he lacked the naval resources necessary to capture them. Instead, he embarked upon a bold strategy of securing his communications with Italy by destroying Avar power completely, and integrating the interior of the Carpathian Basin politically, militarily, religiously, and economically into his empire. The heartland of the Avar khaganate, the site of the fabled treasure, was in those parts of modern Hungary, Romania, and Serbia for which I have elsewhere coined the term the "Watergate" of the Carpathian Basin, the spot where the rivers Drava, Sava, Tisza, and southern Morava gather the waters of their tributaries to join the Danube.[30] Although this region might seem very distant from the Carolingian heartland, or even from Lombard Italy, the vast Danubian river system plus a network of Roman roads through Pannonia made it relatively easy to support logistically armies invading *Mitteleuropa* from west to east.[31]

Officials in Constantinople sensed immediately that this deep penetration into *Mitteleuropa* threatened the security measures they had carefully crafted over two centuries.[32] Nicephorus I (802–811) responded militarily, but suffered two major reverses that had enduring consequences. In 810, he failed to persuade the Franks to abandon Istria, which they had seized in 788, despite the deployment of a large Byzantine fleet. Istria was of great strategic importance because it constituted the best point of departure for expeditions from Italy into the heart of *Mitteleuropa*.[33] Nicephorus lost his life the next year in an even more serious fiasco, when the Bulgars trapped his force of 70,000 men in the narrows of the Haemus Mountains. The emperor was captured, decapitated, and his skull turned into a goblet for the banquet table of the victorious Khan Krum. The debacle of 811 left an indelible mark on Byzantine strategy, discouraging successive emperors from attempting to conquer the northern Balkans. More immediately, it forced the new emperor, Michael I, to make a peace with the Franks in 812 that recognized Carolingian control over Istria, and with it access to the interior. Leo V (813–820) achieved a victory over the Bulgars in 816, but Byzantine officials made no attempt to extend imperial rule northward into *Mitteleuropa*.

The contrasting strategies of the two empires are apparent in the case of Liudewit, a Slav who led a major revolt against Carolingian rule

(818–822). The insurgency originated in the Sava watershed and engulfed parts of the eastern Alps and Dalmatia, prompting Louis the Pious to send out large expeditions year after year until the revolt was finally crushed in 822.[34] Byzantium had a hand in the rebellion, but only diplomatically. Fortunatus, Patriarch of Grado and an opportunist, one of the wealthiest men of his day, abandoned the Franks and was accused of aiding Liudewit by sending him engineers to raise fortifications against the Carolingians. Without answering the charges, Fortunatus fled to Byzantine Dalmatia whence officials conveyed him by ship to Constantinople.[35] The suppression of this insurrection is good evidence that the conquest of *Mitteleuropa* was not just Charlemagne's passing fancy; his successors Louis the Pious, Louis the German, Carloman, and Arnulf of Carinthia all showed great tenacity in holding onto the Watergate at all costs. Whereas the Byzantines relied on diplomacy to encourage indigenous resistance to the Franks, Carolingian commanders doggedly maintained military hegemony in the interior of the Carpathian Basin.

Two reasons explain Byzantine reluctance to use force in this region. First, the rugged geography of the Balkans made it logistically difficult to support an army on the lower Danube. Second, despite a significant revival of the empire's economic and cultural fortunes in the first half of the ninth century, its army continued to practice a military strategy of risk avoidance. Warren Treadgold observed that the Byzantine army's "most impressive ability was to survive military catastrophes without permanently losing either troop strength or territory."[36] Byzantium's conservative strategy toward its northern and western neighbors was effective at stopping conquests south of the Haemus Mountains, though it could not prevent pillaging raids into Thrace, much less halt the deep penetration of the Franks into *Mitteleuropa*.

Following Liudewit's revolt, an embassy from the Bulgar Khan Omortag appeared at the court of Louis the Pious to negotiate border disputes. When these ambassadors were ignored, the Bulgars began raiding Frankish Pannonia. The cause of this conflict was Bulgar concern about Frankish encroachment, for a people known as the Timociani (from the Timok River, a tributary of the Lower Danube east of the Iron Gates) had enlisted Carolingian support against the Bulgars, once again demonstrating the depth of Frankish penetration into *Mitteleuropa*.[37]

Even civil wars and the division of the Carolingian empire in the 830s and 840s failed to halt Frankish aggression in *Mitteleuropa*. When in 838 Lothar I (as king of Italy) attempted to strengthen the march of Friuli, his brother and rival Louis (the German, then king of the Bavarians) sent an army to occupy the Sava watershed and detach this territory from Friuli. At the same time Louis's forces defeated Ratimar, a Slavic chieftain whose power center was located in the watershed of the Drina River, a tributary of the Sava flowing out of the southwestern parts of the Balkan Mountains.[38] Also ca. 838, Louis put a Slavic leader named Pribina in charge of controlling important Roman roads that formed a wedge through southern Pannonia to the Watergate.[39]

For the remainder of the ninth century, Louis, his descendents, and their followers were relentless in their attempts to assert authority throughout the Carpathian Basin and the western Balkans—though they eventually met significant resistance from Slavs named Moravians. In 846, Louis installed Rastislav as the leader (*dux*) of the Moravian Slavs (*Sclavi Margenses*), who had grown restless under Carolingian rule. Thanks to the work of Martin Eggers, we can say with confidence that the realm of the Moravians originated east of the Danube in the heart of the Watergate,[40] near the confluence of the Maros/Mures River with the Tisza. Rastislav did not remain a pliant subordinate of the East Frankish ruler; instead he led an insurgency that resulted in persistent and brutal wars. When Louis's armies finally defeated and captured Rastislav in 870, Franks took over Moravian strongholds and ruled the territory directly. This success was fleeting, however, for Sventibald, Rastislav's nephew and Ratimar's grandson, ambushed the Franks and established himself as Moravian leader. Sventibald already controlled a large chunk of territory in the Balkans, including modern Bosnia and Kosovo.[41] Following his victory over the Franks he expanded his power to the northwest, into modern Slovakia and even (briefly) Bohemia. Thus after 870, a Slavic polity emerged that stretched from the southwestern Balkans to the northern Carpathians. But these territories were strung out and difficult to defend, and Sventibald's "empire" collapsed completely in little more than a decade, following his death in 894. The Carolingian ruler Arnulf (887–899) enticed Hungarians to enter Moravia from the east, while he attacked Sventibald's realm from the west.

Arnulf's attempts to use Hungarians to regain control over the Carpathian Basin ultimately backfired when the nomads crossed the mountains *en masse* to settle in the Carpathian Basin; yet these events illustrate once again just how determined the Franks were to hold the region. Liutpold, the margrave of the eastern marches and the most powerful military leader in the East Frankish kingdom, was attempting to drive the Magyars out when he died in an ambush near Lake Balaton in 907.[42] Since Liutpold was familiar with Hungarian warfare, his defeat cannot be attributed to ignorance of their tactics. In the Carolingian tradition, Liutpold believed that he could defeat an army of mounted archers in Pannonia. His failure halted East Frankish attempts to dominate the region. Instead, his son Duke Arnulf of Bavaria (910–937) successfully practiced a defense-in-depth strategy against the Hungarians similar to that of the Byzantines.[43]

Liutpold's defeat in 907, though, only temporarily halted the East Frankish drive to organize *Mitteleuropa*. Otto the Great revived earlier Carolingian interest in conquering the Carpathian Basin even before his victory at the so-called battle of Lechfeld in 955. Preoccupations with Italy and the early death of Otto II (973–983) prevented a resumption of conquests, however, and bought the Hungarians, whose armies had been annihilated in 955, some time to settle down, regroup, and accept Christianity. King Steven I (1000–1038) married the sister of Emperor Henry II (1002–1024) and invited immigrants from other lands into his realm.[44] Yet the Hungarian kingdom remained politically independent of the empires east and west. The northern parts of the kingdom became Latin Christian, whereas Byzantium eventually exercised its influence in the south, in the region of the Watergate, where an eastern orthodox ecclesiastical organization prevailed.

How this happened is a complicated story that began with a belated Byzantine attempt to promote its brand of Christianity in *Mitteleuropa*.[45] Rastislav, we are told, sent a legation to Constantinople requesting teachers of proper Christian worship. This legation also sought diplomatic assistance against the East Franks who, now allied with the Bulgars, were posed to invade Moravian territory.[46] Byzantine officials, though encouraged by Rastislav's insurgency, had neither the ability nor the inclination to offer direct military support. The eastern emperor responded in 863 by sending the brothers Constantine and Methodius, who at that moment were not yet missionaries, but rather diplomats. They had been ordered first to go to Moravia, assess the situation there, and subsequently continue on to Rome to negotiate with Pope Nicholas I issues involving the so-called Photian Schism and ecclesiastical jurisdiction in Illyricum. They were armed with a precious gift for Nicholas, the relics of Saint Clement, which Constantine believed he had discovered in Cherson while on a diplomatic mission to the Khazars. Traveling overland via routes through Sventibald's realm in the Balkans, they reached Rastislav's court where they hoped to gather information that could be used to persuade Nicholas to restrain Louis.

In 864, Byzantine forces made a rare but important military foray into Bulgaria that relieved the pressure on Rastislav.[47] Khan Boris, who was in the western portions of his realm campaigning against the Moravians, hurried back to his capital, submitted to the Byzantines, and converted to eastern Christianity. However, the defeat of the Bulgars and their conversion did not lead to a Byzantine occupation of Bulgaria. Eastern imperial forces withdrew. Two years later, the khan expelled Greek priests and sent envoys to the West requesting churchmen from Nicholas and Louis.

The dynamic processes that were transforming Mitteleuropa are illustrated by the circumstances surrounding an exceptionally long papal letter dated 866, a response to the khan's request for guidance.[48] Two distinguished bishops, Paul of Pomplona and Formosus of Porto (later a pope himself), headed the Roman delegation and conveyed Nicholas's epistle to the Bulgar ruler. The version of this letter edited in the Monumenta Germaniae Historica (MGH) is thirty-two pages long and contains one hundred and six chapters giving detailed responses to Boris's questions. Nicholas obviously believed that the opportunity should be seized to establish in Bulgaria a Christian ecclesiastical organization obedient to Rome. Nicholas's interest in the region is also illustrated by his massive correspondence dealing with Byzantine relations with the Latin church. Nicholas's portion of the "papae epistolae ad res orientales pertinentes" (letters of the pope pertaining to eastern matters) consists of twenty letters that take up almost two hundred pages in the MGH edition. A lively correspondence concerning matters in the east continued during the pontificates of Hadrian II and John VIII, adding almost forty epistles to this pool.[49]

In this voluminous correspondence, Nicholas I and his successors insisted on massive territorial claims for Roman ecclesiastical jurisdiction in southeastern Europe, including all of Illyricum, Thessalonica, the provinces of Thessaly, Epirus, Macedonia, Attica, Dacia south of the Danube, Moesia, and even the Dardanelles.[50] These claims, if realized, would have carried Roman ecclesiastical authority (potentially backed by Frankish military power) to the very gates of Constantinople. Dvornik has argued that for the papacy and the Franks, this extension was "only a matter of prestige, but for the Byzantines it was a matter of life and death."[51] There is reason, though, to believe that the expansion of the authority of the Latin Church and the Frankish Empire to the Bosporus was a serious goal both for the Franks and for the papacy, in spite of its failure in the long run. The principal aim of Nicholas is clear throughout the correspondence: Byzantine recognition of papal authority over all of Illyricum, understood in Rome to include the Carpathian Basin, the Balkans, and the plain of the Lower Danube. The tenacity with which his successors, Hadrian II and John VIII, pursued this goal indicates that we are dealing with a papal strategy, rather than just Nicholas I's tendency to overreach.

Although based on Charlemagne's conquest, this assertive papal policy also shows the Roman bishopric in the process of emancipating itself from the Frankish monarchy, another hallmark of the Latin Middle Ages.

In the period 791–860, Carolingian rulers had played the leading roles in organizing southeastern Europe politically, militarily, and also ecclesiastically. For instance, Charlemagne and his successors had drawn the lines between the jurisdictions of Salzburg and Aquileia, not the pope. From Nicholas I on, the papacy became actively involved. Despite their efforts, Carolingian political and Roman ecclesiastical authorities failed to incorporate distant Bulgaria into the Latin West. Sheltered behind the Iron Gates of the Danube, Boris's Bulgaria was much more difficult to reach by armies from the west than was Rastislav's Moravia. Yet the perseverance and enormous dedication of human and material resources in pursuit of this goal on the part of ninth-century popes are remarkable.

The Bulgars eventually accepted eastern Christianity, yet it was not forced upon them. Byzantine forces failed to occupy Bulgaria, and the eastern Church had to acquiesce to a semi-independent Bulgarian ecclesiastical organization. Meanwhile, in 870 Nicholas's successor Hadrian II established a Pannonian archdiocese independent of Salzburg, Aquileia, and Passau, the sees that Charlemagne had designated to oversee eastern mission efforts. The pope appointed Methodius archbishop of Sirmium to head this ecclesiastical organization; however, the Franks captured and held him incommunicado for three years.[52] Only after Sventibald's military victories did the papacy have enough leverage to insist on the archbishop's release and reinstatement. Even so, the relationship between the Moravian ruler and Methodius developed badly, and, following this archbishop's death in 885, Sventibald incarcerated his disciples, some of whom managed to escape to Bulgaria, where they played a major role in the creation of an independent Bulgarian church that served as a model for Slavic orthodox ecclesiastical structures throughout much of eastern Europe. Eastern orthodoxy continued to survive in the southern corner of the Hungarian kingdom.

In Pannonia, the struggle continued between the papacy and Bavarian bishops for the prerogative of organizing a Latin ecclesiastical infrastructure. In the early years of the tenth century when the Hungarians were settling in *Mitteleuropa*, Archbishop Theotmar of Salzburg drafted a long letter to Pope John IX in which he complained that the pope had sent a delegation of bishops into the land of the Moravians (*Maraui*), who rightfully came under the ecclesiastical jurisdiction of Passau.[53] Although this petition fell on deaf ears, not even the Hungarian conquests diminished Passau's demands for episcopal jurisdiction in the region of the Watergate. At the end of the tenth century, Bishop Pilgrim (971–990) made extravagant claims for the primacy of his see in a series of forgeries, which were matched by demands by his uncle and rival, Frederick of Salzburg.[54] The problem was only solved at the turn of the millennium when Otto III joined with Pope Silvester II to restructure the ecclesiastical situation in *Mitteleuropa*, by creating independent episcopal organizations in Hungary and Poland.[55]

Throughout the tenth century the Byzantine Empire continued to rely on diplomacy rather than its army, which was generally on the defensive against the now Christian Bulgars. In mid-century a significant treatise, the so-called *De administrando imperii*, attributed to Constantine VII (913–959), was compiled. This source, a Byzantine survival manual, focuses on diplomacy, not military strategy and tactics.[56] For example, it informs us that officials subsidized Serbs and Hungarians to hold the Bulgars in check.[57] According to Constantine, the Serbs and Hungarians were situated in approximately the same territory as the earlier Moravian realm of Sventibald. Although the Magyars had occupied most of the Carpathian Basin, Constantine concerns himself only with those Hungarians who had settled around the Watergate, "old" (*megale*) Moravia.

It has been assumed that Byzantium became more aggressive in the Balkans following Constantine's death. While the emperors Nicephorus II Phocas (963–969) and John I Tzimisces (969–976) cultivated reputations as military leaders, both in fact relied heavily on diplomacy, and their conquests on the European side of the Bosporus were ephemeral. Tzimisces did use his army to drive the Rus from the lower Danube, but this action did not represent a change in strategy, for the emperor did not have in mind the systematic conquest and occupation of the Balkans.[58] Byzantium's defensive posture even continued into the reign of Basil II (975–1025), "the Bulgar slayer," whose reign was putatively the "apogee" of the empire. Paul Stephenson recently published a convincing revision of Basil's rule, suggesting that this emperor should henceforth be known as "the peace maker."[59] Basil's reputation has previously rested on a myth that originated approximately a half-century after his death. Although the situation in the eastern Mediterranean and on the steppes north of the Black Sea gave this emperor an unprecedented opportunity to turn his attention to the Balkans, the "real" Basil reluctantly became involved there militarily. When he did intervene, he exercised his influence, not by means of overwhelming military force, but rather by winning over local elites to whom he distributed patronage and on whom he lavished the splendid fruits of Byzantine workshops as diplomatic gifts. For this emperor, like his predecessors, diplomacy was the continuation of war by other means.

Stephenson's revisionism supports his more general thesis concerning the main currents of Byzantine strategy during the so-called middle period (ca. 950–1180). Emperors pursued a consistent defensive strategy in the western peripheral regions of the empire to ensure stability and security, "so that they might continue to control and exploit the productive lands which provisioned the principal cities, most importantly Constantinople."[60] The emperors, their generals, and bureaucrats were also determined to control land and sea communications, the corridors that allowed them to pursue diplomacy, channel commerce, and, when necessary, intervene militarily in the periphery in order to protect the core. Peripheral regions (the mountainous interior of the Balkans, the northern plains along the Danube, and the littoral of the Adriatic) were concerns primarily because of the "stabilizing influence" they exercised. This was a defensive strategy, a viewpoint that challenges George Ostrogorsky's expansionist paradigm.[61]

Stephenson recognizes that fears of the Latin West motivated this defensive grand strategy, which focused on preventing western expansion into a region that included the Frangochorion (Fruska Gora) and the modern Vojvodina as far north as Szeged, the region that I call the Watergate. During the reign of Basil II, the ancient city of Sirmium (now Sremska Mitrovica) became the anchor of this defensive network. Byzantine influence in the region was based primarily on patronage and the support of the eastern orthodox (largely Slavic) population residing near the Watergate, a population dating from the Byzantine missions of the ninth century. Stephenson's interpretation of Byzantine diplomacy in southeastern Europe during the so-called middle period is compelling, but he does not push back the origins of this defensive posture far enough chronologically. It rested ultimately on Byzantine military and diplomatic practices predating Charlemagne's conquest of *Mitteleuropa*.

This essay began with Pirenne's famous dictum linking Islamic expansion to the isolation of the west from the east, the rise of the Carolingians, and the beginnings of the Middle Ages. I then cited Dvornik, who insisted that the intrusions of Avars and Slavs into Illyricum had already divided west from east. Both paradigms posit that forces (barbarians and Muslims) external to the Roman Empire divided the ancient world and ended classical civilization. In the body of the essay I developed the argument that western aggression caused the rupture between east and west. Charlemagne initiated the expansion/making of *Mitteleuropa* by conquering the Avar khaganate. When his forces crossed the Enns River in 791, the Frankish ruler had a conquest strategy in mind to govern and organize *Mitteleuropa* politically and ecclesiastically. The reason for Carolingian successes lay in Charles's ability to call up and support large armies (heavy cavalry, light cavalry, infantry, siege engineers, and so on.) year after year, employing an offensive strategic doctrine of overwhelming force. In *Mitteleuropa*, Carolingian tactical operations focused on controlling the logistically important Watergate, so that huge invasion arrays could be provisioned. Meanwhile, Carolingian intellectuals pieced together Roman geographical texts to create a conquest ideology. According to Natalia Lozovsky, "Carolingian ideology represented all lands and peoples conquered by the Romans as the rightful legacy of the Christian Frankish empire."[62]

In contrast, Byzantium took over a different aspect of the Roman heritage: the defensive military strategy of the late empire designed primarily to protect the capital. Its tactics were defense-in-depth and the use of diplomacy to play barbarians off against one another. Through ceremonies, gifts, trade, and subsidies, the empire exercised influence, but rarely did it use military force for conquests. Furthermore, although numerous artifacts offer testimony that Christianity did not completely disappear in *Mitteleuropa*, after 600, the Byzantines made no determined effort to Christianize the region by establishing an organized church with an episcopal hierarchy. The massive Frankish intrusion into *Mitteleuropa*, however, forced a reluctant Byzantium to respond slowly in the course of the ninth and tenth centuries, and eventually to transplant its civilization beyond the pale. Byzantium responded to the Carolingian challenge with diplomacy rather than by military force.

Centuries before the beginnings of the Spanish *Reconquista*, the Norman conquest of southern Italy, the origins of the Crusades, Anglo-Norman attempts to subdue the Celtic fringe, and the expansion of the Teutonic knights along the Baltic littoral, Charlemagne and his descendants began, in *Mitteleuropa*, the process of transforming the world in the image of the west. European expansion started with Charlemagne. Throughout the Middle Ages it was taken for granted that the great man had set this process in motion.[63] Although late medieval tales of his military exploits overseas are legends (implanted memories, to use Johannes Fried's terminology) the overall impression they convey is correct.[64] If we equate the expansion of Europe with the making of Europe, then Charlemagne was indeed *pater Europae* (father of Europe).

At the end of the reigns of Henry II (1024) in the west and Basil II (1025) in the east, two empires claiming to be Roman eyed one another suspiciously over a huge geographic space. By then each had extended its influence well beyond *Mitteleuropa* and greatly enlarged Christendom in the process. The formation of new realms such as Hungary, Poland, and Russia that stretched from the Black Sea and the Balkan Mountains to the Baltic marks a major transition in world historical terms, for these polities became buffers protecting Latin Christendom from incursions on the part of peoples living further east. As Nora Berend has recently pointed out, "Hungary developed its own frontier ideology in the thirteenth century, centering on the claim that the kingdom was essential to the defence of Christendom."[65] After 1025 the Latin West, its Inner-Eurasian frontier secure, began expanding in other directions. By the same token, Basil II secured his northwestern frontier by reluctantly extending Byzantium's sphere of interest to the Watergate. It is thus strictly correct to say that without Charlemagne, Basil II is inconceivable.

Notes

1. Richard Hodges and David Whitehouse, *Mohammed, Charlemagne & The Origins of Europe: Archaeology and the Pirenne Thesis* (London: Duckworth, 1983), p. 4.

2. Francis Dvornik, *The Slavs, Their Early History and Civilization* (New Brunswick: Rutgers University Press, 1962), pp. 44–45.

3. Robert I. Moore, *First European Revolution, c. 970–1215* (Oxford: Blackwell, 2000).

4. Richard E. Sullivan, "The Carolingian Age: Reflections on Its Place in the History of the Middle Ages," *Speculum* 6 (1989): 267–308.

5. *Late Antiquity: A Guide to the Postclassical World*, ed. G.W. Bowersock, Peter Brown, and Oleg Grabar (Cambridge, MA: The Belknap Press of Harvard University, 1999), p. ix.

6. Robert Bartlett, *The Making of Europe: Conquest, Colonization and Cultural Change, 950–1350* (Princeton: Princeton University Press, 1993).

7. For example, John France, *The Crusades and the Expansion of Catholic Christendom, 1000–1714* (London: Routledge, 2005); Tomaz Mastnak, *Crusading Peace: Christendom, the Muslim World, and Western Political Order* (Berkeley: University of California Press, 2002). However, Michael Mitterauer, *Warum Europa? Mittelalterliche Grundlagen eines Sonderwegs* (Munich: C.H. Beck, 2003), believes the expansion that "made" Europe began in the Carolingian era.

8. Bernard S. Bachrach, *Early Carolingian Warfare: Prelude to Empire* (Philadelphia: University of Pennsylvania Press, 2003); Bernard S. Bachrach and Charles R. Bowlus, "Heerwesen," *Reallexikon der Germanischen Altertumskunde*, 28 vols. (Berlin: Walter de Gruyter, 2001), 14: 120–36.

9. Bernard S. Bachrach, "Pirenne and Charlemagne," in *After Rome's Fall: Narrators and Sources of Early Medieval History: Essays presented to Walter Goffart*, ed. Alexander Murray (Toronto: Toronto University Press, 1998), pp. 214–31.

10. Charles R. Bowlus, *Franks, Moravians, and Magyars: The Struggle for the Middle Danube, 788–907* (Philadelphia: University of Pennsylvania Press, 1995).

11. Walter Kaegi, *Heraclius: Emperor of Byzantium* (Cambridge, UK: Cambridge University Press, 2003).

12. Edward N. Luttwak, *The Grand Strategy of the Roman Empire: From the First Century A.D. to the Third* (Baltimore: John Hopkins University Press, 1976).

13. John F. Haldon, *Byzantium in the Seventh Century: The Transformation of a Culture* (Cambridge, UK: Cambridge University Press, 1990), p. 444.

14. *Die Awaren am Rand der byzantinischen Welt: Studien zu Diplomatie, Handel und Technologietransfer im Frühmittelalter*, ed. Falco Daim (Innsbruck: Wagner, 2000).

15. Florin Curta, *The Making of the Slavs: History and Archaeology of the Lower Danube Region, c. 500–700 A.D.* (Cambridge, UK: Cambridge University Press, 2001).

16. For contrasting views of relations with the Avars, see Attila Kiss, "Die 'barbarischen' Könige des 4.–7. Jahrhunderts im Karpatenbecken als Verbündete des römischen bzw. byzantinischen Reiches," *Archaeologica Hungarica* 15 (1991): 115–28; Heinz Winter, "Die byzantinischen Fundmünzen aus dem österreichischen Bereich der Awaria," in Daim, *Die Awaren am Rand*, pp. 45–66.

17. Despite the claims of Averil Cameron, "Remaking the Past," in Bowersock et al., *Late Antiquity*, p. 16 [1–21], there is no reason to believe that the Byzantine state made concerted efforts to convert Slavs and Bulgars.

18. Joseph Hergenröther, *Photius, Patriarch von Constantinopel: Sein Leben, seine Schriften und das griechische Schisma*, 3 vols. (Regensburg: Georg Joseph Manz, 1867–1869), 1 (1867): 237.

19. Archaeologists are currently skeptical concerning what artifacts tell us about the development of ethnicities. See Sebastian Brather, "Ethnic Identities as Constructions of Archaeology: The Case of the *Alemanni*," in *On Barbarian Identity: Critical Approaches to Ethnicity in the Early Middle Ages*, ed. Andrew Gillett (Turnhout: Brepols, 2002), pp. 149–75; and the essay by Genevra Kornbluth, chapter 2 in this volume.

20. Rosamond McKitterick, *History and Memory in the Carolingian World* (Cambridge, UK: University of Cambridge Press, 2004), pp. 82–83.

21. "...quod ille et animosius quam cetera, et longe maiori apparatu administravit": Einhard, *Vita Karoli Magni*, ed. G. Waitz, MGH, SSrG 25 (Hannover: Hahn, 1911), pp. 15–16.

22. Rudolf Schieffer, "Karl der Große–Intentionen und Wirkungen," in *Karl der Große und das Erbe der Kulturen*, ed. F.-R. Erkens (Berlin: Akademie Verlag, 2001), p. 7 [3–14]; he bases his statement on Timothy Reuter, "Plunder and Tribute in the Carolingian Empire," *Transactions of the Royal Historical Society*, 5th ser., 35 (1985): 75–94. Cf. Charles R. Bowlus, "Carolingian Military Hegemony in the Carpathian Basin, 791–907," in Erkens, *Karl*, pp. 152–58.

23. Dieter Hägermann, *Karl der Große: Herrscher des Abendlandes* (Berlin: Propyläen, 2000), pp. 354–58.

24. "...utramque Pannoniam, et adpositam in altera Danubii ripa Datiam, Histriam, quoque et Liburniam atque Dalmatiam, exceptis maritimis civitatibus, quas ob amicitiam et iunctum cum eo foedus

Constantinopolitanum imperatorem habere permisit": Einhard, *Vita Karoli*, p. 18.

25. Paulinus, *De Herico duce*, in Einhard, *Vita Karoli: Appendix*, pp. 44–45; see Harald Krahwinkler, *Friaul im Frühmittelalter: Geschichte einer Region vom Ende des fünften bis zum Ende des zehnten Jahrhunderts* (Vienna: Böhlau, 1992), pp. 152–58.

26. Vladimir Georgiev, "Theiß, Temes, Maros, Szamos (Herkunft und Bildung)," *Beiträge zur Namenforschung* 12 (1961): 87–95.

27. Paulinus, *De Herico duce*, p. 45, stanza 7.

28. *Conventus episcoporum ad ripas Danubii*, ed. Albert Werminghoff, MGH, *Conc.* 2.2 (Hannover: Hahn, 1956), pp. 172–78.

29. Charles R. Bowlus, "Italia, Bavaria, Avaria: The Grand Strategy behind Charlemagne's *Renovatio Imperii* in the West," *The Journal of Medieval Military History* 1 (2002): 43–61.

30. Bowlus, *Franks*, pp. 2–5.

31. Bowlus, *Franks*, pp. 26–29, 48–53, 123–33, 227–28.

32. Warren Treadgold, *The Byzantine Revival, 780–842* (Stanford: Stanford University Press, 1988).

33. Krahwinkler, *Friaul*, especially pp. 119–92, 270–300.

34. Bowlus, *Franks*, pp. 60–71.

35. Michael McCormick, *Origins of the European Economy: Communications and Commerce* (Cambridge, UK: Cambridge University Press, 2001), pp. 255–61.

36. Treadgold, *Byzantine Revival*, pp. 347–49.

37. Bowlus, *Franks*, pp. 91–98; Krahwinkler, *Friaul*, pp. 192–98. For the Timocian Slavs, *Annales regni Francorum*, ed. Friedrich Kurze, MGH SSrG 6 (Hannover: Hahn, 1891), pp. 150–51.

38. Martin Eggers, *Das 'Großmährische Reich'–Realität oder Fiktion? Eine Neuinterpretation der Quellen zur Geschichte des mittleren Donauraumes im 9. Jahrhundert* (Stuttgart: Hiersemann, 1995), pp. 296–98.

39. Bowlus, *Franks*, pp. 103–07; Eggers, *Großmährische Reich*, pp. 250–60.

40. For example, Eggers, *Das Großmährische Reich*, one of his many studies on the Moravian problem. Also see Imre Boba, *Moravia's History Reconsidered: A Reinterpretation of Medieval Sources* (The Hague: Nijhoff, 1971); Sergio Bonazza, "Auseinandersetzung über die Grossmährenfrage zwischen Dobrovsky und Kopitar," *Contributi italiani al XIII Congresso internazionale degli Slavisti (15–21 Agosto, 2003)*, ed. A. Alberti, M. Garzaniti, and S. Garzonio (Pisa: Associazione Italiana degli Slavisti, 2003), pp. 627–44; cf. Eric J. Goldberg, *The Struggle for Empire: Kingship and Conflict Under Louis the German, 817–876* (Ithaca, NY: Cornell University Press, 2006); and Eric J. Goldberg, "Ludwig der Deutsche und Mähren: Eine Studie zu karolingischen Grenzkriegen im Osten," in *Ludwig der Deutsche und seine Zeit*, ed. W. Hartmann (Darmstadt: Wissenschaftliche Buchgesellschaft, 2004), pp. 67–94.

41. Eggers, *Großmährische Reich*, pp. 181–243.

42. Bowlus, *Franks*, pp. 235–67.
43. Charles R. Bowlus, *The Battle of Lechfeld and Its Aftermath, August 955: The End of the Age of Migrations in the Latin West* (Aldershot: Ashgate, 2006), pp. 84–88.
44. Gábor Varga, *Ungarn und das Reich vom 10. bis zum 13. Jahrhundert: Das Herrscherhaus der Árpáden zwischen Anlehnung und Emanzipation* (Munich: Ungarisches Institut, 2003), pp. 41–82.
45. Martin Eggers, *Das Erzbistum des Method: Lage, Wirkung und Nachleben der kyrillomethodianischen Mission* (Munich: Sagner, 1996), pp. 17–20.
46. Nickolaos Trunte, "Die römische Mission Konstantinus des Philosophen," *Preslavska knizovna skola* 7 (2004): 256–93; Nicholaos Trunte, "*In quadam civitates, quae lingua gentis illius Dowina dicitur*: Versuch einer Neulokalisierung," *Zeitschrift für slavische Philologie* 61 (2002): 1–24.
47. Martin Eggers and Charles R. Bowlus, "863/864—eine 'internationale' Konfrontation in Südosteuropa," *Südost-Forschungen* 59/60 (2000/2001): 14–33; Richard Sullivan, "Khan Boris and the Conversion of Bulgaria: A Case Study of the Impact of Christianity on a Barbarian Society," *Studies in Medieval and Renaissance History* 3 (1966): 53–141; Francis Dvornik, *The Photian Schism: History and Legend* (Cambridge, UK: Cambridge University Press, 1948), pp. 91–237; Francis Dvornik, *Byzantine Missions among the Slavs: SS. Constantine-Cyril and Methodius* (New Brunswick: Rutgers University Press, 1970), pp. 230–58.
48. Nicholas I, *Ep.* 99, ed. E. Perels, MGH Epp 6, Epp Karolini Aevi 4 (Hannover: Weidmann, 1925), pp. 568–600.
49. See *Nicolai I. papae epistolae*, ed. E. Perels, MGH Epp 6, Epp Karolini Aevi 4 (Hannover: Weidmann, 1925), pp. 433–610 [257–690]; *Hadriani II. papae epistolae*, ed. E. Perels, MGH Epp 6, pp. 747–62 [691–765]; *Registrum Iohannis VIII. papae*, ed. E. Caspar, MGH Epp 7, Epp Karolini Aevi 5 (Hannover: Weidmann, 1928), pp. 121–260 [1–272]. Also see *Epistolae ad res orientales spectantes*, ed. E. Caspar and G. Laehr, MGH Epp 7, pp. 371–84.
50. Nicholas I, *Ep.* 82, MGH Epp 6, Epp Karolini Aevi 4: 438.
51. Dvornik, *Photian Schism*, p. 94.
52. Eggers, *Erzbistum des Method*.
53. Fritz Losek, *Die Conversio Bagoariorum et Carantanorum und der Brief des Erzbischofs Theotmar von Salzburg* (Hannover: Hahn, 1997), pp. 139–57.
54. Martin Eggers, "Die Slawenmission Passaus: Bischof Pilgrim und die Lorcher Fälschungen," *Südost-Forschungen* 57 (1998): 13–36; Charles R. Bowlus, "Archbishop Theotmar of Salzburg's Letter to Pope John IX: A Forgery of Bishop Pilgrim of Passau?" *Südost-Forschungen* 57 (1998): 1–11.
55. Johannes Fried, *Otto III. und Boleslaw Chrobry: Das Widmungsbild des Aachener Evangeliars, der 'Akt von Gnesen' und das frühe polnische und ungarische Königtum*, 2nd ed. (Stuttgart: Steiner, 2001); Varga, *Ungarn*, pp. 65–82.

56. Constantine Porphyrogenitus, *De administrando imperio*, ed. Guyla Moravcsik, trans. R. Jenkins, 2nd ed. (Washington, DC: Dumbarton Oaks, 1967).

57. Constantine Porphyrogenitus, *De administrando imperio* 32, 40, pp. 152–61, 174–79.

58. Paul Stephenson, *Byzantium's Balkan Frontier: A Political Study of the Northern Balkans, 900–1204* (Cambridge, UK: Cambridge University Press, 2000), pp. 51–55.

59. Paul Stephenson, *The Legend of Basil the Bulgar-Slayer* (Cambridge, UK: Cambridge University Press, 2003).

60. Stephenson, "Byzantium's Balkan Frontier, 900–1204: A Political Overview," *Byzantium and the North: Acta Byzantina Fennica* 10 (1999–2000): 167 [153–67].

61. George Ostrogorsky, *History of the Byzantine State*, trans. Joan Hussey (Oxford: Oxford University Press, 1963).

62. Natalia Lozovsky, "Roman Geography in the Carolingian Empire," *Speculum* 81 (2006): 354 [325–64].

63. Nikolas Jaspert, "Von Karl dem Großen bis Kaiser Wilhelm: Die Erinnerung an vermeintliche und tatsächliche Kreuzüge in Mittelalter und Moderne," in *Konfrontation der Kulturen? Saladin und die Kreuzfahrer*, ed. H. Gaube, B. Schneidmüller, and S. Weinfurter (Mainz: Philipp von Zabern, 2005), pp. 136–59.

64. Johannes Fried, *Der Schleier der Erinnerung: Grundzüge einer historischen Memorik* (Munich: C.H. Beck, 2004), pp. 153–71, 252–55.

65. Nora Berend, *At the Gate of Christendom: Jews, Muslims and 'Pagans' in Medieval Hungary, c. 1000–c. 1300* (Cambridge, UK: Cambridge University Press, 2001), p. 270.

CHAPTER 12

PERIOD TROUBLE: THE
IMPOSSIBILITY OF TEACHING
FEMINIST MEDIEVAL HISTORY

Lisa M. Bitel

Critique of linear narrative for teaching medieval women's history, proposing instead a scheme grounded in the kabbalistic concept of ordering the world by gathering dispersed fragments of divinity.

Thirty years ago, historian Joan Kelly Gadol asked a now-celebrated historiographical question: Did women have a Renaissance? Kelly answered negatively, arguing that major intellectual and cultural changes of the fourteenth and fifteenth centuries had happened only for men.[1] She implied further that men had effectively denied women full participation in the major developments of western history. Since then, three decades of historiographical response have helped historians rethink women's participation in every period of the European past. Some scholars have pointed out the exceptional women who took part in and even helped direct mainstream trends and events. Others have responded to Kelly with a discrete history of mothers, wives, workers, servants, and other females who dwelt beyond the direct influence of easily defined political events or intellectual and artistic movements.[2]

Kelly's question and historians' responses have aimed to revise traditional timelines. Yet both traditional periodization and feminist reperiodizing schemes depend on the idea of historical periods joined in sequence. Historical narrative posits purposeful human development from an always inferior past to the salvation of a wiser future. In a similar way, feminist critiques of traditional textbook periodization assume a political evolution from a patriarchal past to a more gender symmetrical society.[3] In a parallel progression, the once-sexist historiographical canon has given way to an increasingly gender-sensitive understanding of the past, thus enabling scholars such as Kelly to pose critical questions. But Kelly and her critics have failed to acknowledge that the historical model of teleology is flawed. For one thing, teleology is impossible to prove since its goal is an unknowable future—we still await the Second Coming and gender symmetry. For another thing, historians continue to haggle over the definitions and boundaries of historical periods. Medievalists have long been annoyed at their imprisonment between Antiquity and Renaissance. One medievalist has suggested that we do away with periods entirely; instead of asking Joan Kelly's question, we should wonder whether anyone had or believes in a Renaissance.[4] At the same time, feminist historians lack practical alternatives for organizing courses, textbooks, curricula, standardized tests, or even professional associations and related historical journals.

If historical periods were governed by some other principle besides succession, they might be more useful to feminist critics. Hence, I suggest an interim consciousness-raising exercise aimed at destabilizing the teleology underlying both traditional periodization and feminist reperiodization. Such an exercise requires varying the pace of historical narratives and introducing an ethical impetus for understanding historical events. By directly addressing the philosophical problems of teleology in the classroom through lecture, discussion, and collective performance, historians might introduce students to completely different concepts of time's movement acquired outside normative western historical tradition. Any non-messianic, non-hegemonic ontology would serve to replace the Christian teleology inherent in familiar history: an animist concept of truth housed in the physical environment, or an Osiran death and rebirth cycle, or a Zen concentration on essentials. In this essay, however, I propose to use the kabbalistic concept of *tikkun olam* or ordering the world by gathering up fragments of dispersed divinity.[5] The goal of this exercise is to counter exclusionary teleological historical frameworks developed in the largely Christian, male academy, thus to practice feminist history and also influence the operations of gender in our academic present.

More than twenty years ago, in the first issue of *Speculum* (America's premier journal of medieval studies) ever devoted to women, Allen Frantzen already argued that feminist scholarship was over. According to Frantzen, feminists had successfully forced most medievalists, first, to realize the lack of women's participation in traditional historical thinking, then to include women, and, finally, to realize that women were not enough. When women are not enough, he suggested, we must turn back to the study of men. Gender systems include more than one gender, thus gender historians cannot study one without the other(s).[6] At a moment when mainstream medievalist scholarship had just acknowledged the importance of including women in the past, some medievalists interested in gender issues were already abandoning the study of women.

Frantzen's mischievous declaration of masculine independence was an early warning about the effects of gendering medieval history too quickly. Even when medievalists wield the constructs of gender and masculinity in nuanced ways, it is still shockingly easy to focus on men. In the largely male-authored and male-oriented texts of the Middle Ages, as in medieval historiography, there will never be enough women. The nature of the evidence and our methodologies too easily assign historical topics according to gender. Kings, Vikings, crusades, knights, universities, laws, philosophy, theology, and the mind are masculine; mysticism, heresy, music, love, sex, the body, feminine. The dichotomy of gender also helps naturalize false historical dichotomies of male/female, as well as Straight/Gay, European/not European, and Christian/Unchristian (Jew, Muslim, heretic, pagan). Even studies of queerness in the medieval past coincide in dismaying numbers with studies of masculinity, whereas feminist examinations of medieval topics are too often heterosexist.[7]

The infusion of gender has not always helped the cause of feminist pedagogy, perhaps because academics, like the general public, tend to conflate the study of gender with the study of sexuality, and feminism with queer studies.[8] Furthermore, Vivian May notes that "even though Women's Studies has its roots in constructivist, liberatory approaches to learning and social change, it is simultaneously embedded in the academy, which functions according to disciplinary divisions and institutional structures shaped by rationalist definitions of knowledge and the knower."[9] The debate about the naming and content of academic programs—Women's Studies, Gender Studies, Feminist Studies, or combinations of these—raged through the 1990s.[10] For many programs, the study of gender was a strategy for salvation in response to student demand and administrative pressure to gain majors, as well as a reaction to perceived theoretical developments. The trend toward gender studies also coincided with the backlash against feminism and the renewal of right-wing social policies in America.[11] Whatever the inspiration, the result has been to shift the focus of teachers and students from the politically motivated feminist study of women to the study of gender and sexuality.[12]

Applying the lens of gender to history makes questions like that of Joan Kelly irrelevant, because historians no longer need to identify women's experiences or locate them on existing historical timelines. In a 1996 forum on "gendering the history survey," published in the American Historical Association's *Perspectives*, participants collectively assumed that historians had, in the words of one, "moved well beyond the stage where women's history was introduced, rather awkwardly, in an occasional special lecture." Panelists suggested that history teachers focus instead on "systematic conceptual structure" and the "interactions of women and men."[13] One panelist recounted the evolution of her American survey class. Originally, she had "included material about women, African Americans, and working-class people into almost every class period." But her students responded, "Why has the most interesting history been kept from us?" Appalled by such a reaction to her inclusive narrative, she restructured the course to include a series of debates articulating rival historical positions on such issues as slavery and suffrage. In this relativist approach, all narratives became equally valid, including the cranky narrative of ignorant, biased students trained to prefer traditional political histories—what Bonnie Smith has labeled "men and facts."[14]

The awkwardness of the occasional lecture on women—the intrusiveness of Chick Week—seems preferable to the false objectivity of debates about misogyny, racism, and colonialism. Yet surprisingly few historians are willing to suggest to students that exclusionary historical narratives are wrong and bad. The American academy, as historian Philippa Levine has pointed out, has not delivered on the ideal of pluralism. Its diverse opinions and tolerant perspectives work, as she has put it, "to impose a particular western logic . . . couched in a language of natural rights and utterly indebted to the work of a small group of eighteenth-century European philosophers themselves shaped by the alleged cradle of western thought, ancient Greek philosophy." According to Levine, nineteenth-century builders of our academic curricula institutionalized this particular set of historical knowledges, which still shape the discipline of history.[15] Women can disappear into postfeminist, gender-neutral history the way they used to disappear within heterosexist social scientific studies of kinship, marriage, children, and everyday life. This sort of shift has happened before; once mainstream analysis opened to peasants, laborers, and citizens of non-western cultures, formal Marxist methodology largely disappeared from published historiography.

In response to "objective" history, the brusque interruption of historical narrative with a woman-focused topic may be a useful, old-fashioned tool. Meaningful history in the classroom can be made of striking but artificial juxtapositions: the tender lyric of a poet whose lover has gone off on crusade, set against a Hebrew chronicle of mothers massacred at Speyer; or the diploma of a corrupt papal bureaucracy contrasted with stories of cloistered women mystics. It is useful to set women's unique experiences in conscious comparison to the generalizing effects of gender-neutral history. As the biblical scholar, Esther Fuchs has put it, "In a lopsided world where social, economic, and discursive male hegemony continues to thrive, whose interests are served by the dream of gender neutrality?"[16] It is crucial to remind ourselves of women's diverse experiences of maltreatment, injustice, and subordination, including women's subordination of other women.[17] Feminist histories have typically been driven by a shared political anger at historical evils, a perceived need for justice, and ethical stances opposed to women's continuing subordination. This kind of history is not aimed, teleologically, at arriving in the present, but at changing it. Gender-neutral history too easily forgives the historical evils of sexism and misogyny, just as colorblind history refuses to oppose racism.[18]

So what does all this mean for medievalists seeking to redefine the Middle Ages? The lens of gender is no adequate substitute for the critical feminist eye. Feminisms are many, but none of them are finished. We can refine our interpretation of women's experience with the concepts of postmodernism, queer theory, and multiple feminisms. We must read as widely as possible in the literatures of injustice—colonialism, racism, heterosexism, and other discourses of oppression—in order to justify our manifold interpretations of women in the past. We should try our best to avoid simpleminded truth claims and essentialist equations of women with a particular sex, gender, body, sexuality, race, class, ethnicity, continent, or culture. In the classroom and in research we must resist replacing the master narrative with a *mater* (mother) narrative. Nonetheless, we have a duty to remind all our students about women in the past, whether students like it or not, and to do so we must contest the metamorphosis of women's history into gender history.

None of this is to deny the importance of scholarship on gender, but rather to question its political value in relation to feminism. The task may seem difficult on anything but a rhetorical level because it requires us to reject the seeming progress of historiography over the last thirty years. The question is: how to destabilize the most insidiously gendered assumption that plagues the practice of history, namely, that the latest interpretation is best? The concept of time's movement and thus of history itself—whether traditionally male-exclusive, woman-focused, purportedly gender-neutral, or more inclusively gendered—undermines effective feminist inquiry into women's past. Teleology drives both history and historiography. No single pedagogical technique can help historians escape the race of time. Only a purposeful combination of strategies and devices can stop history.

Medieval textbooks used to convey thousands of years of events in thin-papered, bible-sized volumes of stories about men. Historians marched briskly through the narrative of the Middle Ages, conquering the past with double-columned pages, subduing the evidence with sub-headings, sidebars, and inserts. Although savvy publishers now offer shorter, brightly illustrated, multicultural surveys, written histories of the Middle Ages must still include certain established topics and follow a particular chronology suitable for the classroom, or no teacher will assign them. Medieval textbooks never leave out Charlemagne or ignore the Crusades. Few historians would risk the confusion of students in an introductory survey class by teaching a non-teleological Middle Ages. High school has already instilled in them an official historical journey through facts and figures from Rome to Renaissance. Although textbook-writers such as Barbara Rosenwein and Judith Bennett have striven credibly to infuse gender concepts into this names-and-dates history, observable occurrences make better textbook material than enduring gender ideologies or women's disenfranchisement.[19] How many chapters can an author spend on spinning and weaving to counter the pages lavished on kingdoms and warfare? How many times in one class can a professor remind students that women constantly strategized around the limitations placed on them by patriarchal laws?

Writers of exclusively women's history have been equally unsuccessful at producing satisfactory textbooks, which, at any rate, end up being assigned as books to parallel and correct traditional texts, or as textbooks for history-of-women classes. One early example, Judith Zinsser and Bonnie Anderson's *A History of Their Own* (first published 1988), tried to negotiate between historical narrative and a different kind of topically organized text, focusing early chapters on attitudes and ideologies regarding women and the realities of women's work.[20] Only after setting out the unchanging did the authors treat political and social events involving women. The book's contents reveal the attention to incidental details, "minor" texts, and a few famous personalities that has long characterized women's historical writing.[21] Surveys such as *A History of Their Own* suggest that women's past does not fit into scientific, teleological history; or, alternatively, that women did not participate in enough recognizable (i.e., political) events to fill a more typically gendered history textbook. By definition, then, the experience of women in the period we call medieval was alternative, that is, outside the movement of time that is inherent in conventional definitions of the Middle Ages; or outside the scientific analysis of texts that is the basis of modern historical practice. Similar problems attend sourcebooks of medieval women's writings, which are usually arranged thematically rather than chronologically.[22] The lack of satisfactory textbooks with coherent narratives sends a clear message to students: Women are not suitable subjects for an introductory survey of the Middle Ages but are only relevant in thematic, elective, or peripheral courses.

So, how to teach medieval history with and through women, while taking advantage of developments in gender history and avoiding the limits of chronological narratives, yet sidestepping the dangers of fragmentation and marginalization? How to let the lessons of gender and feminism inform our shaping of medieval pasts while consciously contesting the categories of "medieval" and "women"? Rather than simply criticizing existing historical pedagogies as we continue to teach and unteach them in the classroom (as with Elizabeth Brown's famous approach to feudalism), I suggest some different performances.[23]

To begin with, any feminist history of the Middle Ages must operate on more than one timeline simultaneously. As Bennett and other historians have shown, women's experiences sometimes moved at a different pace than did the history of women and men together. If we keep in mind the artificiality of the chronological Middle Ages, we can play with temporal movements and chronological divides.[24] Continuities—not timeless continuities, but long, slow changes—characterized women's work in the past.[25] The division of labor, political disenfranchisement, and sexual constraints remained fairly stable during the first Christian millennium. But in the fourth and fifth centuries, demographic decline, redistribution of the population, and Christianization, with its profound effects on gender ideologies, shifted some political and social limits on women. Likewise, the demographic catastrophes of the mid-fourteenth and mid-seventeenth centuries marked shifts with arguably greater effect on more women than can be associated with the cultural changes we call Renaissance or Reformation. So long as we also remind our students that it is the evidence itself, not the interpreters, that compels us to treat women as bodies in a landscape, such a demographic approach balances more traditional frameworks of political events and intellectual development. The scientific data of economy, demography, and environment thus counteract the written evidence produced by medieval writers and challenges the historical specificity usually monopolized by chronology.

We can also substitute other kinds of motion for linearity. For instance, a professor might teach the Middle Ages as a map of movement into, within, and outside of Europe. Women's experience gains measurability in a story of overlapping population movements and individual travels, including the circulation of trade goods, armies, documents, pilgrims, marriage partners, and migrants to the internal and external frontiers of Europe. The story has a momentum comprehensible to students via scientific historical analysis. But it is not simply the tale of movement in a single direction. Patrilocal marriage offers a recurring example of gendered mobility, whereas stories of women on Europe's frontiers in the Iberian *Reconquista* (Reconquest) and Iceland complement the more familiar tales of Vikings, crusaders, mendicants, and merchants.

I believe that most students are happy to re-imagine the past. Multiple chronologies will not trouble students if offered as enhancements, rather than replacements, for traditional timelines. Likewise, students have learned to accept multiple pasts that include traditionally underprivileged groups such as women, peasants, racial and religious minorities, or non-Europeans, as long as they can still study male elites. Herein, though, lurks the danger of pluralist objectivity. Students are ready to accept multiple versions of the past but are never eager to judge. Students prefer putatively neutral facts and objective viewpoints. One student told me that we should not condemn the crusaders who killed Jews in Speyer but we should, instead, try to understand them. Wrong! We should do both. Teachers can use simultaneous histories to draw the line against relativism. We can compare different historical perspectives and denounce, on an ethical basis, those that have supported classism, racism, sexism, or other wrongs.

One way to raise ethical historical consciousness is to practice Gramsci for Girls. On a basic level, the concept of cultural hegemony is useful for destabilizing the naturalness of women's subordination in medieval society and offering ways to think about women's collusion in creating those positions.[26] In the classroom, this means showing students that even if most medieval women were silent, we do not need to rely on medieval men to learn about them. Jo Ann McNamara has demonstrated how to identify moments of women's shared consciousness, when people in a particular society became women-as-a-group.[27] Rather than study all Christian women's reactions to ecclesiastical bureaucracy and its rules, McNamara's book constantly points to the choices available to different groups of women in a variety of historical situations. By identifying the many options for women, McNamara explains that religious women were neither always victims nor always agents, but people who worked with, against, and apart from men in the project of Christianity. Religious women were part of a well-known Christian history that included men, but they also experienced other Christian histories simultaneously.

More explicit talk about consciousness helps students see that all historians judge the past, although they rarely admit it. The historian Gerhard Otto Oexle has argued that both popular and scholarly conceptions of the Middle Ages are derived from our own modernity. We moderns are always congratulating ourselves for getting out of the Middle

Ages, or fearing that—in leaving the medieval behind—we have lost something primitive and good. We have gained penicillin, air travel, women's rights; we have lost religion, family, community. Either way we are defining the medieval in terms of modernity while forgetting that the Middle Ages itself is a product of modernity.[28] Whatever their politics, scholars are always choosing not only how to relate to medieval women and men, but how to relate medieval women to medieval men. Teachers select readings and topics of the course, writers of textbooks reduce and arrange facts, and editors of documentary readers collect passages out of context. These professedly neutral mediations take as profoundly political a stance as any blatantly feminist interpretation. Students must learn to suffer the same crises of conscience in articulating their historical positions as teachers do.[29]

Second-wave and radical feminisms offer pedagogical techniques that may be more effective than lecturing students about multiple chronologies and historical judgment. In particular, feminist expositions of language and social practice may prove useful for awakening students to the problem of the inherently anti-feminist Middle Ages and its relation to dwellers in modernity and postmodernity. Several feminist theorists have suggested that language itself is linear; its formation into logical narratives automatically prevents any genuine understanding of women and women's experience.[30] Similarly, Kathleen Biddick has argued that history as we practice it is a "captivating bundle of supersessionary fantasies about temporality," whose influence comes not only from the meaning of words but also from the very appearance of words on a plotted, printed page.[31] From spoken to printed form, history is made of words arranged in linear order. Whether expressed in numerical data, ethnological description, simultaneous multiple perspectives of particular events, purely visual forms, or explicitly non-narrative multimedia forms, historical analysis cannot escape the linearity of language itself.[32]

Theories of social performance also offer challenges to the march of narrative. Judith Butler has argued that all gender identity is created and maintained, but also potentially threatened, by performance.[33] The play's the thing. How might we play with and thus challenge the gender identity of the Middle Ages? Suppose, for example, a teacher begins the semester with a master narrative about the fall of Rome. She could juxtapose that traditional story with a competing feminist tale of women's attraction to Christianity; the medieval would thus become feminized and the declining ancient world would be gendered as impotently male. Alternatively, a professor might cast lectures as a masculine mode of teaching, explaining how the form necessitates a focus on political events in order to seem authoritative. Meanwhile, in purposely informal discussion groups imitative of second-wave feminist consciousness-raising sessions, students could offer opinions about both canonical and less famous authors from Late Antiquity, such as Perpetua, Jerome, Sulpicius Severus, and Egeria. Then teacher and students together could collectively contest the authority of lectures, textbook, and Christian discourse as a way to begin the course. Or, as a third option, a class might examine texts and images to understand multiplicity in historical representation: How many medieval Europes were there? Where were they? Which ones are we studying? How many masculinities and femininities existed in any given place or medieval subperiod? How did these interrelate? Any of these exercises could help the students gain critical distance from their own assumptions.

The simple feminist tricks suggested here purport to offer improved techniques and more conscientious conclusions. Of course, in making these pedagogic suggestions I, too, am abiding by the hegemony of the classroom, the textbook, the syllabus, and time's arrow. By suggesting better ways to teach medieval history, I am not only suggesting the superiority of one feminist stance—my own—but I am also colluding in the concept of medieval, forerunner of modernity, even as I criticize the established parameters of the Middle Ages. The problem is that even a theoretically informed, multimedia-enhanced, gender-enlightened story, carried out as described above, still operates as a traditional salvific narrative. The goal is better history. All classroom enterprises are focused on a single objective: higher understanding of the medieval past brought by passage through the Middle Ages to the end of the course. Even if the students engaged with me in multiple dramatic techniques for critical deconstruction of the evidence and multiple feminist evaluations of people and events in the past, thus exemplifying consciousness-as-a-group and acknowledging our gendered positions vis-à-vis the linear past, we would remain victims of the same forced teleology that I have been complaining about during this entire essay. Something begins—the group, the reading, the lesson, the semester—and then ends, because the teacher, the university administration, and the structure of education collectively decree the finish. One class ends so that students may take another, more advanced, class.

So long as we live at the far end of history, we cannot avoid privileging ourselves by comparison to our medieval objects of study because we have collectively defined those objects in relation to ourselves within a specific ontological and teleological framework. Even the rejection of reperiodization cannot liberate historians from linearity until we redefine our own temporal position in relation to the so-called medieval past. Just as we play with the boundaries and markers of historical time, so we might experiment with alternative movements of time. Many novelists write nonlinear fiction; recently, historians have begun experimenting with nonlinear expressions of history in electronic publications.[34] Such alternatives need not be less flawed or arbitrary than the traditional western, text-driven, teleological model—they need only be different.

As one way to destabilize linearity, I propose substituting a different philosophical and moral basis for the Christian-inspired teleology of modern historical interpretation. Specifically, I suggest the Jewish theological concept called *tikkun ha-Olam* (roughly translated as "repair the world," from *tikkun*, a biblical term meaning ordering or straightening, and *olam,* the world), derived originally from *halakhah*, traditional law.[35] *Halakhah* challenges linear historical frameworks in several ways. Although Judaism's ancient founding text, Torah, is basically linear in structure, diasporic Jewish interpretation has always insisted on interpreting Torah outside of time. Jewish laws, for instance, elaborated in Talmud and its medieval commentaries offer explications of biblical events that purposefully adapt ancient scripture to contemporary situations. Outside the explicit historicism of the biblical books, the Jewish canon operates on the assumption that time does not always move forward. On the Sabbath and particular holy days, for instance, time becomes sacred space and ordinary temporal change is invalid.[36] In addition, as one modern interpreter of Jewish law maintains, the methods of halakhic interpreters are sympathetic to feminist scholarship simply because both feminists and rabbis have existed historically on the peripheries of power. Both groups are socialized to privilege human communities and individuals over strict rules.[37] Hence, halakhic and feminist strategies are inherently critical of history, teleology, and existing power structures.

Tikkun olam provides an apt model for the impossibility of history. Although rabbis of the Talmudic period used the phrase to mean the observance of law and practice of good deeds (*mitzvot*), medieval Jewish mystics discovered additional explanatory possibilities of *tikkun olam* as a creation myth. Medieval interpretations became part of a compilation of kabbalistic texts from Iberia called the *Zohar,* but *tikkun olam* only became central to kabbalah when Isaac Luria (1534–1572) explained it.[38] Luria told how, at some catastrophic point in timeless creation after God had purposely contracted (*tzimtzum*) and hence left a metaphysically empty space wherein the cosmos might be formed, the essential elements of the cosmos were captured as divine lights in vessels. But—calamity!—the divine emanations could not be contained by material vessels, which shattered. Sparks of divinity trapped in shards of the vessels were scattered throughout the created world. Entities that should have been whole—god, humanity, life, knowledge, time, male, female—divided into binary principles. After creation and throughout time, these opposite entities have always been in tension. As each human travels through the cosmic dialectic that is life, s/he encounters particular sparks. Our job is to gather them again. Only the finished collection of sparks can reunite binary principles, restore the divine, and complete history. The myth of *tikkun olam* offers hope of human reunion with the divine yet suggests no foreseeable end to our task of regathering divine knowledge. Human existence is itself the task; history is not the purpose but the context for our job.[39]

Kabbalistic *tikkun olam* can function as a simple parable, a meditative device, or an inspiration for theology. Furthermore, *tikkun olam* suggests at once a guide for ethical action, a historical model beyond the simple dialectic of gender analysis, and a comprehensive theory of historical interpretation. *Tikkun olam* scripts the reconciliation of past with present and future without privileging particular periods, trends, or individuals. In this script, every day offers another chance to destabilize the binaries of past/present, medieval/modern, male/female. All students of history are able and obliged to join in the task, for no single individual can find all the pieces. Yet each individual who practices history with explicit consciousness of gender, class, race, religion, and other codes for dispossession, oppression, and hurt contributes to the larger historical project. Still, as in the larger metanarrative of kabbalah, the most important truths of the project remain elusive because they are by nature secret. Everyone knows that the past has reality in time, but that past is ultimately inaccessible to historians, just as God's transcendence is both real and unattainable to the mystic.[40] Both historian and mystic face the problem of conveying a truth that is hidden. The paradoxical concept of *tikkun olam* explains why we should continue to search for the unattainable revelation of life in the past.

I have yet to translate this impossible obligation into effective pedagogy, although I have begun the experiment. I remind my students that my voice is but one of many historical authorities that also include the primary sources, modern scholarship, artworks, films and novels, and their own interpretations of historical evidence. Who owns the past, I ask them: Those who study history objectively or those to whom it has some personal meaning? Those who find the Middle Ages romantic, or those who decry its oppressions? I try to help students understand the many ways that we relate individually and collectively to the experiences of individuals and groups at specific points in particular pasts. Doctrinaire objectivism has no place in this task. To paraphrase Rabbi Hillel, if they do not take the past for themselves, who will take it to them? But the personal past has limits, too. If a student reads the past only through her own limited experience, what will she discover?

While I try to teach many viable views of history, I also plead with my students, like an old-time prophet, to judge among those views. Historians are the chosen people: our special burden is not simply to collect the shards of the past but to reconstruct them in a luminous, meaningful whole. The more shards of the past we find, the better chance we have of recreating history. Those who refuse to discriminate among the shards will find no logic in their picture of the past. Those who judge too harshly will never have enough pieces for a complete picture; future generations will find their work biased and simplistic. Finally, we must reveal our reconstruction of the past to future generations of judges via our research and writing. Luria neglected this task. He left his student, Rabbi Chaim Vital, to record and popularize his discoveries. We who lack disciples have a duty to perform our methodological consciousness in the classroom, enact it in syllabi, and write it into authoritative textbooks.

Ultimately kabbalistic Judaism offers no more reliable model for practicing feminist history than the redemptive scheme of Christian teleology. Without an underlying commitment to the spiritual principles of kabbalah, the fable of *tikkun olam* is rudimentary and relentlessly pious. Compared with postmodern methodologies, it is folkloric and flawed. For most casual interpreters, the scripture of Judaism, like that of Christianity and many other religions, continues to operate as a linear narrative. It proposes a cosmic chronology that begins with creation— whether in the Garden or the Void—and transcends human history, just as Christianity does. Judaism too has promoted eschatology, although aimed at a different savior and a different end-time. Chaim Vital believed that Luria himself was the savior and that the end of history was near, and one of Luria's own students proposed an even more famous messianic failure, Shabbatai Z'vi.[41]

But *tikkun olam*'s metaphor of timeless scrounging has other heuristic advantages over mainstream salvific teleology. First, simply by substituting another self-conscious model, awkward because of its difference, we make students rethink their relation to the past. They are forced to distance themselves from the dominant supersessionist narratives of medieval history, including the pervasive influence of Christian doctrine on gender ideologies and historical models. Modern Christianities, particularly fundamentalist Protestantisms, preach the increasing momentum of the end of history (a vision derived from, but not the same as, medieval ideas about paradise and the afterlife.)[42] By rejecting the Armageddon-driven chronology developed during the Middle Ages, we show how medieval people and their ideas continue to influence the way that

moderns live their own history. By rejecting the medieval Christian teleology implicit in modern historical narrative, students may be able to
consider other theoretical relations of present to past, such as Biddick's
"passages, thresholds, gaps, intervals, in-betweenness" or Donna
Haraway's interstices.[43]

Another advantage for feminist medievalists is the urgent political
meaning of *tikkun olam*. For Jews of the last half century, the concept of
world healing has become synonymous with social activism.[44] Applied to
the teaching of history and historiography, this means fighting moral
amnesia. We situate our knowledges as admittedly imperfect and consciously derived from particular political, cultural, and religious stances.
We bring these conscious stances and oppositions into the classroom,
explicitly and visibly challenging students to work together to articulate
their own ethical relations to people and events long ago. Our pedagogical mission is to identify bad and good in the past, suggest how to choose
between the two, and encourage students to choose the good—including
feminism—in thoughts and actions. As the liberal Catholic theologian
Rosemary Ruether put it, "For me, feminism itself is a prophetic social
justice ethic."[45]

Finally, the paradox of *tikkun olam* constantly reminds us that the feminist and the medieval are eternally opposing constructs reconcilable only
outside of historical time. The problem is not time's periods and boundaries, but the imbalanced relation of past to present. We cannot give up
on either feminist history or the Middle Ages precisely because of their
troubled relationship. Past and present exist only together. The tension
between feminism and medievalism is exactly what gives meaning to our
work. History teachers need to use any and every critical trick that can
help derail the teleology driving mainstream historical pedagogy. In the
future, a different performance with different tricks may help us teach the
past. For now, while we hurtle through history with the job of feminism
unfinished, let's perform a little period trouble.

Notes

1. Joan Kelly Gadol, "Did Women Have a Renaissance?," in *Becoming Visible:
   Women in European History, ed.* Renata Bridenthal, Claudia Koonz, and
   Susan Mosher Stuard, 2nd ed. (Boston: Houghton Mifflin, 1987), pp.
   175–201. Cf. Marilyn Frye, "The Possibility of Feminist Theory," in
   Theoretical Perspectives on Sexual Difference, ed. Deborah L. Rhode (New
   Haven: Yale University Press, 1990), pp. 174–84.
2. *Rewriting the Renaissance: The Discourses of Sexual Difference in Early Modern
   Europe,* ed. Margaret W. Ferguson, Maureen Quilligan, and Nancy

J. Vickers (Chicago: University of Chicago Press, 1986); Judith Bennett, "Feminism and History," *Gender & History* 1 (1989): 252–53; *Sisters and Workers in the Middle Ages*, ed. Judith Bennett et al. (Chicago: University of Chicago Press, 1989).

3. Some classic feminist interpretations of world history posit an original pre-patriarchal or even matriarchal situation prior to patriarchy. See, for example, Friedrich Engels, *The Origin of the Family, Private Property, and the State* (New York: Pathfinder Press, 1972), pp. 120–21; Gerda Lerner, *The Creation of Patriarchy* (New York: Oxford University Press, 1986); Rhiane Eisler, *The Chalice and the Blade: Our History, Our Future* (San Francisco: Harper, 1988).

4. Felice Lifshitz, "Differences, (Dis)appearances and the Disruption of the Straight Telos: Medievalology as a History of Gender," in *Mediävistik im 21. Jahrhundert: Stand und Perspektiven*, ed. Jörg Jarnut and Hans-Werner Goetz (Munich: Wilhelm Fink Verlag, 2003), p. 304 [295–312].

5. Many scholars have suggested similar destabilizing techniques. Kathleen Biddick called for "a nonfoundational medieval studies that articulates rather than re-presents the Middle Ages as a historical category," in *The Shock of Medievalism* (Durham, NC: Duke University Press, 1998) p. 85. Felice Lifshitz pointed out the "medieval dystopia" posited by Western Civilization survey courses, in "Differences, (Dis)appearances and the Disruption of the Straight Telos," pp. 295–312. Jo Ann McNamara argued for a long millennium including Late Antiquity and the early Middle Ages, in "Women and Power Through the Family Revisited," in *Gendering the Master Narrative: Women and Power in the Middle Ages*, ed. Mary C. Erler and Maryanne Kowaleski (Ithaca: Cornell University Press, 2003), pp. 17–30. Timothy Reuter suggested a concept of the Middle Ages based on informed consensus, in "Medieval: Another Tyrannous Construct?," *The Medieval History Journal* 1 (1998): 25–45.

6. Alan Frantzen, "When Women Aren't Enough," *Speculum* 68 (1993): 445–71; repr. in *Studying Medieval Women: Sex, Gender, Feminism*, ed. Nancy F. Partner (Cambridge, MA: Medieval Academy of America, 1993), pp. 143–70. See also Elizabeth Clark, "Women, Gender and the Study of Christian History," *Church History* 70 (2001): 395 [395–426].

7. Kathleen Biddick, *The Typological Imaginary: Circumcision, Technology, History* (Philadelphia: University of Pennsylvania Press, 2003); but also see the Introduction to *Queering the Middle Ages*, ed. Glenn Burger and Steven F. Kruger (Minneapolis: University of Minnesota Press, 2001). See the articles collected in *Medieval Feminist Forum* 36 (Fall 2003); Jane Flax, "Postmodernism and Gender Relations in Feminist Theory," in *Feminism/ Postmodernism*, ed. Linda J. Nicholson (New York: Routledge, 1990), pp. 39–62; *Medieval Masculinities: Regarding Men in the Middle Ages*, ed. Clare Lees (Minneapolis: University of Minnesota Press, 1994); *Becoming Male in the Middle Ages*, ed. Jeffrey Jerome Cohen and Bonnie Wheeler (New York: Palgrave, 2000). For an elegant understanding of gender via

masculinity, see Ruth Mazo Karras, *From Boys to Men: Formations of Masculinity in Late Medieval Europe* (Philadelphia: University of Pennsylvania Press, 2003).

8. Joan W. Scott, "Some More Reflections on Gender and Politics," in Joan W. Scott, *Gender and the Politics of History*, rev. ed. (New York: Columbia University Press, 1999), pp. 199–222; Madeline Caviness, *Reframing Medieval Art: Differences, Margins, Boundaries* (Tufts University Electronic Book, 2001), Chapter 4: "Edging Out Difference: Revisiting the Margins as a Post Modern Project" <http://nils.lib.tufts.edu/Caviness>.

9. Vivian May, "Disciplinary Desires and Undisciplined Daughters: Negotiating the Politics of a Women's Studies Doctoral Education," *National Women's Studies Association Journal* 14 (2002): 134–59.

10. For lists of relevant programs, see <http://research.umbc.edu/~korenman/wmst/programs.html> and <http://www.artemisguide.com>. For the 1990s debate, see <http://research.umbc.edu/~korenman/wmst/womvs-gen.html> and Tania Modleski, *Feminism without Women: Culture and Criticism in a Postfeminist Age* (New York: Routledge, 1991).

11. Bennett, "Feminism and History," 252–53.

12. Karen S. Rowan, "Women's Studies, the Institution, and Interdisciplinarity: The Women's Studies Department at the University of Maryland," *On Campus With Women* 32 (Spring/Summer 2003), at: <http://www.aacu.org/ocww/volume32_3/feature.cfm?section=3>.

13. Kathi L. Kern, Tracey Rizzo, Judith P. Zinsser, and Peter N. Stearns, "Teaching Innovations: Gendering the History Survey Course," *Perspectives* (May–June, 1996), at <http://www.historians.org/teaching/articles/htm>.

14. Bonnie Smith, *The Gender of History: Men, Women and Historical Practice* (Cambridge, MA: Harvard University Press, 1998), pp. 130–56.

15. Philippa Levine, "Peripheries and Centers: The Challenge of the Interdisciplinary," paper presented at 2003 University of Utah Humanities Graduate Conference. Many thanks to Professor Levine for sharing this paper with me.

16. Esther Fuchs, "Men in Biblical Feminist Scholarship," *Journal of Feminist Studies in Religion* 19 (2003): 103 [93–114].

17. Joan Hoff, "Gender as a Postmodern Category of Paralysis," *Women's History Review* 3 (1994): 149–68; Robert Scholes, *Protocols of Reading* (New Haven: Yale University Press, 1989), pp. 93–105; Caroline Ramazanoglu, "Unravelling Postmodern Paralysis: A Response to Joan Hoff," *Women's History Review* 5 (1996): 19–23; Clare Lees and Gillian Overing, eds., *Journal of Medieval and Early Modern Studies* 34.1 (2004).

18. Thomas Hahn, "The Difference the Middle Ages Makes: Color and Race before the Modern World," *Journal of Medieval and Early Modern Studies* 31 (2001): 1–36.

19. Barbara Rosenwein, *A Short History of the Middle Ages* (Peterborough, Ontario: Broadview Press, 2002); C. Warren Hollister and Judith M. Bennett, *Medieval Europe: A Short History* (Boston: McGraw-Hill, 2002).

20. Bonnie S. Anderson and Judith P. Zinnser, *A History of Their Own: Women in Europe from Prehistory to the Present*, 2 vols. (New York: Harper and Row, 1988).

21. Smith, *Gender of History*, pp. 130–56, 202–03.

22. *Women and Writing in Medieval Europe: A Sourcebook*, ed. Carolyne Larrington (New York: Routledge, 1995); *Women's Lives in Medieval Europe: A Sourcebook*, ed. Emily Amt (New York: Routledge, 1993).

23. Elizabeth Brown, "The Tyranny of a Construct: Feudalism and Historians of Medieval Europe," *American Historical Review* 79 (1974): 1063–88.

24. My thanks to discussants on the medfem-l discussion list for tips about playing with timelines in the classroom.

25. Judith M. Bennett, "History that Stands Still: Women's Work in the European Past," *Feminist Studies* 14 (1988): 269–83; Maryanne Kowaleski, "Singlewomen in Medieval and Early Modern Europe: The Demographic Perspective," in *Singlewomen in the European Past 1250–1800*, ed. Judith M. Bennett and Amy M. Froide (Philadelphia: University of Pennsylvania Press, 1999), pp. 38–81.

26. Susanne B. Dietzel and Polly Pagenhart, "Teaching Ideology to Material Girls: Pedagogy in the 'Postfeminist' Classroom," *Feminist Teacher* 9 (1995): 129–36.

27. Jo Ann McNamara, *Sisters in Arms: Catholic Nuns Through Two Millennia* (Cambridge, MA: Harvard University Press, 1996).

28. Otto Gerhard Oexle, "The Middle Ages through Modern Eyes. A Historical Problem," *Transactions of the Royal Historical Society* 6th ser., 9 (1999): 128 [121–42].

29. Caviness, *Reframing Medieval Art, Introduction* <http://nils.lib.tufts.edu/Caviness>.

30. Julia Kristeva, "Stabat Mater," trans. Arthur Goldhammer, *Poetics Today* 6 (1985): 133–52.

31. Biddick, *Typological Imaginary*, p. 2.

32. Robert William Fogel and Stanley L. Engerman, *Time on the Cross: The Economics of American Negro Slavery* (Boston: Little, Brown, 1974); Jacques Le Goff, *Time, Work, and Culture in the Middle Ages*, trans. Arthur Goldhammer (Chicago: University of Chicago Press, 1980); Natalie Zemon Davis, *The Return of Martin Guerre* (Cambridge, MA: Harvard University Press, 1983).

33. Judith Butler, *Gender Trouble: Feminism and the Subversion of Identity* (New York: Routledge, 1999).

34. Philip J. Ethington, "Los Angeles and the Problem of Urban Historical Knowledge," A Multimedia Essay to Accompany the December Issue of *The American Historical Review*, published by the <historycooperative.org> December 2000 <http://cwis.usc.edu/dept/LAS/history/history-lab/LAPUHK/index.html>.

35. Eccl. 1: 5, 7: 13, 12: 9.

36. Abraham Joshua Heschel, *Sabbath: Its Meaning for Modern Man* (New York: Farrar, Straus and Young, 1951), p. 8; Emmanuel Lévinas, *Au-delà du*

verset: lectures et discours talmudiques (Paris: Editions du Minuit, 1982), p. 33.

37. Tikva Frymer-Kensky, "The Feminist Challenge to Halakhah" (copyright 1994, Tikva Frymer-Kensky), at <http://www.law.harvard.edu/programs/Gruss/frymer.html>.

38. *Contemporary Jewish Religious Thought: Original Essays on Critical Concepts, Movements, and Beliefs,* ed. Arthur A. Cohen and Paul Mendes-Flohr (New York: Free Press, 1987), p. 1095; *The Zohar,* 5 vols., trans. Harry Sperling and Maurice Simon (London: The Soncino Press, 1931–1934); Chayyim Vital, *The Tree of Life: Chayyim Vital's Introduction to the Kabbalah of Isaac Luria,* trans. Donald Wilder Menzi and Zwe Padeh (Northvale, NJ: Jason Aronson Inc., 1999).

39. Lawrence Fine, *Physician of the Soul, Healer of the Cosmos: Isaac Luria and His Kabbalistic Fellowship* (Stanford: Stanford University Press, 2003).

40. David Biale, "Gershom Scholem's 'Ten Unhistorical Aphorisms on Kabbalah': Text and Commentary," *Modern Judaism* 5 (1985): 67–93; Lyle M. Eslinger, "Ezekiel 20 and the Metaphor of Historical Teleology: Concepts of Biblical History," *Journal for the Study of Old Testament* 81 (1998): 93–125.

41. Gershom Scholem, *Sabbatai Sevi: The Mystical Messiah, 1626–1676* (Princeton: Princeton University Press, 1973).

42. Caroline Walker Bynum, *Resurrection of the Body in Western Christianity, 200–1336* (New York: Columbia University Press, 1995).

43. Biddick, *Typological Imaginary,* p. 2; Donna J. Haraway, "A Cyborg Manifesto: Science, Technology, and Socialist-Feminism in the Late Twentieth Century," in eadem, *Simians, Cyborgs, and Women: The Reinvention of Nature* (New York: Routledge, 1991), pp. 149–81.

44. Sanford Drob, "The Metaphors of Tikkun Haolam: Their Traditional Meaning and Contemporary Significance," *Jewish Review* 3 (1990).

45. Rosemary Radford Ruether, *Goddesses and the Divine Feminine: A Western Religious History* (Berkeley: University of California Press, 2005), p. 5.

CONTRIBUTORS

Bernard S. Bachrach received his Ph.D. from the University of California at Berkeley in 1966. Professor of History at the University of Minnesota-Twin Cities, he is author of *Early Carolingian Warfare: Prelude to Empire* (Philadelphia: University of Pennsylvania Press, 2001), *Armies and Politics in the Early Medieval West* (Aldershot:Variorum, 1993), and *Fulk Nerra-the Neo Roman Consul: A Political Biography of the Angevin Count (987–1040)* (Berkeley: University of California Press, 1993).

Lisa M. Bitel received her Ph.D. from Harvard University in 1987. She is currently Professor of History and Gender Studies at the University of Southern California and is author of *Isle of the Saints: Monastic Settlement and Christian Community in Early Ireland* (Ithaca: Cornell University Press, 1990), *Land of Women: Tales of Sex and Gender from Early Ireland* (Ithaca: Cornell University Press, 1996), and *Women in Early Medieval Europe* (Cambridge, UK: Cambridge University Press, 2002).

Constance Brittain Bouchard received her Ph.D. from the University of Chicago in 1976. Distinguished Professor of History at the University of Akron, she is the author of *"Those of My Blood": Constructing Noble Families in Medieval Francia* (Philadelphia: University of Pennsylvania Press, 2001), *"Every Valley Shall Be Exalted": The Discourse of Opposites in Twelfth-Century Thought* (Ithaca: Cornell University Press, 2003), and *"Strong of Body, Brave and Noble": Chivalry and Society in Medieval France* (Ithaca: Cornell University Press, 1998).

Charles R. Bowlus received his Ph.D. from the University of Massachusetts in 1973. Emeritus Professor of History as the University of Arkansas-Little Rock, he is author of *Franks, Moravians, and Magyars: The Struggle for the Middle Danube 788–907* (Philadelphia: University of Pennsylvania Press, 1995) and *The Battle of Lechfeld and Its Aftermath, August 955: The End of the Age of Migrations in the Latin West* (Aldershot: Ashgate, 2006).

Celia Chazelle received her Ph.D. from Yale University in 1985. Professor of History at the College of New Jersey, she is the author of *The Crucified God in the Carolingian Era: Theology and the Art of Christ's Passion* (Cambridge, UK: Cambridge University Press, 2001), and the editor of *The Study of the Bible in the Carolingian Era* (with Burton Van Name Edwards) (Turnhout: Brepols, 2003) and *Literacy, Politics, and Artistic Innovation in the Early Medieval West* (Lanham, MD: University Press of America, 1992).

Florin Curta received his Ph.D. from Western Michigan University in 1998. Associate Professor of History and Archaeology at the University of Florida, he is the author of *The Making of the Slavs. History and Archaeology of the Lower Danube Region, c. 500–700* (Cambridge, UK: Cambridge University Press, 2001) and *Southeastern Europe in the Middle Ages, ca. 500– 1250* (Cambridge, UK: Cambridge University Press, 2006).

Jason Glenn received his Ph.D. from the University of California at Berkeley in 1997. He is Associate Professor of History at the University of Southern California, and is the author of *Politics and History in the Tenth Century: The Work and World of Richer of Reims* (Cambridge, UK: Cambridge University Press, 2004).

Genevra Kornbluth received her Ph.D. from the University of North Carolina at Chapel Hill in 1986. An Independent Scholar, she is the author of *Engraved Gems of the Carolingian Empire* (University Park, PA: Penn State University Press, 1995) and *Amulets, Power and Identity in Early Medieval Europe* (forthcoming, Oxford University Press).

Michael Kulikowski received his Ph.D. from the University of Toronto in 1998. Associate Professor of History at the University of Tennessee-Knoxville, he is the author of *Late Roman Spain and Its Cities* (Baltimore: The Johns Hopkins University Press, 2004) and *Rome's Gothic Wars from the Third Century to Alaric* (Cambridge, UK: Cambridge University Press, 2006).

Felice Lifshitz received her Ph.D. from Columbia University in 1988 and is Professor of History and Fellow of the Honors College at Florida International University. She is the author of *The Norman Conquest of Pious Neustria: Historiographic Discourse and Saintly Relics, 684–1090* (Toronto: Pontifical Institute of Mediaeval Studies Press, 1995) and *The Name of the Saint: The Martyrology of Jerome and Access to the Sacred in Francia, 627–827* (Indiana: University of Notre Dame Press, 2005).

Lawrence Nees received his Ph.D. from Harvard University in 1977. Professor of Art History at the University of Delaware, he is the author of *Early Medieval Art* (Oxford: Oxford University Press, 2002), *A Tainted Mantle: Hercules and the Classical Tradition at the Carolingian Court* (Philadelphia: University of Pennsylvania Press, 1991), and *The Gundohinus Gospels* (Cambridge, MA: Medieval Academy of America, 1987).

SELECT BIBLIOGRAPHY

Aitchison, N.B. "The Ulster Cycle: Heroic Image and Historical Reality." *Journal of Medieval History* 13 (1987): 87–116.

Adams, Henry. *Mont St. Michel and Chartres*, intro. and notes Raymond Carney. New York: Penguin Books, 1986.

Alexander, Jonathan J.G. *Insular Manuscripts, 6th to the 9th Century*. London: Harvey Miller, 1978.

Algazi, Gadi, Valentin Groebner, and Bernhard Jussen, eds. *Negotiating the Gift: Pre-Modern Figurations of Exchange*. Veröffentlichungen des Max-Planck-Instituts für Geschichte 188. Göttingen: Vandenhoeck & Ruprecht, 2003.

Allen, Terry. *Five Essays on Islamic Art*. Manchester, MI: Solipsist Press, 1988.

Amory, Patrick. *People and Identity in Ostrogothic Italy, 489–554*. Cambridge, UK: Cambridge University Press, 1997.

Antliff, Mark and Patricia Leighten. "Primitive." In *Critical Terms for Art History*, ed. Robert S. Nelson and Richard Shiff, 170–84. Chicago: University of Chicago Press, 1996.

Bachrach, Bernard S. "Anthropology and Early Medieval History: Some Problems." *Cithara* 34 (1994): 3–10.

————. "Charlemagne and the Carolingian General Staff." *The Journal of Military History* 66 (2002): 313–57.

————. "Charlemagne's Cavalry: Myth and Reality." *Military Affairs* 47 (1983): 181–87. Reprinted in Bernard S. Bachrach, *Armies and Politics in the Early Medieval West*, XIV, 1–20. Aldershot: Variorum, 1993.

————. *Early Carolingian Warfare: Prelude to Empire*. Philadelphia: University of Pennsylvania Press, 2001.

————. "Early Medieval Europe." In *War and Society in the Ancient and Medieval Worlds: Asia, the Mediterranean, Europe, and Mesoamerica*, ed. Kurt Raaflaub and Nathan Rosenstein, 271–307. Cambridge, MA: Center for Hellenic Studies, Trustees for Harvard University, 1999.

————. *A History of the Alans in the West: From Their First Appearance in the Sources of Classical Antiquity through the Early Middle Ages*. Minneapolis: University of Minnesota Press, 1973.

————. *Merovingian Military Organization, 481–751*. Minneapolis: University of Minnesota Press, 1972.

Bachrach, Bernard S. "Pirenne and Charlemagne." *After Rome's Fall: Narrators and Sources of Early Medieval History: Essays Presented to Walter Goffart*, ed. Alexander Murray, 214–31. Toronto: Toronto University Press,1998.

Bachrach, Bernard S. and Charles R. Bowlus. "Heerwesen." In *Reallexikon der Germanischen Altertumskunde*, ed. Heinrich Beck et al., vol. 14: 122–36. Berlin: De Gruyter, 2000.

Backhouse, Janet. *The Lindisfarne Gospels*. Oxford: Phaidon, 1981.

Baer, Eva. *Islamic Ornament*. New York: New York University Press, 1998.

Barford, Paul M. "Identity and Material Culture: Did the Early Slavs Follow the Rules or Did They Make Up Their Own?" *East Central Europe* 31 (2004): 99–123.

Bartlett, Robert. *The Making of Europe: Conquest, Colonization and Cultural Change, 950–1350*. Princeton: Princeton University Press, 1993.

———. "Medieval and Modern Concepts of Race and Ethnicity." *The Journal of Medieval and Early Modern Studies* 31 (2001): 39–56.

Beck, C.W., E. Wilbur, S. Meret, D. Kossove, and K. Kermani. "The Infrared Spectra of Amber and the Identification of Baltic Amber." *Archaeometry* 8 (1965): 96–109.

Beidelman, Thomas O. *The Cool Knife: Imagery of Gender, Sexuality and Moral Education in Kaguru Initiation Ritual*. Washington: Smithsonian Books, 1997.

Bell, Catherine. *Ritual: Perspectives and Dimensions*. New York: Oxford University Press, 1997.

Bennett, Judith M. "Feminism and History." *Gender & History* 1 (1989): 251–72.

———. "History that Stands Still: Women's Work in the European Past." *Feminist Studies* 14 (1988): 269–83.

Bennett, Judith M., Elizabeth A. Clark, Jean F. O'Barr, and B. Anne Vilen, eds. *Sisters and Workers in the Middle Ages*. Chicago: University of Chicago Press, 1989.

Berend, Nora. *At the Gate of Christendom: Jews, Muslims and 'Pagans' in Medieval Hungary, c. 1000–c. 1300*. Cambridge, UK: Cambridge University Press, 2001.

Berkhofer, Robert F. *Beyond the Great Story: History as Text and Discourse*. Cambridge, MA: Harvard University Press, 1995.

Biddick, Kathleen. *The Shock of Medievalism*. Durham, NC: Duke University Press, 1998.

———. *The Typological Imaginary: Circumcision, Technology, History*. Philadelphia: University of Pennsylvania Press, 2003.

Bliujienė, Audronė. "Lithuanian Amber Artifacts from the Roman Iron Age to Early Medieval Times." In *Amber in Archaeology: Proceedings of the Fourth International Conference on Amber in Archaeology, Talsi 2001*, ed. Curt W. Beck, Ilze B. Loze, and Joan M. Todd, 47–71. Riga: Institute of the History of Latvia, 2003.

———. "Lithuanian Amber Artifacts in the Middle of the First Millennium and Their Provenance within the Limits of the Eastern Baltic Region." In *Proceedings of the International Interdisciplinary Conference: Baltic Amber in Natural*

Sciences, Archaeology, and Applied Arts, ed. Adomas Butrimas, 171–86. Vilnius: Vilniaus Dailes Akademijos Leidykla, 2001.

Boba, Imre. *Moravia's History Reconsidered: A Reinterpretation of Medieval Sources.* The Hague: Nijhoff, 1971.

Bober, Harry. "On the Illumination of the Glazier Codex: A Contribution to Early Coptic Art and Its Relation to Hiberno-Saxon Interlace." In *Homage to a Bookman: Essays on Manuscripts, Books and Printing Written for Hans P. Kraus on His Sixtieth Birthday*, ed. Hellmut Lehmann-Haupt, 31–49. Berlin: Mann, 1967.

Bouchard, Constance Brittain. *"Those of My Blood": Constructing Noble Families in Medieval Francia.* Philadelphia: University of Pennsylvania Press, 2001.

Bowlus, Charles R. *The Battle of Lechfeld and Its Aftermath, August 955: The End of the Age of Migrations in the Latin West.* Aldershot: Ashgate, 2006.

———. *Franks, Moravians, and Magyars: The Struggle for the Middle Danube 788–907.* Philadelphia: University of Pennsylvania Press, 1995.

———. "Italia, Bavaria, Avaria: The Grand Strategy behind Charlemagne's Renovatio Imperii in the West." *The Journal of Medieval Military History* 1 (2002): 43–61.

Branner, Robert. "The Art of the Scriptorium at Luxeuil." *Speculum* 29 (1954): 678–90.

Brather, Sebastian. "Ethnic Identities as Constructions of Archaeology: The Case of the Alemanni." In *On Barbarian Identity: Critical Approaches to Ethnicity in the Early Middle Ages*, ed. Andrew Gillett, 149–75. Turnhout: Brepols, 2002.

Brown, Elizabeth. "The Tyranny of a Construct: Feudalism and Historians of Medieval Europe." *American Historical Review* 79 (1974): 1063–88.

Brown, Katharine Reynolds, Dafydd Kidd, and Charles T. Little, eds. *From Attila to Charlemagne: Arts of the Early Medieval Period in The Metropolitan Museum of Art.* New York: Metropolitan Museum of Art, 2000.

Brown, Michelle P. *The Lindisfarne Gospels: Society, Spirituality and the Scribe.* London: British Library, 2003.

Brown, Peter R.L. *The Rise of Western Christendom: Triumph and Diversity, A.D. 200–1000*, 2nd ed. Oxford: Blackwell, 2003.

———. *The World of Late Antiquity, AD 150–750.* New York: Harcourt Brace Jovanovich, 1971.

Brown, Thomas S. *Gentlemen and Officers: Imperial Administration and Aristocratic Power in Byzantine Italy, A.D. 554–800.* London: British School at Rome, 1984.

Bruce-Mitford, R.L.S. *The Art of the Codex Amiatinus.* Jarrow: The Rectory, 1966.

Buc, Philippe. *The Dangers of Ritual: Between Early Medieval Texts and Social Scientific Theory.* Princeton: Princeton University Press, 2001.

Buckler, F.W. *Harunu'l-Rashid and Charles the Great.* Cambridge, MA: Medieval Academy of America, 1931.

Burger, Glenn and Steven F. Kruger, eds. *Queering the Middle Ages.* Minneapolis: University of Minnesota Press, 2001.

Butler, Judith. *Gender Trouble: Feminism and the Subversion of Identity.* New York: Routledge, 1999.

Byer, Glenn C.J. *Charlemagne and Baptism: A Study of Responses to the Circular Letter of 811/812.* San Francisco: International Scholars Press, 1999.

Bynum, Caroline Walker. *Resurrection of the Body in Western Christianity, 200–1336.* New York: Columbia University Press, 1995.

Caviness, Madeline. *Reframing Medieval Art: Differences, Margins, Boundaries.* Tufts University Electronic Book, 2001, <http://nils.lib.tufts.edu/Caviness>.

Chazelle, Celia. "Amalarius's *Liber Officialis*: Spirit and Vision in Carolingian Liturgical Thought." In *Seeing the Invisible in Late Antiquity and the Early Middle Ages,* ed. Giselle de Nie, Karl F. Morrison, and Marco Mostert, 327–57. Turnhout: Brepols, 2005.

———. "Ceolfrid's Gift to St. Peter: The First Quire of the Codex Amiatinus and the Evidence of Its Roman Destination." *Early Medieval Europe* 12 (2003): 129–57.

———, ed. *Literacy, Politics and Artistic Innovation in the Early Medieval West.* Lanham, MD: University Press of America, 1992.

———. "The Three Chapters Controversy and the Biblical Diagrams of Cassiodorus's Codex Grandior and *Institutions*." In *The Crisis of the Oikoumene: The Three Chapters and the Failed Quest for Unity in the Sixth-Century Mediterranean,* ed. Celia Chazelle and Catherine Cubitt. Turnhout: Brepols, 2007, pp. 161–205.

Chibnall, Marjorie. "'Clio's Legal Cosmetics': Law and Custom in the Work of Medieval Historians." *Anglo Norman Studies* 20 (1998): 31–43.

Christie, Neil and S.T. Loseby, eds. *Towns in Transition: Urban Evolution in Late Antiquity and the Early Middle Ages.* Aldershot: Ashgate, 1996.

Clark, Elizabeth A. *History, Theory, Text: Historians and the Linguistic Turn.* Cambridge, MA: Harvard University Press, 2004.

———. "Women, Gender and the Study of Christian History." *Church History* 70 (2001): 395–426.

Cohen, Jeffrey Jerome and Bonnie Wheeler, eds. *Becoming Male in the Middle Ages.* New York: Palgrave, 2000.

Collins, Roger. *Charlemagne.* Toronto: University of Toronto Press, 1998.

Cormack, Margaret. *The Saints in Iceland: Their Veneration from the Conversion to 1400.* Subsidia Hagiographica 78. Brussels: Société des Bollandistes, 1994.

Cramer, Peter. *Baptism and Change in the Early Middle Ages, c. 200–c. 1150.* Cambridge, UK: Cambridge University Press, 1993.

Crocker, Richard L. *The Early Medieval Sequence.* Berkeley: University of California Press, 1977.

Curta, Florin. "From Kossinna to Bromley: Ethnogenesis in Slavic Archaeology." In *On Barbarian Identity: Critical Approaches to Ethnicity in the Early Middle Ages,* ed. Andrew Gillett, 201–18. Turnhout: Brepols, 2002.

———. *The Making of the Slavs: History and Archaeology of the Lower Danube Region, c. 500–700.* Cambridge, UK: Cambridge University Press, 2001.

———. "Merovingian and Carolingian Gift-Giving." *Speculum* 81(2006): 671–99.

Davis, Natalie Zemon. *The Return of Martin Guerre*. Cambridge, MA: Harvard University Press, 1983.

Davis, R.H.C. "Domesday Book: Continental Parallels." In *Domesday Studies: Papers Read at the Novocentenary Conference of the Royal Historical Society and the Institute of British Geographers: Winchester, 1986*, ed. J.C. Holt, 15–39. Woodbridge, UK: Boydell Press, 1987.

———. *The Medieval Warhorse: Origin, Development and Redevelopment*. New York: Thames and Hudson, 1989.

DeGregorio, Scott. "Bede's *In Ezram et Neemiam* and the Reform of the Northumbrian Church." *Speculum* 79 (2004): 1–25.

———. "'*Nostrorum socordiam temporum*': The Reforming Impulse of Bede's Later Exegesis." *Early Medieval Europe* 11 (2002): 107–22.

Downs, Laura Lee. *Writing Gender History*. London: Arnold Press, 2004.

Drew, Katherine Fischer, trans. and intro. *The Burgundian Code*. Philadelphia: University of Pennsylvania Press, 1972.

———. trans. and intro. *The Lombard Laws*. Philadelphia: University of Pennsylvania Press, 1973.

Duby, Georges. *The Chivalrous Society*. Translated from the French by Cynthia Postan. Berkeley: University of California Press, 1977.

———. *Love and Marriage in the Middle Ages*. Translated from the French by Jane Dunnett. Chicago: University of Chicago Press, 1994.

Dvornik, Francis. *Byzantine Missions among the Slavs: SS. Constantine-Cyril and Methodius*. New Brunswick: Rutgers University Press, 1970.

———. *The Photian Schism: History and Legend*. Cambridge, UK: Cambridge University Press, 1948.

———. *The Slavs, Their Early History and Civilization*. New Brunswick: Rutgers University Press, 1962.

Effros, Bonnie. "Art of the 'Dark Ages': Showing Merovingian Artefacts in North American Public and Private Collections." *Journal of the History of Collections* 17 (2005): 85–113.

———. "Dressing Conservatively: Women's Brooches as Markers of Ethnic Identity?" In *Gender in the Early Medieval World: East and West, 300–900*, ed. Leslie Brubaker and Julia M.H. Smith, 165–84. Cambridge, UK: Cambridge University Press, 2004.

———. *Merovingian Mortuary Archaeology and the Making of the Early Middle Ages*. Berkeley: University of California Press, 2003.

Eisler, Rhiane. *The Chalice and the Blade: Our History, Our Future*. San Francisco: Harper, 1988.

Engels, Friedrich. *The Origin of the Family, Private Property, and the State*. New York: Pathfinder Press, 1972.

Eslinger, Lyle M. "Ezekiel 20 and the Metaphor of Historical Teleology: Concepts of Biblical History." *Journal for the Study of Old Testament* 81 (1998): 93–125.

Evans, Helen C. and William D. Wixom, eds. *The Glory of Byzantium: Art and Culture of the Middle Byzantine Era, A.D. 843–1261*. New York: Metropolitan Museum of Art, 1997.

Evergates, Theodore, ed. *Aristocratic Women in Medieval France.* Philadelphia: University of Pennsylvania Press, 1999.

Fanning, Steven C. "Emperors and Empires in Fifth-Century Gaul." In *Fifth-Century Gaul: A Crisis of Identity?,* ed. John Drinkwater and Hugh Elton, 288–97. Cambridge, UK: Cambridge University Press, 1992.

———. "Tacitus, Beowulf and the *Comitatus.*" *The Haskins Society Journal* 9 (2001): 17–38.

Farmer, Sharon. *Communities of Saint Martin: Legend and Ritual in Medieval Tours.* Ithaca: Cornell University Press, 1991.

Farrell, Robert and Carol Neuman de Vegvar, eds. *Sutton Hoo: Fifty Years After,* American Early Medieval Studies 2. Oxford, OH: Miami University of Ohio, 1992.

Ferguson, Margaret W., Maureen Quilligan, and Nancy J. Vickers, eds. *Rewriting the Renaissance: The Discourses of Sexual Difference in Early Modern Europe.* Chicago: University of Chicago Press, 1986.

Fernández-Ochoa, Carmen and Ángel Morillo Cerdán. "Walls in the Urban Landscape of Late Roman Spain." In *Hispania in Late Antiquity: Current Approaches,* ed. Kim Bowes and Michael Kulikowski, 299–340. Leiden: Brill, 2005.

Fine, Lawrence. *Physician of the Soul, Healer of the Cosmos: Isaac Luria and His Kabbalistic Fellowship.* Stanford: Stanford University Press, 2003.

Flam, Jack and Miriam Deutch, eds. *Primitivism and Twentieth-Century Art: A Documentary History.* Berkeley: University of California Press, 2003.

Flax, Jane. "Postmodernism and Gender Relations in Feminist Theory." In *Feminism/Postmodernism,* ed. Linda J. Nicholson, 39–62. New York: Routledge, 1990.

Foerster, Norman. "The Future of the Humanities in State Universities." In *A State University Surveys the Humanities,* ed. L.C. MacKinney, Nicholas B. Adams, and Harry K. Russell, 205–62. Chapel Hill: University of North Carolina Press, 1945.

Foot, Sarah. " 'By Water in the Spirit': The Administration of Baptism in Early Anglo-Saxon England." In *Pastoral Care before the Parish,* ed. John Blair and Richard Sharpe, 171– 92. Leicester: Leicester University Press, 1992.

———. "Finding the Meaning of Form: Narrative in Annals and Chronicles." In *Writing Medieval History,* ed. Nancy Partner, 88–108. London: Hodder Arnold, 2005.

Forsyth, Ilene H. *The Throne of Wisdom: Wood Sculptures of the Madonna in Romanesque France.* Princeton: Princeton University Press, 1972.

Fouracre, Paul and Richard A. Gerberding. *Late Merovingian France: History and Hagiography, 640–720.* Manchester: Manchester University Press, 1996.

France, John. *The Crusades and the Expansion of Catholic Christendom, 1000–1714.* London: Routledge, 2005.

Frank, Roberta. "Scaldic Verse and the Date of Beowulf." In *The Dating of Beowulf,* ed. Colin Chase, 123–39. Toronto: University of Toronto Press, 1981.

Frantzen, Alan. "When Women Aren't Enough." *Speculum* 68 (1993): 445–71. Reprinted in *Studying Medieval Women: Sex, Gender, Feminism,* ed. Nancy Partner, 143–70. Cambridge, MA: Medieval Academy of America, 1993.

Freeman, Ann, ed. *Opus Caroli regis contra synodum (Libri Carolini),* MGH, *Concilia* II, *Supplementum* I, Unter Mitwirkung von Paul Meyvaert. Hannover: Hahn, 1998.

Frojmovic, Eva. "Messianic Politics in Re-Christianized Spain: Images of the Sanctuary in Hebrew Bible Manuscripts." In *Imagining the Self, Imagining the Other,* ed. Eva Frojmovic, 91–128. Leiden: Brill, 2002.

Frye, Marilyn. "The Possibility of Feminist Theory." In *Theoretical Perspectives on Sexual Difference,* ed. Deborah L. Rhode, 174–84. New Haven: Yale University Press, 1990.

Fuchs, Esther. "Men in Biblical Feminist Scholarship." *Journal of Feminist Studies in Religion* 19 (2003): 93–114.

Gadol, Joan Kelly. "Did Women Have a Renaissance?" In *Becoming Visible: Women in European History,* ed. Renata Bridenthal, Claudia Koonz, and Susan Mosher Stuard, 2nd ed., 175–201. Boston: Houghton Mifflin, 1987.

Ganshof, F.L. "Charlemagne." *Speculum* 24 (1949): 520–27.

———. "Charlemagne and the Administration of Justice." In F.L. Ganshof, *Frankish Institutions Under Charlemagne,* translated from the French by Bryce and Mary Lyon, 71–97. Providence, RI: Brown University Press, 1968.

———. "Charlemagne and the Institutions of the Frankish Monarchy." In F.L. Ganshof, *Frankish Institutions Under Charlemagne,* translated from the French by Bryce and Mary Lyon, 3–55. Providence, RI: Brown University Press, 1968.

Ganz, David. *Corbie in the Carolingian Renaissance.* Sigmaringen: Thorbecke, 1990.

Geary, Patrick J. *Aristocracy in Provence: The Rhône Basin at the Dawn of the Carolingian Age.* Philadelphia: University of Pennsylvania Press, 1985.

———. "Barbarians and Ethnicity." In *Interpreting Late Antiquity: Essays on the Postclassical World,* ed. G.W. Bowersock, Peter Brown, and Oleg Grabar, 107–29. Cambridge, MA: Belknap Press of Harvard University Press, 2001.

———. "Ethnic Identity as a Situational Construct in the Early Middle Ages." *Mitteilungen der Anthropologischen Gesellschaft in Wien* 113 (1983): 15–26.

———. *The Myth of Nations: The Medieval Origins of Europe.* Princeton: Princeton University Press, 2002.

Gerberding, Richard A. *The Rise of the Carolingians and the "Liber historiae Francorum."* Oxford: Oxford University Press, 1987.

Gillett, Andrew. "Was Ethnicity Politicized in the Earliest Medieval Kingdoms?" In *On Barbarian Identity: Critical Approaches to Ethnicity in the Early Middle Ages,* ed. Andrew Gillett, 85–121. Turnhout: Brepols, 2002.

Glenn, Jason. *Politics and History in the Tenth Century: The Work and World of Richer of Reims.* Cambridge, UK: Cambridge University Press, 2004.

Goffart, Walter. *Barbarian Tides: The Migration Age and the Later Roman Empire.* Philadelphia: University of Pennsylvania Press, 2006.

Goffart, Walter. *Caput and Colonate: Towards a History of Late Roman Taxation.* Toronto: University of Toronto Press, 1974.

———. *The Le Man Forgeries: A Chapter from the History of Church Property in the Ninth Century.* Cambridge, MA: Harvard University Press, 1966.

———. *The Narrators of Barbarian History (A.D. 550–800): Jordanes, Gregory of Tours, Bede, and Paul the Deacon.* Princeton: Princeton University Press, 1988.

———."Paul the Deacon's *Gesta episcoporum Mettensium* and the Early Design of Charlemagne's Succession." *Traditio* 42 (1986): 59–93.

Goldberg, Eric J. *The Struggle for Empire: Kingship and Conflict under Louis the German, 817–876.* Ithaca, NY: Cornell University Press, 2006.

Gombrich, Ernst H. *The Preference for the Primitive: Episodes in the History of Western Taste and Art.* London: Phaidon, 2002.

Gorman, Michael. "The Myth of Hiberno-Latin Exegesis." *Revue bénédictine* 110 (2000): 42–85.

Grabar, Oleg. *The Mediation of Ornament.* Princeton: Princeton University Press, 1992.

Grane, Thomas. "Roman Sources for the Geography and Ethnography of *Germania.*" In *The Spoils of Victory: The North in the Shadow of the Roman Empire,* ed. Lars Jørgensen, Birger Storgaard, and Lone Gebauer Thomson, 126–47. Copenhagen: Nationalmuseet, 2003.

Greene, Kevin. "Gothic Material Culture." In *Archaeology as Long-Term History,* ed. Ian Hodder, 117–31. Cambridge, UK: Cambridge University Press, 1987.

Grierson, Philip. "Commerce in the Dark Ages: A Critique of the Evidence." *Transactions of the Royal Historical Society* 5 (1959): 123–40.

———. "The Date of Theoderic's Gold Medallion." *Hikuin* 11 (1985): 19–26.

Hahn, Thomas. "The Difference the Middle Ages Makes: Color and Race before the Modern World." *Journal of Medieval and Early Modern Studies* 31 (2001): 1–36.

Haldon, John F. *Byzantium in the Seventh Century: The Transformation of a Culture.* Cambridge, UK: Cambridge University Press, 1990.

———. *Warfare, State, and Society in the Byzantine World, 565–1204.* London: University College London Press, 1999.

Halsall, Guy. *Warfare and Society in the Barbarian West.* London: Routledge, 2003.

Harden, Donald B. et al. *Glass of the Caesars: The Corning Museum of Glass, Corning, the British Museum, London, Römisch-Germanisches Museum, Cologne.* Milan: Olivetti, 1987.

Haraway, Donna J. "A Cyborg Manifesto: Science, Technology, Socialist-Feminism in the Late Twentieth Century." In idem., *Simians, Cyborgs and Women: The Reinvention of Nature,* 149–81. New York: Routledge, 1991.

Head, Thomas F. *Hagiography and the Cult of Saints: The Diocese of Orléans, 800–1200.* Cambridge, UK: Cambridge University Press, 1990.

Heather, Peter. "The Creation of the Visigoths." In *The Visigoths from the Migration Period to the Seventh Century: An Ethnographic Perspective,* ed. Peter Heather,

41–92. Studies in Historical Archaeoethnology 4. Woodbridge: Boydell Press, 1999.

———. *The Fall of the Roman Empire*. London: Macmillan, 2005.

———. *The Goths*. Oxford: Blackwell, 1996.

Heather, Peter and John Matthews. "The Sîntana de Mureş-Černjachov Culture." In *The Goths of the Fourth Century*, ed. Peter Heather and John Matthews, 51–101. Translated Texts for Historians. Liverpool: Liverpool University Press, 1991.

Hedeager, Lotte. "Warrior Economy and Trading Economy in Viking-age Scandinavia." *Journal of European Archaeology* 2 (1994): 130–48.

Heene, Katrien. *The Legacy of Paradise: Marriage, Motherhood and Woman in Carolingian Edifying Literature*. Frankfurt: Peter Lang, 1997.

Hen, Yitzhak. "The *Annales* of Metz and the Merovingian Past." In *The Uses of the Past in the Early Middle Ages*, ed. Yitzhak Hen and Matthew Innes, 175–90. Cambridge, UK: Cambridge University Press, 2000.

———. *The Royal Patronage of Liturgy in Frankish Gaul, to the Death of Charles the Bald (877)*. Henry Bradshaw Society. London: Boydell Press, 2001.

Henderson, George. *From Durrow to Kells: The Insular Gospel-books, 650–800*. London: Thames and Hudson, 1987.

———. *Vision and Image in Early Christian England*. Cambridge, UK: Cambridge University Press, 1999.

Henry, Françoise. *Irish Art in the Early Christian Period (to 800 A.D.)*. Ithaca: Cornell University Press, 1965.

———. *The Book of Kells*. London: Thames and Hudson, 1974.

Herbert, Eugenia W. *Iron, Gender and Power: Rituals of Transformation in African Societies*. Bloomington, IN: Indiana University Press, 1993.

Hines, John. *The Scandinavian Character of Anglian England in the Pre-Viking Period*. BAR British Series 124. Oxford: British Archaeological Reports, 1984.

Hodder, Ian. *Symbols in Action: Ethnoarchaeological Studies of Material Culture*. New Studies in Archaeology. Cambridge, UK: Cambridge University Press, 1982.

Hodges, Richard. *Dark Age Economics: The Origins of Towns and Trade, A.D. 600–1000*. London: St. Martin's Press, 1982.

———. "Henri Pirenne and the Question of Demand in the Sixth Century." In *The Sixth Century: Production, Distribution, and Demand*, ed. Richard Hodges and William Bowden, 3–14. Leiden: Brill, 1998.

———. *Towns and Trade in the Age of Charlemagne*. London: Duckworth, 2000.

Hodges, Richard and David Whitehouse. *Mohammed, Charlemagne and The Origins of Europe: Archaeology and the Pirenne Thesis*. London: Duckworth 1983.

Hoff, Joan. "Gender as a Postmodern Category of Paralysis." *Women's History Review* 3 (1994): 149–68.

Holsinger, Bruce W. *The Premodern Condition: Medievalism and the Making of Theory*. Chicago: University of Chicago Press, 2005.

Howell, Martha and Walter Prevenier. *From Reliable Sources: An Introduction to Historical Methods*. Ithaca: Cornell University Press, 2001.

Hummer, Hans J. "Franks and Alamanni: A Discontinuous Ethnogenesis." In *Franks and Alamanni in the Merovingian Period: An Ethnographic Perspective*, ed. Ian Wood, 9–32. Studies in Historical Archaeoethnology 3. Woodbridge: Boydell Press, 1998.

Hyams, Paul. *Rancor and Reconciliation in Medieval England*. Ithaca: Cornell University Press, 2003.

Hyland, Ann. *The Medieval Warhorse from Byzantium to the Crusades*. Conshohocken, PA: Combined Books, 1994.

Innis, Matthew. *State and Society in the Early Middle Ages: The Middle Rhine Valley, 400–1000*. Cambridge, UK: Cambridge University Press, 2000.

Jackson, Kenneth. *The Oldest Irish Tradition: A Window on the Iron Age*. Rede Lectures. Cambridge, UK: Cambridge University Press, 1964.

James, Edward, ed. "Origins of the European Economy: A Debate with Michael McCormick." *Early Medieval Europe* 12 (2003): 259–323.

Johnson, Edgar Nathaniel. *The Secular Activities of the German Episcopate, 919–1024* (Lincoln: University of Nebraska Press, 1932).

Jones, Christopher A. "The Book of the Liturgy in Anglo-Saxon England." *Speculum* 73 (1998): 659–702.

Jones, Siân. *The Archaeology of Ethnicity: Constructing Identities in the Past and Present*. London: Routledge, 1997.

———. "Historical Categories and the Praxis of Identity: The Interpretation of Ethnicity in Historical Archaeology." In *Historical Archaeology: Back from the Edge*, ed. Pedro Paulo A. Funari, Martin Hall, and Siân Jones, 219–32. London: Routledge, 1999.

Kaegi, Walter. *Heraclius: Emperor of Byzantium*. Cambridge, UK: Cambridge University Press, 2003.

Karkov, Catherine and Robert Farrell, eds. *Studies in Insular Arts and Archeology*, American Early Medieval Studies 1. Oxford, OH: Miami University of Ohio, 1991.

Karkov, Catherine, Kelley M. Wickham-Crowley, and Bailey K. Young, eds. *Spaces of the Living and the Dead*. American Early Medieval Studies 3. Oxford, OH: Miami University of Ohio, 1999.

Karras, Ruth Mazo. *From Boys to Men: Formations of Masculinity in Late Medieval Europe*. Philadelphia: University of Pennsylvania Press, 2003.

Keefe, Susan A. *Water and the Word: Baptism and the Education of the Clergy in the Carolingian Empire*, 2 vols. Notre Dame, IN: University of Notre Dame Press, 2002.

Kerber, Linda K. "We Are All Historians of Human Rights." *Perspectives* October, 2006, <http://www.historians.org/Perspectives/issues/2006/0610/0610pre1.cfm>.

Kitzinger, Ernst. "Anglo-Saxon Vinescroll Ornament." *Antiquity* 10 (1936): 61–71.

———. *Early Medieval Art with Illustrations from the British Museum Collection*. London: British Museum, 1941. Revised edition by David Buckton. London: British Museum, 1983.

————. "The Sutton Hoo Finds: The Silver." *Antiquity* 14 (1940): 40–63.

Kobyliński, Zbigniew and Zdisław Hensel. "Imports or Local Products? Trace Elements Analysis of Copper-Alloy Artefacts from Haćki, Białystok Province, Poland." *Archaeologia Polona* 31 (1993): 129–40.

Kornbluth, Genevra. *Engraved Gems of the Carolingian Empire.* University Park, PA: Penn State University Press, 1995.

Kowaleski, Maryanne. "Singlewomen in Medieval and Early Modern Europe: The Demographic Perspective." In *Singlewomen in the European Past, 1250–1800,* ed. Judith M. Bennett and Amy M. Froide, 38–81. Philadelphia: University of Pennsylvania Press, 1999.

Koziol, Geoffrey. "The Dangers of Polemic: Is Ritual Still an Interesting Topic of Historical Study?" *Early Medieval Europe* 11 (2002): 367–88.

Kühnel, Bianca. "Jewish Symbolism of the Tabernacle and Christian Symbolism of the Holy Sepulchre and the Heavenly Tabernacle." *Jewish Art* 12–13 (1986–1987): 147–68.

Kuhn, Thomas S. *The Structure of Scientific Revolutions,* 3rd ed. Chicago: University of Chicago Press, 1996.

Kulikowski, Michael. "Cities and Government in Late Antique Hispania: Recent Advances and Future Research." In *Hispania in Late Antiquity: Current Approaches,* ed. Kim Bowes and Michael Kulikowski, 31–70. Leiden: Brill, 2005.

————. *Late Roman Spain and Its Cities.* Baltimore: The Johns Hopkins University Press, 2004.

La Monte, John, ed. *Anniversary Essays in Mediaeval History, By Students of Charles Homer Haskins, Presented on His Completion of Forty Years of Teaching.* Boston and New York: Houghton Mifflin, 1929.

Larick, Roy. "Age Grading and Ethnicity in the Style of Loikop (Samburu) Spears." *World Archaeology* 18 (1986): 269–83.

Lavan, Luke, ed. *Recent Research in Late-Antique Urbanism.* Journal of Roman Archaeology Supplement 42. Portsmouth, RI: Journal of Roman Archaeology, 2001.

Le Goff, Jacques. *Time, Work, and Culture in the Middle Ages,* translated from the French by Arthur Goldhammer. Chicago: University of Chicago Press, 1980.

Lees, Clare, ed. *Medieval Masculinities: Regarding Men in the Middle Ages.* Minneapolis: University of Minnesota Press, 1994.

Lerner, Gerda. *The Creation of Patriarchy.* New York: Oxford University Press, 1986.

Lewis, A.R. *The Development of Southern French and Catalan Society, 718–1050.* Austin: University of Texas Press, 1965.

————. *The Northern Seas: Shipping and Commerce in Northern Europe, A.D. 300–1100.* Princeton: Princeton University Press, 1958.

Leyser, Karl J. *Rule and Conflict in an Early Medieval Society: Ottonian Saxony.* Bloomington, IN: Indiana University Press, 1978.

Liebeschuetz, J.H.W.G. *The Decline and Fall of the Roman City.* Oxford: Oxford University Press, 2001.

Lifshitz, Felice. "Demonstrating Gun(t)za: Women, Manuscripts, and the Question of Historical 'Proof,' " In *Vom Nutzen des Schreibens: Soziales Gedächtnis, Herrschaft, und Besitz*, ed. Walter Pohl and Paul Herold, 67–96. Vienna: Österreichische Akademie der Wissenschaften, 2002.

———. "Differences, (Dis)appearances and the Disruption of the Straight Telos: Medievalology as a History of Gender." In *Mediävistik im 21. Jahrhundert: Stand und Perspektiven*, ed. Jörg Jarnut and Hans-Werner Goetz, 295–312. Munich: Wilhelm Fink Verlag, 2003.

———. "Gender, Exegesis and Exemplarity East of the Middle Rhine: Jesus, Mary and the Saints in Manuscript Context." *Early Medieval Europe* 9 (2000): 325–44.

Lincoln, Bruce. *Emerging from the Chrysalis: Studies in Rituals of Women's Initiation.* Cambridge, MA: Harvard University Press, 1981.

Lowden, John. "The Beginnings of Biblical Illustration." In *Imaging the Early Medieval Bible*, ed. John Williams, 9–59. University Park, PA: Pennsylvania State University Press, 1999.

———. *The Making of the Bibles Moralisées.* University Park, PA: Pennsylvania State University Press, 2000.

Lozovsky, Natalia. "Roman Geography in the Carolingian Empire." *Speculum* 81 (2006): 325–64.

MacKinney, Loren C. *Early Medieval Medicine: With Special Reference to France and Chartres.* Baltimore: Johns Hopkins University Press, 1937.

Maldonado, Pedro Castillo. "*Angelorum participes*: The Cult of the Saints in Late Antique Spain." In *Hispania in Late Antiquity: Current Approaches*, ed. Kim Bowes and Michael Kulikowski, 151–88. Leiden: Brill, 2005.

Mango, Marlia Mundell. "Silver Plate among the Romans and among the Barbarians." In *La Noblesse romaine et les chefs barbares du IIIe au VIIe siècle*, ed. Françoise Vallet and Michel Kazanski, 77–88. Mémoires publiées par l'Association Française d'Archéologie Mérovingienne 9. Rouen: Association Française d'Archéologie Mérovingienne and Musée des Antiquités Nationales, 1995.

Marcus, Ivan G. *Rituals of Childhood: Jewish Acculturation in Medieval Europe.* New Haven: Yale University Press, 1996.

Mastnak, Tomaz. *Crusading Peace: Christendom, the Muslim World, and Western Political Order.* Berkeley: University of California Press, 2002.

Mathisen, Ralph. "*Peregrini, Barbari*, and *Cives Romani*: Concepts of Citizenship and the Legal Identity of Barbarians in the Later Roman Empire." *American Historical Review* 111 (2006): 1011–40.

McCone, Kim. *Pagan Past and Christian Present in Early Irish Literature.* Maynooth: An Sagart, 1991.

McCormick, Michael. *Origins of the European Economy: Communications and Commerce, A.D. 300–900.* Cambridge, UK: Cambridge University Press, 2001.

McKitterick, Rosamond. *The Carolingians and the Written Word.* Cambridge, UK: Cambridge University Press, 1989.

———. *History and Memory in the Carolingian World*. Cambridge, UK: Cambridge University Press, 2004.

McNamara, Jo Ann. *Sisters in Arms: Catholic Nuns through Two Millennia*. Cambridge, MA: Harvard University Press, 1996.

———. "Women and Power through the Family Revisited." In *Gendering the Master Narrative: Women and Power in the Middle Ages*, ed. Mary C. Erler and Maryanne Kowaleski, 17–30. Ithaca: Cornell University Press, 2003.

Meaney, Audrey L. *Anglo-Saxon Amulets and Curing Stones*. Oxford: British Archaeological Reports, 1981.

Meyvaert, Paul. "Bede, Cassiodorus, and the Codex Amiatinus." *Speculum* 71 (1996): 827–83.

———. "The Date of Bede's *In Ezram* and His Image of Ezra in the Codex Amiatinus." *Speculum* 80 (2005): 1087–33.

———. "'In the Footsteps of the Fathers': The Date of Bede's *Thirty Questions on the Book of Kings* to Nothelm." In *The Limits of Ancient Christianity: Essays on Late Antique Thought and Culture in Honour of R.A. Markus*, ed. W.E. Klingshirn and Mark Vessey, 267–86. Ann Arbor: University of Michigan Press, 1997.

Mitchell, Kathleen and Ian Wood, eds. *The World of Gregory of Tours*. Leiden: Brill, 2002.

Modleski, Tania. *Feminism without Women: Culture and Criticism in a Postfeminist Age*. New York: Routledge, 1991.

Moore, Robert I. *First European Revolution c. 970–1215*. Oxford: Blackwell, 2000.

Moreland, John. *Archaeology and Text*. London: Duckworth, 2001.

———. "What Is Archaeology? An Essay on the Nature of Archaeological Research." *History and Theory* 30 (1991): 246–61.

Morey, Charles Rufus. *Early Christian Art: An Outline of the Evolution of Style and Iconography in Sculpture and Painting from Antiquity to the Eighth Century*. Princeton: Princeton University Press, 1942.

———. "Medieval Art and America," *Journal of the Warburg and Courtauld Institutes* 7 (1944): 1–6.

———. "The Sources of Medieval Style." *Art Bulletin* 7 (1924): 35–50.

Morrissey, Robert. *Charlemagne and France: A Thousand Years of Mythology*, trans. Catherine Tihanyi. Notre Dame, IN: University of Notre Dame Press, 2003.

Morrison, Karl F. *The Two Kingdoms: Ecclesiology in Carolingian Political Thought*. Princeton: Princeton University Press, 1964.

Mostert, Marco. "Celtic, Anglo-Saxon or Insular? Some Considerations on 'Irish' Manuscript Production and Their Implications for Insular Latin Culture, c. AD 500–800." In *Cultural Identity and Cultural Integration: Ireland and Europe in the Early Middle Ages*, ed. Doris Edel, 92–115. Dublin: Four Courts Press, 1995.

Murray, Alexander Callander, ed. *After Rome's Fall: Narrators and Sources of Early Medieval History, Essays Presented to Walter Goffart*. Toronto: University of Toronto Press, 1998.

Murray, Alexander Callander, ed. *Germanic Kinship Structure: Studies in Law and Society in Antiquity and the Early Middle Ages*. Toronto: University of Toronto Press, 1983.

————. "Reinhard Wenskus on 'Ethnogenesis', Ethnicity, and the Origin of the Franks." In *On Barbarian Identity: Critical Approaches to Ethnicity in the Early Middle Ages*, ed. Andrew Gillett, 39–68. Turnhout: Brepols, 2002.

Nees, Lawrence. *Early Medieval Art*. Oxford: Oxford University Press, 2002.

————. "The Originality of Early Medieval Artists." In *Literacy, Politics, and Artistic Innovation in the Early Medieval West*, ed. Celia M. Chazelle, 77–109. Lanham MD: University Press of America, 1992.

————. "Problems of Form and Function in Early Medieval Illustrated Bibles From Northwest Europe." In *Imaging the Early Medieval Bible*, ed. John Williams, 121–77. University Park, PA: Pennsylvania State University Press, 1999.

————. "Weaving Garnets: Thoughts about Two 'Excessively Rare' Belt Mounts from Sutton Hoo." In *Making and Meaning: Proceedings of the Fifth International Conference on Insular Art*, ed. Rachel Moss. Dublin: Four Courts Press, 2006.

Nelson, Janet L. *Charles the Bald*. London: Longman, 1992.

————. "Literacy in Carolingian Government." In *The Uses of Literacy in Early Medieval Europe*, ed. Rosamond McKitterick, 258–96. Cambridge, UK: Cambridge University Press, 1990.

————. *Politics and Ritual in Early Medieval Europe*. London: Hambledon Press, 1986.

Netzer, Nancy. "The Book of Durrow: The Northumbrian Connection." In *Northumbria's Golden Age*, ed. Jane Hawkes and Susan Mills, 315–26. Newcastle-upon-Tyne: Sutton Publishing, 1999.

Neuman de Vegvar, Carol. "In the Shadow of the Sidhe: Arthur Kingsley Porter's Vision of an Exotic Ireland." *Irish Arts Review Yearbook* 17 (2001): 48–60.

Noble, Thomas F.X. "From Brigandage to Justice: Charlemagne, 785–794." In *Literacy, Politics, and Artistic Innovation in the Early Medieval West*, ed. Celia M. Chazelle, 49–75. Lanham, MD: University Press of America, 1992.

————, ed. *From Roman Provinces to Medieval Kingdoms*. Rewriting Histories. New York: Routledge, 2006.

Noble, Thomas F.X. and John J. Contreni, eds. *Religion, Culture and Society in the Early Middle Ages: Studies in Honor of Richard E. Sullivan*. Kalamazoo: Western Michigan University, 1987.

Noonan, Thomas S. "The Fur Road and the Silk Road: The Relations between Central Asia and Northern Russia in the Early Middle Ages." In *Kontakte zwischen Iran, Byzanz und der Steppe im 6.–7. Jahrhundert*, ed. Csanád Bálint, 285–302. Budapest: Akadémiai kiadó, 2000.

Nordenfalk, Carl. "Before the Book of Durrow." *Acta Archaeologica* 18 (1947): 141–74.

————. *Celtic and Anglo-Saxon Painting*. New York: Braziller, 1977.

————. "An Illustrated Diatessaron." *Art Bulletin* 50 (1968): 119–40.

————. "The Persian Diatessaron Once More." *Art Bulletin* 55 (1973): 534–46.

Nordhagen, Per Jonas. "C.R. Morey and His Theory on the Development of Early Medieval Art." *Konsthistorisk Tidsskrift* 61 (1992): 1–7.

Ó Cróinín, Dáibhí. "Bischoff's *Wendepunkte* Fifty Years On." *Revue bénédictine* 110 (2000): 204–37.

———. "The Irish as Mediators of Antique Culture on the Continent." In *Science in Western and Eastern Civilization in Carolingian Times*, ed. Paul Leo Putzer and Dietrich Lohrmann, 41–52. Basel: Birkhauser, 1993.

O'Reilly, Jennifer. "The Art of Authority." In *After Rome*, ed. Thomas Charles-Edwards, 141–89. Oxford: Oxford University Press, 2003.

———. "The Library of Scripture: Views from Vivarium and Wearmouth-Jarrow." In *New Offerings, Ancient Treasures: Studies in Medieval Art for George Henderson*, ed. Paul Binski and William Noel, 3–39. Stroud: Sutton, 2001.

Odegaard, Charles E. *Vassi and Fideles in the Carolingian Empire*. Cambridge, MA: Harvard University Press, 1945.

Oexle, Otto Gerhard. "The Middle Ages through Modern Eyes: A Historical Problem." *Transactions of the Royal Historical Society* 6 ser., 9 (1999): 121–42.

Okoye, Ikem Stanley. "Architecture, History and the Debate on Identity in Ethiopia, Ghana, Nigeria and South Africa." *Journal of the Society of Architectural Historians* 61 (2002): 381–96.

———. "Tribe and Art History." *Art Bulletin* 78 (1996): 610–15.

Osteen, Mark, ed. *The Question of the Gift: Essays across Disciplines*. Routledge Studies in Anthropology 2. London: Routledge, 2002.

Panofsky, Erwin. *Renaissance and Renascences in Western Art*. 2 vols. Stockholm: Almqvist & Wiksell, 1960.

Pirenne, Henri. *Mohammed and Charlemagne*. Translated from the French of the 10th ed. by Bernard Miall. New York: Norton, 1939.

Piterberg, Gabriel. *An Ottoman Tragedy: History and Historiography at Play*. Berkeley: University of California Press, 2003.

Pohl, Walter. "Conceptions of Ethnicity in Early Medieval Studies." *Archaeologia Polona* 29 (1991): 39–49.

———. "The Empire and the Lombards: Treaties and Negotiations in the Sixth Century." In *Kingdoms of the Empire: The Integration of Barbarians in Late Antiquity*, ed. Walter Pohl, 75–133. Leiden: Brill, 1997.

———. "Telling the Difference: Signs of Ethnic Identity." In *Strategies of Distinction: The Construction of Ethnic Communities, 300–800*, ed. Walter Pohl and Helmut Reimitz, 17–69. Leiden: Brill, 1998.

Polanyi, Karl. "The Economy as Instituted Process." In *Trade and Market in the Early Empires: Economies in History and Theory*, ed. Karl Polanyi, Conrad M. Arensberg, and Harry W. Pearson, 243–70. Glencoe: Free Press, 1957.

Post, Gaines, ed. *Medieval Statecraft and the Perspectives of History: Essays by Joseph R. Strayer*. Princeton: Princeton University Press, 1971.

Ramazanoglu, Caroline. "Unravelling Postmodern Paralysis: A Response to Joan Hoff." *Women's History Review* 5 (1996): 19–23.

Renfrew, Colin. "Alternative Models for Exchange and Spatial Distribution." In *Exchange Systems in Prehistory*, ed. Timothy K. Earle and Jonathan E. Ericson, 71–90. New York: Academic Press, 1977.

Reuter, Timothy. "Medieval: Another Tyrannous Construct?" *The Medieval History Journal* 1 (1998): 25–45.

———. "Plunder and Tribute in the Carolingian Empire." *Transactions of the Royal Historical Society* 5th ser., 35 (1985):75–94.

Reynolds, Paul. "Hispania in the Late Roman Mediterranean: Ceramics and Trade." In *Hispania in Late Antiquity: Current Approaches*, ed. Kim Bowes and Michael Kulikowski, 369–486. Leiden: Brill, 2005.

———. *Settlement and Pottery in the Vinalopó Valley (Alicante, Spain), A.D. 400–700*. British Archaeological Reports, International Series 588. Oxford: Tempus Reparatum, 1993.

———. *Trade in the Western Mediterranean, AD 400–700: The Ceramic Evidence*. British Archaeological Reports, International Series 604. Oxford: Tempus Reparatum, 1995.

Ripoll López, Gisela. "Symbolic Life and Signs of Identity in Visigothic Times." In *The Visigoths from the Migration Period to the Seventh Century: An Ethnographic Perspective*, ed. Peter Heather, 401–46. Studies in Historical Archaeoethnology 4. Woodbridge: Boydell Press, 1999.

Ritvo, Harriet. *The Platypus and the Mermaid and Other Figments of the Classifying Imagination*. Cambridge, MA: Harvard University Press, 1997.

Rouse, Mary and Richard Rouse. *Authentic Witnesses: Approaches to Medieval Texts and Manuscripts*. South Bend, IN: Notre Dame University Press, 1991.

Rubin, William, ed. *"Primitivism" in 20th-Century Art: Affinity of the Tribal and the Modern*. 2 vols. New York: Museum of Modern Art, 1984.

Ruether, Rosemary Radford. *Goddesses and the Divine Feminine: A Western Religious History*. Berkeley: University of California Press, 2005.

Ruiz, Teofilo. "Medieval Europe and the World: Why Medievalists Should Also be World Historians." *History Compass* 4 (2006), <http://www.history-compass.com>.

Russell, Charles Edward. *Charlemagne, First of the Moderns*. Boston and New York: Houghton Mifflin, 1930.

Sánchez, Fernando López. "Coinage, Iconography and the Changing Political Geography of Fifth-Century Hispania." In *Hispania in Late Antiquity: Current Approaches*, ed. Kim Bowes and Michael Kulikowski, 487–518. Leiden: Brill, 2005.

Schapiro, Meyer. *The Language of Forms: Lectures on Insular Manuscript Art*. New York: Pierpont Morgan Library, 2005.

Schapiro, Meyer and Seminar. "The Miniatures of the Florence Diatessaron (Laurentian MS. Or. 81): Their Place in Late Medieval Art and Supposed Connection with Early Christian and Insular Art." *Art Bulletin* 55 (1973): 494–533.

Scholem, Gershom. *Sabbatai Sevi: The Mystical Messiah, 1626–1676*. Princeton: Princeton University Press, 1973.

Scholes, Robert. *Protocols of Reading*. New Haven: Yale University Press, 1989.

Schor, Naomi. *Reading in Detail: Aesthetics and the Feminine*. New York: Methuen, 1987.

Scott, Joan W. "Some More Reflections on Gender and Politics." In Joan W. Scott, *Gender and the Politics of History*, rev. ed., 199–222. New York: Columbia University Press, 1999.

Shanzer, Danuta. "Two Clocks and a Wedding: Theodoric's Diplomatic Relations with the Burgundians." *Romanobarbarica* 14 (1996–1997): 225–28.

Shennan Stephen, ed. *Archaeological Approaches to Cultural Identity*. London: Unwin Hyman, 1989.

———. "Exchange and Ranking: The Role of Amber in the Earlier Bronze Age of Europe." In *Ranking, Resource, and Exchange: Aspects of the Archaeology of Early European Society*, ed. Colin Renfrew and Stephen Shennan, 33–45. Cambridge, UK: Cambridge University Press, 1982.

Siegmund, Frank. "Social Structure and Relations." In *Franks and Alamanni in the Merovingian Period: An Ethnographic Perspective*, ed. Ian Wood, 177–212. Studies in Historical Archaeoethnology 3. Woodbridge: Boydell Press, 1998.

Sims-Williams, Patrick. "The Visionary Celt: The Construction of an Ethnic Preconception." *Cambridge Medieval Celtic Studies* 11 (1986): 70–96.

Smith, Bonnie. *The Gender of History: Men, Women and Historical Practice*. Cambridge, MA: Harvard University Press, 1998.

Smith, Julia M.H. *Europe after Rome: A New Cultural History, 500–1000*. Oxford: Oxford University Press, 2005.

Spiegel, Gabrielle. *The Past as Text: The Theory and Practice of Medieval Historiography*. Baltimore: Johns Hopkins University Press, 1997.

———. "Towards a Theory of the Middle Ground: Historical Writing in the Age of Postmodernism." In *Historia a Debate: actas del Congreso Internacional "A Historia a Debate" celebrado el 7–11 de Julio de 1993 en Santiago de Compostela*, ed. Carlos Barros, Vol. 1: 169–763. 3 vols. Santiago de Compostela: Historia a Debate, 1995. Reprinted in Gabrielle Spiegel. *The Past as Text: The Theory and Practice of Medieval Historiography*, 44–56. Baltimore: Johns Hopkins Press, 1997.

Sprincz, Emma. "Amber Artifacts of Hungary from the Middle Bronze Age to the Hungarian Conquest (from 1600 BC to 896 AD)." In *Amber in Archaeology: Proceedings of the Fourth International Conference on Amber in Archaeology, Talsi 2001*, ed. Curt W. Beck, Ilze B. Loze, and Joan M. Todd, 203–12. Riga: Institute of the History of Latvia, 2003.

Stein, Robert. "Literary Criticism and the Evidence for History." In *Writing Medieval History*, ed. Nancy Partner, 67–87. London: Hodder Arnold, 2005.

Stephenson, Paul. *Byzantium's Balkan Frontier: A Political Study of the Northern Balkans, 900–1204*. Cambridge, UK: Cambridge University Press, 2000.

———. *The Legend of Basil the Bulgar-Slayer*. Cambridge, UK: Cambridge University Press, 2003.

Stevick, Robert. *The Earliest Irish and English Bookarts: Visual and Poetic Forms before A.D. 1000*. Philadelphia: University of Pennsylvania Press, 1994.

Sullivan, Richard E. "The Carolingian Age: Reflections on Its Place in the History of the Middle Ages." *Speculum* 6 (1989): 267–308.

Sullivan, Richard E. "Khan Boris and the Conversion of Bulgaria: A Case Study of the Impact of Christianity on a Barbarian Society." *Studies in Medieval and Renaissance History* 3 (1966): 53–141.

Thacker, Alan. "Bede's Ideal of Reform." In *Ideal and Reality in Frankish and Anglo-Saxon Society*, ed. Patrick Wormald et al., 130–53. Oxford: Basil Blackwell, 1983.

———. "Memorializing Gregory the Great: The Origin and Transmission of a Papal Cult in the Seventh and Early Eighth Centuries." *Early Medieval Europe* 7 (1998): 59–84.

Theuws, Frans and Janet L. Nelson, eds. *Rituals of Power: From Late Antiquity to the Early Middle Ages*. The Transformation of the Roman World 8. Leiden: Brill, 2000.

Thompson, E.A. *The Visigoths in the Time of Ulfila*. Oxford: Clarendon Press, 1966.

Treadgold, Warren. *The Byzantine Revival, 780–842*. Stanford: Stanford University Press, 1988.

Trigger, Bruce G. *A History of Archaeological Thought*. Cambridge, UK: Cambridge University Press, 1990.

Trilling, James. *The Language of Ornament*. London: Thames and Hudson, 2001.

Wallace-Hadrill, John Michael. *The Long-Haired Kings, and Other Studies in Frankish History*. London: Methuen and Co., 1962.

Ward-Perkins, Bryan. *The Fall of Rome and the End of Civilization*. Oxford: Oxford University Press, 2005.

Warner, David. "Ritual and Memory in the Ottonian Reich: The Ceremony of *Adventus*." *Speculum* 76 (2001): 255–83.

Weitzmann, Kurt, ed. *Age of Spirituality: A Symposium*. New York: Metropolitan Museum of Art, in association with Princeton University Press, 1980.

———. *Illustrations in Roll and Codex: A Study of the Origin and Method of Text Illustration*. Princeton: Princeton University Press, 1947.

Werner, Martin. "The Cross-Carpet Page in the Book of Durrow: The Cult of the True Cross, Adomnán and Iona." *Art Bulletin* 72 (1990): 174–223.

White, Hayden. *The Content of the Form: Narrative Discourse and Historical Representation*. Baltimore: John Hopkins University Press, 1987.

White, Stephen D. *Custom, Kinship, and Gifts to Saints: The "Laudatio Parentum" in Western France, 1050–1150*. Chapel Hill: University of North Carolina Press, 1988.

Wickham, Chris. *Early Medieval Italy: Central Power and Local Society 400–1000*. Ann Arbor: University of Michigan Press, 1981.

———. *Framing the Early Middle Ages: Europe and the Mediterranean, 400–800*. Oxford: Oxford University Press, 2005.

Williams, John, ed. *Imaging the Early Medieval Bible*. University Park, PA: Pennsylvania State University Press, 1999.

Wolfram, Herwig. *History of the Goths*, rev. ed., translated from the German by Thomas J. Dunlap. Berkeley: University of California Press, 1988.

Wood, Ian. "Genealogy Defined by Women: The Case of the Pippinids." In *Gender in the Early Medieval World: East and West, 300–900*, ed. Leslie Brubaker and Julia M. H. Smith, 234–56. Cambridge: Cambridge, University Press, 2004.

———. *The Most Holy Abbot Ceolfrid*. Jarrow: The Rectory, 1995.

———. "A Prelude to Columbanus: The Monastic Achievement in the Burgundian Territories." In *Columbanus and Merovingian Monasticism*, ed. H.B. Clarke and Mary Brown, 3–32. British Archaeological Reports, International Series 113. Oxford: BAR, 1981.

Wozniak, Frank E. "Byzantine Diplomacy and the Lombard-Gepidic Wars." *Balkan Studies* 20 (1979): 139–58.

Zerubavel, Eviatar. *Time Maps: Collective Memory and the Social Shape of the Past.* Chicago: University of Chicago Press, 2003.

INDEX